Facts, Not Fear

Facts, Not Fear

Teaching Children About the Environment

Revised Edition

Michael Sanera
and Jane S. Shaw

REGNERY
PUBLISHING, INC.
An Eagle Publishing Company • Since 1947

Library of Congress Cataloging-in-Publication Data

Sanera, Michael, 1947–
     Facts, Not Fear : teaching children about the environment /
Michael Sanera and Jane S. Shaw. —2nd ed.
        p.   cm.
     Includes bibliographical references and index.
     ISBN 0-89526-293-2 (paperback)
     1. Environmental education. 2. Environmental sciences—Study and teaching.
  I. Title.   II. Shaw, Jane S., 1944–
  GE70.S26 1999
  363.7—DC21   99-040214

Published in the United States by
Regnery Publishing, Inc.
An Eagle Publishing Company
One Massachusetts Avenue, N.W.
Washington, D.C. 20001

Distributed to the trade by
National Book Network
4720-A Boston Way
Lanham, MD 20706

Designed by Dori Miller

Printed on acid-free paper.
Manufactured in the United States of America

10 9 8 7 6 5 4 3 2 1

Books are available in quantity for promotional or premium use. Write to Director of Special Sales, Regnery Publishing, Inc., One Massachusetts Ave., NW, Washington, DC 20001, for information on discounts and terms or call 202-216-0600.

To Wendy:
Thank you for bringing your joy,
happiness and love into my life.
M.S.

To Rick and David, who taught me that the future can
be better than the past.
J.S.S.

Contents

....

Foreword

by Diane Lanier

Huntsville Middle School
Huntsville, Alabama

....

AS A FORMER research chemist now teaching middle-school science, I am concerned about the scientific ignorance underlying much of what now passes for environmental education. I am concerned that a social and political agenda is being promoted in the cloak of "unbiased" science. That is the reason I am pleased to recommend *Facts, Not Fear,* a concise and easy-to-use alternative resource. Because it offers accurate information in a user-friendly format, *Facts, Not Fear* can be used by parents, teachers, and other citizens concerned about education.

Children are vitally interested in the environment, and rightly so. When offered accurate information, they not only learn facts, but they also begin to develop the critical thinking skills required by the scientific method.

But if key elements of existing scientific information are ignored, students will jump to unfounded conclusions and the scientific method will be subverted. All too often this is the case.

Many environmental issues today, from global warming to the use of pesticides, have been discussed widely in the media, and children have picked up perspectives that reflect "conventional wisdom" rather than scientific fact. Frequently, these oversimplified perceptions are repeated in textbooks.

For example, children are taught that "organically grown" vegetables are safer than those grown by modern agricultural means. Yet this is a misperception, as prominent scientists have pointed out. Similarly, children worry about the depletion of stratospheric ozone without understanding that the amount of ozone varies considerably even from day to day. And they don't learn that air pollution has been decreasing, not increasing, in the United States for many years.

Children are often encouraged in our society to emote uncritically. Many educational texts fail to correct this tendency. Instead, they rely on emotional questions to stimulate discussion without introducing any real science. But science is not based on emotions, no matter how deeply felt or well-intentioned; it is based on knowledge. Teachers should not indoctrinate students but help them acquire accurate information and teach them to reason with it effectively.

Too frequently, we all fall into the trap of presenting science to young people as a completed product with no questions left unanswered. Environmental science provides an opportunity for showing them that science is constantly evolving. Continually, as new data on the environment are being discovered, our analysis changes. But we cannot analyze accurately when so much educational literature is devoted to presenting a portion of data that adheres to one particular interpretation.

With the many time constraints we all face, it is difficult to evaluate environmental materials to determine if they are presenting just one side of an issue. Yet we want to present all the relevant information and encourage children to think critically for themselves. Ultimately, our goal is to help produce mature, reasoning adults. *Facts, Not Fear* is a tool that can help us achieve that goal.

Acknowledgments

·····························

FACTS, NOT FEAR IS the product of many people's efforts. Our special thanks go to Gary Palmer of the Alabama Family Alliance for the inspiration for this book. Gary's steadfast efforts and patience in helping bring it to fruition are deeply appreciated. We thank Fred Smith of the Competitive Enterprise Institute for helping us launch the project, and we appreciate the contributions of many CEI staff members, especially Jonathan Adler and Helen Hewitt, in completing it.

In Arizona, we are grateful to Marcia Sielaff and Bob Dean for their research assistance, and to Michael's students at Northern Arizona University, who provided a welcome "reality check."

In Montana, we thank the staff and associates of PERC (the Political Economy Research Center). Terry Anderson, Donald Leal, and Richard Stroup have helped us look afresh at many environmental issues. The staff, under the direction of Monica Lane Guenther, worked carefully without complaint and under great pressure. We especially thank Dianna Rienhart, Michelle Johnson, and Pamela Malyurek for their administrative and word processing contributions.

The Earhart Foundation, the Hume Foundation, and several individuals provided support at critical times. Finally, we thank those scientists and other specialists who took the time to read our chapters and correct our errors. Additional thanks go to Sandy Stimpson and Daniel K. Benjamin. We appreciate the patience and perseverance of the staff at Regnery Publishing, Inc., and we especially thank Charlotte Hays for her superb editing. Any errors that remain are ours.

Michael Sanera
Jane S. Shaw

Academic and Scientific Advisory Panel

....

THE FOLLOWING EXPERTS HAVE reviewed the issue-specific chapters indicated below (chapters 4–17). They agree that the content of the specific chapter they reviewed accurately reflects scientific understanding of the issues discussed and the surrounding debate. Organizations are listed for identification purposes only. Their listing does not imply in any way the organizations' endorsement or approval of this book. The authors, and not these experts, are solely responsible for any errors or omissions in this book.

CHAPTER 4: WILL BILLIONS STARVE?

Nicholas Eberstadt
Visiting Scholar,
American Enterprise Institute
Washington, DC
and Visiting Fellow
Harvard Center for Population and
Development Studies

Thomas Poleman
Professor of International Food
Economics
Cornell University

CHAPTER 5: NATURAL RESOURCES—ON THE WAY OUT?

James Gwartney
Chief Economist,
Jont Economic
Committee, U.S. Congress

Murray Weidenbaum
Chairman, Center for the Study
of American Business
and Professor of Economics
Washington University
St. Louis, Missouri

CHAPTER 6: ARE OUR FORESTS DYING?

Ronald N. Johnson
Professor of Economics
Montana State University

Gary Libecap
Professor of Economics and Law
and Director, Karl Eller Center
University of Arizona

Douglas W. MacCleery
Assistant Director, Timber
Management
U.S. Forest Service
Washington, DC

CHAPTER 7: THE RAIN FOREST— ONE HUNDRED ACRES A MINUTE?

Sandra Brown
Senior Program Officer
Winrock International
Corvallis, Oregon

Ariel E. Lugo
Director
International Institute of Tropical
Forestry
U.S. Forest Service, Puerto Rico

Roger Sedjo
Senior Fellow
Resources for the Future
Washington, DC

CHAPTER 8: AMERICAN WILDLIFE—ON THE EDGE?

Dean Lueck
Assistant Professor of Economics
of Agricultural and Resource
Economics
North Carolina State University

Jack T. Wenders
Former Professor of Economics
University of Idaho

CHAPTER 9: WHERE HAVE ALL THE SPECIES GONE?

David G. Cameron
Former Professor of Biology and
Genetics
Montana State University

Matthew Cronin
Senior Research Biologist
LGL Alaska Research Associates, Inc.
and former Research Geneticist,
U.S. Fish and Wildlife Service

CHAPTER 10: THE AIR WE BREATHE

Mikhail S. Bernstam
Senior Research Fellow
Hoover Institution
Stanford University

Robert W. Crandall
Senior Fellow in Economic Studies
The Brookings Institution
Washington, DC

D. H. Stedman
Phillipson Chair Professor of
Chemistry and Biochemistry
University of Denver

CHAPTER 11: A HOTTER PLANET?

Robert Balling
Director, Office of Climatology
and Professor of Geography
Arizona State University

Roy W. Spencer
Engineer
NASA Marshall Space Flight Center
Huntsville, Alabama

CHAPTER 12: SORTING OUT OZONE

Sallie Baliunas
Senior Scientist
George C. Marshall Institute
Washington, DC

D. H. Stedman
Phillipson Chair Professor of
Chemistry and Biochemistry
University of Denver

Fred Seitz
President Emeritus
Rockefeller University
Past President
National Academy of Sciences

CHAPTER 13: ACID RAIN

Patricia Irving
Manager, Environmental Science
Department
Pacific Northwest Laboratory,
Richland, Washington.
Former Director, National Acid
Precipitation Assessment Program
(NAPAP)

J. Laurence Kulp
Affiliate Professor of Civil
Engineering
University of Washington
and former Director of Research,
National Acid Precipitation
Assessment Program (NAPAP)
and former Professor of
Geochemistry, Columbia University

CHAPTER 14: NOT A DROP TO DRINK

Indur M. Goklany
Manager, Science and Engineering
Office of Policy Analysis
Department of the Interior
Washington, DC

Roger E. Meiners
Professor of Economics and Law
University of Texas-Arlington

Bruce Yandle
Alumni Distinguished Professor of
Economics and Legal Studies
Clemson University

CHAPTER 15: DON'T EAT THAT APPLE!

Gordon W. Gribble
Professor of Chemistry
Dartmouth University

Joseph D. Rosen
Professor of Food Chemistry
and Director of the Graduate
Program
Cook College, Rutgers University

Steven Safe
Distinguished Professor of
Veterinary Physiology and
Pharmacology
Texas A & M University

CHAPTER 16: A GARBAGE CRISIS?

M. B. Hocking
Professor of Chemistry
University of Victoria

William Rathje
Professor of Anthropology
Director, The Garbage Project
University of Arizona

Clark Wiseman
Professor of Economics
Gonzaga University

CHAPTER 17: THE RECYCLING MYTH

M. B. Hocking
Professor of Chemistry
University of Victoria

Clark Wiseman
Professor of Economics
Gonzaga University

William Rathje
Professor of Anthropology
Director, The Garbage Project
University of Arizona

CHAPTER ONE

Too Few Facts

....

IN SCHOOLS TODAY, it is typical to see walls covered with posters depicting endangered animals. Students hold T-shirt sales to raise money to save the rain forest. Children write letters to government officials, pleading to save the planet. In math class, students may solve word problems about deforestation or air pollution as well as multiply fractions. Environmental issues are part and parcel of children's education.

This emphasis could be a good thing. When taught well, environmental education can be informative and absorbing. It can bring to life the scientific principles and information that underlie ecology, for example. Children can learn about how plants grow and how different kinds of vegetation foster different ecological communities. And making children aware of environmental problems can encourage them to think critically and creatively.

Too often, however, environmental education skips the basics, pushing students into complex and controversial topics such as endangered species and global warming without establishing a scientific basis of knowledge. Education can play second fiddle to emotionalism and political activism.

❦ Shortly after Earth Day in 1997, a parent wrote a letter to the *New York Times:* "I have noticed a disturbing trend. With each passing school year, my children are more convinced that humans and technology are bad for the planet.... While teachers are helping to insure a 'greener' future, I do not think they understand that children may infer a condemnation of humanity."[1]

❦ To celebrate Earth Week in 1998, the Sierra Club took a group of fourth graders on a field trip to downtown Denver. After encouraging the children to use sidewalk chalk to draw pictures of endangered animals, the Sierra Club organizers gathered the children around a podium and began denouncing the voting record of a Colorado senator.[2]

Because environmental issues are emotional and complicated, sometimes it is easier for parents and teachers to let emotions, rather than facts, guide their discussion. Sometimes it's easier to let outsiders, even those who may be biased, present information. And, unfortunately, many of the materials in schools, including textbooks published by the leading national publishers, are unreliable. They echo the views expressed by the media or by politicians or by an uninformed public. It is difficult for parents and teachers to sort the facts from the fiction.

The purpose of this book is twofold: To raise some questions about the way environmental issues are being taught and to offer information to balance the biased presentations that are so prevalent.

We, the authors of this book, believe we have the background to help teachers and parents correct misinformation found in the materials. Michael spent seventeen years as a political science professor teaching at Northern Arizona University. He also has started two research institutes and published two books. Jane was a journalist for many years before she began to write and edit articles for a research institute in Montana. Our research has been aided by people familiar with each environmental issue we write about. In addition, we are both parents of preteens, and we know from personal experience the conflicts between emotion and fact that crop up in environmental education.

Before we can help, you need to understand the nature of the problem.

APOCALYPSE TOMORROW

"Our Earth is getting hotter every minute and the only way we can stop it is to stop burning Styrofoam," wrote Catherine Mitchell, then a student at Percy Priest Elementary School in Nashville, Tennessee. "I'm also too young to die, might I add, so stop burning the Earth!"[3]

Catherine worried about dying because she had learned that global warming and a thinning ozone layer threaten her life. Never mind that the greenhouse effect and the so-called "hole" in the ozone layer have little to do with each other, or that burning Styrofoam has little to do with either one. Catherine's environmental knowledge was scientifically weak but emotionally potent.

Consider the following:

🍂 Global warming will cause polar ice caps to melt, says a junior high school text. "New York City would almost be covered with water. Only the tops of very tall buildings will be above the water."[4] But most scientists believe that if the world gets warmer, the sea level might increase only by between six and forty inches.[5]

🍂 *Rainforest,* a storybook for small children, tells how a man on a bulldozer destroys the rain forest and its animal life. Justice is done when the rains come and wash the bulldozer over a cliff, killing the man. (A drawing shows the man falling to his death.) "The Machine was washed away!" the book concludes. "But the creatures of the rain forest were safe."[6]

🍂 The National Wildlife Federation tells students to pour highly acidic water on potted plants to simulate acid rain. When the plants die, students conclude that acid rain kills forests.[7] Yet the largest scientific study of acid rain ever conducted (at a cost of more than $500 million) couldn't find convincing evidence that acid rain is destroying forests.[8]

🌿 An environmental supplement to the *Weekly Reader* states that CFCs (chlorofluorocarbons) "break down and go directly to the ozone layer and destroy it." These CFCs "are found in the plastic foam from which cups, plates, and some fast food containers are made."[9] But by 1992, when this issue appeared, plastic foam products had been CFC-free for two years.[10]

These are just some of the many examples found during a review of more than 130 textbooks, 170 environmental books for children, and examples of curriculum materials from environmental and business groups. Unbiased materials are a rare exception. Most materials either present only one side of an issue, select worst-case examples, or omit important information.

ARMAGEDDON IN THE PRESS

These materials echo the messages conveyed by the mass media.

🌿 "Let there be no illusions," wrote *Time* magazine in its "Planet of the Year" special issue. "Taking effective action to halt the massive injury to the earth's environment will require a mobilization of political will, international cooperation and sacrifice unknown except in wartime." Sprinkled through the issue were statements such as: "Nearly every habitat is at risk," "Greenhouse gases could create a climatic calamity," and "Swarms of people are running out of food and space."[11]

🌿 Actress Meryl Streep appeared on the "Phil Donahue Show" to warn mothers about a substance called Alar, a growth regulator used on apples. CBS's "60 Minutes" presented the charges, too. Both were part of a public relations campaign conducted in 1989 for the Natural Resources Defense Council (NRDC). The group claimed that one out of every five thousand preschoolers exposed to Alar residues was likely to get cancer. Parents were terrified. Schools stopped selling apples in their vending machines. (The NRDC's claims were never substantiated.)[12]

🐝 "Captain Planet," a cartoon seen on the Cartoon Network, begins a typical episode with this narration: "Our world is in peril. Gaia, the spirit of the Earth, can no longer stand the terrible destruction plaguing our planet." One of the shows features "Hoggish Greedly" and "Dr. Blight," who are trying to destroy the rain forest and make it into a golf course.[13]

REINFORCING THE MESSAGE

Some scientists and other prominent citizens reinforce the message conveyed by the media. In fact, they often speak through the media. While scientists must be objective and careful when they publish articles in scientific journals, they can speak dramatically for popular consumption.

🐝 Stephen Schneider, a scientist at Stanford University and the National Center for Atmospheric Research in Boulder, Colorado, told *Good Housekeeping* readers that "world global warming would mean that food and water supplies would be threatened (temporarily, at least), that certain diseases might go haywire, that numerous species of animals or plants—even whole ecosystems—would be endangered, and that both the temperature and the level of the oceans would rise, leading to more likelihood of severe storms and flooding of the coastlines."[14] Each of these statements is questioned by equally reputable scientists.

🐝 James E. Hansen, who directs the Goddard Institute for Space Studies, told *Newsweek* that even the deep snow blanketing the East in the winter of 1995–96 was caused by global warming. "As you get more global warming, you should see an increase in the extremes of the hydrologic cycle—droughts and floods and heavy precipitation," he explained.[15]

For scientists and government officials, "crisis" can mean bigger budgets.

Since so much scientific research is funded by government grants, some scientists often improve their access to funds if they can show politicians that their work may "save the planet." In fact, other scientists who downplay crises may find themselves in hot water because they are threatening the budgets of their colleagues.

🐝 Melvyn Shapiro, the chief of research at a laboratory of the National Oceanic and Atmospheric Administration, told *Insight* magazine that much of the reason for alarm about ozone depletion was budgetary. "If there were no dollars attached to this game, you'd see it played on intellect and integrity," he said. "When you say the ozone threat is a scam, you're not only attacking people's scientific integrity, you're going after their pocketbook as well. It's money, purely money." But soon after the article appeared, Shapiro stopped accepting calls from the press. Word circulated that his superiors had told him to quit talking.[16]

Government officials recognize that environmental "crises" mean bigger budgets, too.

🐝 When the Superfund law, designed to clean up hazardous waste sites, was passed in 1980, the Environmental Protection Agency's (EPA) budget went up almost instantly by hundreds of millions of dollars—and ultimately by billions. The EPA administrator at the time actively campaigned for the Superfund law. He made sure that the EPA, not some other agency, would be in charge, and, in fact, the law that emerged was largely written by members of his agency.[17]

But perhaps the most accomplished promoters of crisis are environmental groups. Many environmental groups were born out of genuine alarm about air and water pollution or other issues. But advocacy has become big business. Multimillion-dollar organizations are housed in skyscrapers and managed by well-paid executives who spend much of their time as Washington lobbyists. If these organizations are to continue to exist in their comfortable style and maintain their political power, they must keep donations coming.

> **By most measures the environment in North America has improved substantially.**

So their fund-raising letters are calculated to grip the reader's attention.

- "It is entirely possible that we may be the last generation of humans to know this wondrous earth as it was meant to be," warns the Sierra Club Legal Defense Fund.[18]

- "In the time it takes you to read this letter, nine hundred acres of rainforest will have been destroyed forever," says the Rainforest Action Network.[19]

- "Without firing a shot, we may kill one-fifth of all species of life on this planet in the next 20 years," shouts the World Wildlife Fund.[20]

Ironically, fear about the environment does not mean that the environment is significantly worse than it used to be. As this book will show, by most measures the environment in North America has improved substantially.

- Air quality has dramatically improved in the last few decades. According to the Environmental Protection Agency, for example, national emissions of carbon monoxide declined by 14.8 percent between 1975 and 1994, and emissions of sulfur dioxide declined by 24.6 percent during the same period. These declines occurred in spite of substantial economic growth.[21]

- The United States has more standing timber now than it did in 1920, and more timber grows each year than is cut.[22]

🐝 Many wildlife populations are greater than they were 80 or 100 years ago.[23]

So, just as the texts are often irresponsible in predicting the future, they are often negligent in describing the past and present.

CHIEF SEATTLE

In our review of children's environmental literature we found many instances of exaggeration and half truth. In most cases, the misinformation children receive is more a matter of emphasis than outright falsehood. An exception is the tale of Chief Seattle.

The subject of a 1991 best-selling children's book entitled *Brother Eagle, Sister Sky: A Message from Chief Seattle* by Susan Jeffers, the chief is a favorite of authors who write about the environment. Chief Seattle, a nineteenth century leader of Puget Sound Indian tribes, is credited with delivering a speech in 1855 that resonated with environmental relevance. "The earth is our mother.... What befalls the earth befalls all the sons and daughters of the earth," he is often quoted as having said. These and other lines attributed to him seem perfect expressions of the environmentalist message.

As it happens, a little too perfect. According to a front page *New York Times* story that appeared in April 1992, Chief Seattle did not address himself to environmental issues in that speech, or on any other occasion, as far as anyone knows.

The "quotes" come from Ted Perry, a university professor hired to write a documentary about pollution for the Southern Baptist Convention's Radio and Television Commission. For this 1972 film, Perry decided to create a fictional version of Seattle's response to territorial officials' offer to buy tribal land. He intended the speech to be allegorical, and he thought that putting "written by Ted Perry" at the end of the film would make clear his use of poetic license.

SAVING THE PLANET WITHOUT SCARING KIDS

How can parents and teachers give students a balanced view of environmental problems? One way is to expand the information they receive. In this book, you will read the facts that are not covered in textbooks and the scientific controversies that are not explained.

Unfortunately, that's not the way it worked out. The film's producer changed the credit to "researched by Ted Perry" and Perry's protests about the change were ignored, as were his many subsequent efforts to correct the record.

The speech took on a life of its own, showing up in U.S. Supreme Court Justice William Douglas's autobiography, in Al Gore's book *Earth in the Balance*, and in other articles; it has also been broadcast in at least six foreign countries. According to a 1993 report in *Reader's Digest,* Perry's fictional account continues to be read as fact in elementary school classrooms across the country.

Even a minimal amount of checking should have raised questions about the authenticity of the speech, because Perry put words in the chief's mouth that he could not possibly have uttered. For example, he described "a thousand rotting buffaloes on the prairie," shot by white men from a passing train. Yet buffalo did not roam near where Chief Seattle lived, and trains did not run there until years after the speech was delivered. The chief also referred to "ripe hills being blotted out by talking wires," but the telephone was not invented until after his death.

At the very least, these anomalies ought to have been detected by the presumably well-educated authors of children's textbooks. But neither Perry's disclaimers nor subsequent exposés have diminished the frequency with which Chief Seattle's faked words are quoted.

(The full story is told in "The Little Green Lie," by Mary Murray, *Reader's Digest*, July 1993, 100-104. A more scholarly source is "What Chief Seattle Said" by Paul S. Wilson, *Environmental Law*, Vol. 22, 1992, 1451–68.)

Simply learning that reputable scientists often disagree with the claims of imminent catastrophe will keep children from blindly fearing the future. Such information will also help them see that environmental science is a discipline that reflects scientific uncertainty and is open to continual discovery. Students can learn about environmental issues and develop their critical thinking skills at the same time. As scientists do, they can collect the facts and see whether the theories that have been advanced actually fit the facts.

With this greater objectivity, students can also begin to think critically about why we have environmental problems and can become more aware of human nature. They won't be so quick to accept the simplistic claims of catastrophic global destruction. Children will probably stop pestering parents to take up the cause of the day, or at least they will be willing to consider that their crusade may not be for everyone.

Each chapter about a specific environmental topic concludes with a few questions and answers that will help summarize the information in the chapter. Each also has activities that children may like to read and perhaps try out with the help of their teachers and parents. The activities offer concrete evidence that supports the points in the chapter. These are suggestions that may make a trip to the lumberyard, say, or to the supermarket a richer experience.

Part One

....

CHAPTER TWO

At Odds With Science

....

DON'T BE MISLED BY TITLES like *Environmental Science* or *Earth Science*. Despite their names, these books may not be teaching science at all.

Science sets out to discover what "is." Many environmental texts skip past the "what is" to arrive at the "what ought to be."

For example, scientists don't know whether greenhouse gases are causing the Earth to get warmer. But *Earth Science: The Challenge of Discovery* tells children what to do about it, anyway: "Reduce greenhouse gases by using less fossil fuel. Walk, ride a bike, or take a bus instead of a car for short trips. Turn off appliances when you are not using them."[1]

While global warming is treated as a fact in classrooms, scientists themselves are still exploring it as a question. They are using the existing body of scientific knowledge, from geology to atmospheric chemistry, to figure it out. Bit by bit, week by week, writing in specialized journals, their latest findings accumulate.

Scientists tell us, for example, that temperature measurements taken from satellites show warmer than normal temperature in recent years. But in the mid-1980s and the early 1990s, temperatures were much cooler than normal.

Bore holes (dug deep into the ground) in the United States and Canada show signs of warming temperatures over the past century. Another study suggests that air pollution might be cooling the Earth, and another examines how ocean currents affect temperatures. So, while it is too early to tell if the greenhouse effect will cause substantial warming, gradually the pieces of the puzzle are being put together.

Unfortunately, this discovery process is largely neglected in the textbooks when environmental issues are discussed. A typical textbook would lead you to believe that on most environmental issues scientific knowledge is settled. But it is not. As a result:

- Children learn that one hundred species of plants and animals may be going extinct each day. In fact, no one even knows how many species there are now, and the estimates are guesses, partly based on studies of how many species disappear when the habitats of small islands are destroyed.

- Organic farming is considered safe because it doesn't use pesticides. But the fruits and vegetables we eat have many more natural toxins than are ever added through pesticides.

- Overpopulation is often pegged as the root of environmental problems. Yet economic studies have failed to show that rapid population growth causes famine or depletion of natural resources.

THE SCIENTIFIC METHOD

To understand where environmental science veers from science, we need to recognize that over the years scientists have developed a process for learning what "is." This is the scientific method, and it works like this:

Scientists start by being curious about something. To use a simplistic example, suppose that they want to know the cause of fire. Gradually, they develop a hypothesis, a statement about the physical world that can be tested.

For example, a scientist might develop a hypothesis about one piece of the puzzle: The scientist might propose that fire needs oxygen to burn.

To test hypotheses, scientists devise experiments. The scientist studying fire and oxygen might use three closed chambers. In each, the scientist might start a fire and then replace the air in each chamber with a different gas: in the first, carbon dioxide; in the second, nitrogen; and in the third, oxygen.

Over the years, scientists have developed a process for learning what "is"— the scientific method.

The scientist then observes the results. The fires in the chambers with carbon dioxide and nitrogen go out, but the fire in the oxygen chamber continues to burn. The experiment supports the hypothesis that fire needs oxygen to burn.

Scientists document their experiments and results precisely and submit their findings to scientific journals. If other scientists (their professional peers) find a paper to be of high caliber, it is published and becomes part of the scientific literature. More scientists can then review the experiments and perhaps repeat them.

If an experiment is repeated many times and produces the same results, scientists have established a scientific fact. The accumulation of many scientific facts leads to the development of a theory. This is a statement about the physical world that is supported by scientific experiments and other forms of verification but does not have sufficient evidence to establish it as a scientific law.

Ultimately, a theory may lead to the recognition of a scientific law. Sir Isaac Newton, the famous seventeenth century British scientist, for example, first stated the theory of gravity. However, only after many experiments did other scientists agree with Newton and consider the theory a scientific law.

THE WORLD AS LABORATORY

Of course, real science is rarely as simple or straightforward as this outline suggests. For one thing, not all scientific questions are testable in carefully controlled laboratory experiments.

So scientists have developed techniques to discover facts "in the field." While these techniques are not as good as a controlled experiment, they can, when used rigorously, lead to greater understanding.

Some years ago people began to notice that trees in Western Europe, including England, were dying. Many people thought that the cause was "acid rain" (excessive sulfur dioxide and nitrogen oxides in the atmosphere).

When scientists examined the forests more closely, however, they found that acid rain couldn't explain very much of the damage. Forests are affected by many factors—different kinds of pollution, cold weather, poor management, and insects. They concluded that abnormal weather had caused some damage. More important, they found that the diseased trees were exceptions. European forests were, in general, fairly healthy. The amount of wood they produced each year was rising steadily.[2] (We will look more carefully at acid rain in chapter 13.)

In the mid-1980s, scientists developed a theory that chlorine from CFCs was reducing ozone in the upper atmosphere over the Antarctic. To test this theory, NASA scientists made expeditions into the stratosphere over the Antarctic in specially fitted high-flying airplanes. There they measured the levels of ozone and other chemicals. These expeditions supported the theory that chlorine from CFCs is depleting ozone, but they also supported the view that other factors, such as cold polar temperatures and winds known as the polar vortex, affect ozone levels, too.[3] (We will look at ozone more closely in chapter 12.)

WHY SCIENCE ISN'T EASY

Other factors make environmental science difficult, but also stimulating. They include:

Cause and Effect or Just Correlation?

Scientists want to understand what causes things to happen. Often it is possible to detect two things happening at the same time but it is difficult to know if one caused the other. The two events may be "correlated" but not linked by "cause and effect."

Over the past hundred years, the average global temperatures rose about half a degree centigrade. Over the same period, the amount of carbon dioxide in the atmosphere went up about 25 percent. Did the carbon dioxide cause the warming? Did the warming cause the rise in CO_2? Or did the carbon dioxide and temperatures just happen to go up at the same time? Scientists are still grappling with this question, as we shall see in chapter 11.

Scientists have also looked back at the distant record, hundreds of thousands of years ago, by drilling deep holes in the ice. The ancient ice contains the carbon dioxide that was present in the atmosphere at that time, long before any greenhouse gases were unleashed by humans. Scientists can also estimate past temperatures from this ice.

Many global warming predictions are based on models that attempt to simulate the workings of the Earth's atmosphere. This is an enormous task, since thousands of factors, from ocean currents to water vapor, influence the Earth's atmospheric and weather conditions.

Again, there is a correlation between carbon dioxide levels and temperature. But in many cases the carbon dioxide came after the warming![4]

Computers—Shedding Light but also Confusion

One way to cope with the complexity of the real world is to use computers. Scientists enter vast amounts of data about the real world and use sophisticated mathematical programs to simulate the complexity of weather and climate.

Many global warming predictions are based on models that attempt to simulate the workings of the entire Earth's atmosphere. This is an enormous task, since thousands of factors, from ocean currents to water vapor, influence the Earth's atmospheric and weather conditions. But how? Do clouds cool the Earth or warm it? They can do both. If greenhouse gases lead to an increase in clouds (as they might), the clouds could either warm or cool the Earth. Predictions are thus rather shaky.

Furthermore, simply because the Earth is so large, computer models treat large stretches of the Earth as if they were the same. For example, some computer models can't distinguish between the forests of Oregon and the deserts of Nevada.[5] And one prominent scientist, Richard Lindzen, points out that the computer models cannot even successfully calculate the present average global temperature—let alone predict the temperature of the atmosphere ten or twenty years from now.[6]

Theories in Conflict

The existence of conflicting scientific theories is normal. For every scientific theory, usually several others exist that conflict with it. Scientists are constantly refining their theories in light of increased knowledge and experience.

For example, physics was full of uncertainty about fundamental theories and laws for more than half a century. When Marie Curie, late in the nineteenth century, observed that a rock containing the element radium (supposedly inert matter) could create an image on a sealed photographic plate, she realized that matter was more complex than scientists had thought. At the time, physicists believed that matter reacted only at the chemical level, not at the atomic level. But, in fact, alpha particles from the radioactive radium had traveled through the protective cover and exposed the photographic plate.

> Vice President Al Gore wrote that paying too much attention to doubters "undermines the effort to build a solid base of support for the difficult actions we must take." His message: Agree or be quiet.

The existing scientific theories could not explain what had happened, so Curie set out to discover the answer. She and her husband Pierre proposed a mysterious source of energy within the atoms. Others, however, identified the alpha particle as the nucleus of the helium atom. And in 1905 Albert Einstein explained the source of the apparently enormous energy with his famous equation $E=mc^2$. It took about thirty more years to establish the theory firmly, and it led to the development of the atomic bomb.

CONTINUING THE SEARCH FOR TRUTH

When properly conducted, scientists' search for truth is governed by strict rules of conduct and ethics. Scientists make hypotheses, test them, and submit their findings for review and replication by other scientists. These scientific debates, while lively, are supposed to be conducted free of political interference.

Environmental issues, however, are different. There *is* political interference. In 1992, Vice President Al Gore (then Senator) concluded that global warming was a fact. He wrote in his book *Earth in the Balance* that paying too much attention to the doubters "undermines the effort to build a solid base of public support for the difficult actions we must soon take."[7] His message: Agree with him or be quiet. Because of his prominence, scientists had to listen.

But neither Al Gore nor any other politician is going to quash the scientific method. Ultimately, science, not politics, will answer the scientific questions surrounding global warming, species extinction, and other environmental issues.

A politically motivated "rush to judgment" is not the way to settle scientific disputes. Good science often takes time. In 1912, Alfred Wegener suggested that the Earth's continents, which nearly everyone thought were static, actually moved. At first, this idea was rejected by most geological experts. It took Wegener and his followers forty years to gather the supporting evidence for this theory. Faced with a massive accumulation of scientific evidence, the scientific community accepted the theory of plate tectonics in the early 1950s.

CHAPTER THREE

What Are the Costs?

....

OUT IN MONTANA, where Jane lives, many people are trying to preserve the beauty of the land and the diversity of wildlife. David Cameron is a friend of hers who used to be a biology professor at Montana State University. He is also a third-generation rancher. In addition to raising cattle and sheep, his family has a long tradition of protecting wildlife. Elk, deer, mountain lions, and bears thrive on his ranch.

A few years ago Dave decided to improve the wildlife in the area by bringing back the grayling. This is a native Montana fish that disappeared from nearby streams many years ago. Dave consulted with specialists and found a suitable place on the ranch to reintroduce the fish.

But then he learned that the U.S. Fish and Wildlife Service was considering listing the Montana grayling as an endangered species. Almost instantly, he changed his mind.

Once Dave had an endangered fish on his property, federal agents could prevent him from using his pastures for grazing. They could simply claim

David Cameron decided to improve wildlife in his area by bringing back the grayling. But then he learned that the U.S. Fish and Wildlife service was considering listing the Montana grayling as an endangered species. Almost instantly, he changed his mind.

that his cattle would pollute the stream or otherwise harm the endangered fish. "I sadly bowed out," he says.[1]

Textbooks routinely support the Endangered Species Act and recommend making it stronger. Because the authors have little or no grounding in economics, they don't recognize that its severe penalties may have an effect exactly the opposite of its intention.

Without an understanding of economic principles, texts don't tell "the rest of the story." Here are a few more examples.

BAN CFCS

On January 1, 1996, production of chemicals known as CFCs became illegal in the United States. (Freon is the best-known of these chemicals.) The Montreal Protocol, an agreement by thirty-one nations to phase out the chemicals, had taken effect.

The Montreal Protocol was "one of the most significant environmental agreements ever attempted," says the National Wildlife Federation.[2] And other materials praise the agreement just as highly. But the textbooks leave out some important information. They don't tell children that:

- There is now a black market in illegally imported CFCs. "Law enforcement officials say the refrigerant has become the most lucrative contraband after illicit drugs," reported the *New York Times*.[3]

- It can cost hundreds of dollars to have an automobile air conditioner fixed so that it can use the new substitutes.

- The ban makes all kinds of cooling (not just air conditioning) more expensive. In the Third World, more children are likely to die of infectious diseases because it will be more difficult to keep vaccines cold.[4]

- By raising the price of refrigeration, the ban will cause more people to get sick from food poisoning.

RECYCLE OR ELSE

Recycling, too, is universally supported by environmental textbooks. But the textbooks leave out some facts:

🐝 In 1987, when the state of New Jersey made recycling newspapers mandatory, so many people were trying to sell their papers that the price per pound fell below zero. Recyclers had to pay $25 per ton to have newspapers hauled away![5]

🐝 In Los Angeles, curbside recycling meant that the city had to have eight hundred rather than four hundred trucks to pick up trash.[6] And that city already has air pollution from its traffic.

🐝 Recycling paper doesn't necessarily save trees. If recycling paper increased dramatically, people who now grow trees for paper pulp would plant fewer trees. [7]

DON'T DRIVE; USE MASS TRANSIT

And then there is the automobile. Textbooks tell students that it is the bane of Americans' existence. Stop riding in a car, they say, and lobby for more mass transit. They don't tell you that:

🐝 People want to drive cars because they provide door-to-door convenience, especially for transporting young children.

🐝 You can force people to pay for mass transit but you can't make them use it. Even in Washington, DC, which has a beautiful, tax-supported subway system, only 36 percent of commuters use mass transit.[8]

🐝 The advent of the automobile in the early twentieth century brought enormous benefits. Farmland returned to forest because we didn't need so many fields for hay. City streets became clean streets without all that manure.

YES, WE HAVE SOME POLLUTION

The textbooks fail to recognize that people respond to rewards and penalties. Environmental policies change the rewards and penalties, so people's behavior changes, sometimes dramatically.

The texts also fail to help children understand why we have pollution problems in the first place. Yes, some companies and individuals pollute. They do so because it's sometimes cheaper to let waste from their facilities enter the air or stream than to clean it up.

The picture is not entirely grim. Pollution is down:

- Between 1975 and 1989, airborne lead went down, on average, by 93 percent in the U.S., while particulates declined by 20 percent.[9]

- Since the mid-1970s, levels of pesticides, fertilizers, and chemicals called PCBs in the Great Lakes have dropped dramatically.[10]

Laws passed since 1970 have contributed to some of these improvements. But air pollution has been declining for years. Economist Robert Crandall points out that air pollution was declining faster in the United States in the 1960s before passage of the Clean Air Act than it did after passage of the act.[11]

How could this be? Air pollution is often unburned fuel. Profit-making firms have an incentive, over time, to figure out how to use the fuel more efficiently, rather than wasting it by sending it up a smokestack.

Also, even before we had major environmental laws, courts discouraged severe pollution. A person has a right to be free from harm inflicted by others, and that includes injury by pollutants. Polluters can be sued in court by people who are

Textbooks fail to recognize that people respond to rewards and penalties. Environmental policies change the rewards and penalties, so people's behavior changes, sometimes dramatically.

harmed, and in the past they were. Industrial polluters were forced to compensate people whom they harmed by air and water pollution.

This common law system discouraged pollution, but it was not perfect. When there were many sources of pollution (such as thousands of cars driving every day), the courts declined to blame any single individual or company, and left the correction of the problem up to local governments. In any case, today regulation has largely superseded this approach to pollution control.

"THE TRAGEDY OF THE COMMONS"[12]

Have you ever noticed that most homes and yards tend to be clean, while public parks and streets are often dirty? Have you ever wondered why we have no shortage of cats and dogs, while many other species are threatened with extinction?

Economics helps us understand these contrasts. When you or I own something, we have a strong interest in taking care of it. We have much less interest in taking care of things that we don't own or that "everyone" owns.

- We can keep our own yard clean and—usually—prevent people from littering it. But even if we clean up a public park, we can't keep others from making a mess of it as soon as we are done.

- We can take care of our pets. But no one can take care of whales in the ocean. In fact, whale hunters have an incentive to kill whales whenever they see them (rather than let them breed for the future). If they don't, other hunters may come along and kill the whale they avoided.

Many environmental problems, especially in Third World countries, stem from the fact that land is owned in common and anyone can use it. In the Sahel region of Africa south of the Sahara Desert, a person who built a water well in the past could control access to it. But then colonial and national governments began to build wells in the area. Their intentions were good; they wanted the wells to be available to all.

But people were attracted to the land around the government wells and began to graze more livestock than the area could support. So while there was enough water, there wasn't enough grass. Overgrazing destroyed the soil for future pasture.[13]

When private ownership is adopted, environmental problems often diminish. The World Bank found that:

🍂 Soil erosion declined when hill farmers in Kenya obtained secure ownership of their land.

🍂 When slumdwellers in Bandung, Indonesia, owned their own homes, their investment in sanitation tripled.

🍂 Private rights to a portion of the fishing catch reduced overfishing in New Zealand waters.[14]

But these positive examples are rarely discussed in our children's textbooks.

LET THE GOVERNMENT DO IT?

The message in many textbooks is that people should change their behavior. Since only government has the right to force people to change, the textbooks usually recommend that the government adopt a new law or regulation.

As we have seen, governments can't always force the behavior they want. But there are other reasons to question "letting the government do it," too. Governments are often worse polluters than private industry. And government policies actually promote many environmental problems. For example:

🍂 The federal government has caused millions of acres of wetlands to be drained. Programs that encourage wetlands draining include:

flood control projects by the Army Corps of Engineers, loans from the Farmers' Home Administration at below-market interest rates, disaster assistance, and farm support prices.[15]

🐝 There is more hazardous waste on federal land, per acre, than on private land.[16]

🐝 Farm support prices also encourage excessive use of pesticides.[17]

🐝 The federal government is failing to protect the wildlife and habitat in its major national parks. The diversity of animals in our parks is declining.[18]

So, putting your trust in governmental solutions can backfire. That's the "rest of this story."

IS ECONOMIC GROWTH HARMFUL TO THE ENVIRONMENT?

Not far from Jane's home in Bozeman, Montana, outside the city limits, you can buy a homesite in a development called Eagle Rock Reserve. But you must buy twenty acres and then use only three acres for your home. The rest of your twenty acres is set aside as wildlife habitat, primarily for elk.

These homesites cost a lot of money—nearly $200,000 per homesite—because the land is valuable and could be used to build many more homes. But some people are willing to pay the price. Why?

As people become more wealthy, they are willing to spend their money to preserve open space, wildlife, and environmental amenities. Indeed, many economists argue that one of the best ways to improve the environment is to encourage economic growth, which leads to higher incomes throughout society.

Gene Grossman and Alan Krueger, economists at Princeton University,[19] looked at the national incomes of many countries and at the levels of pollution in those countries. They found that when the average income of a country is very low, economic growth puts stress on the environment, initially increasing pollution. But after a certain level of wealth is reached, the environment begins to improve. At that point, people have a greater interest in protection and they have the financial ability to achieve it.

In addition, economic growth leads to conservation of resources. Resources—energy, rare minerals, and other nonrenewable raw materials—turn out to be more plentiful than ever. (We will discuss this more in chapter 5.) For example, the profit motive spurs producers to become more efficient in their use of raw materials. In the 1960s, when most soft-drink cans were made of steel, making one thousand cans required 164 pounds of metal. By 1990, the same number of cans could be made from only thirty-five pounds of aluminum.[20]

Why? Trying to reduce their costs so that they could stay competitive, producers switched from steel to lighter-weight aluminum, and they made many slight changes that allowed them to use less aluminum. (They continue to try to reduce the use of aluminum.) No government regulation had mandated conservation. The pressures of the marketplace caused the change.

Economics teaches us about human behavior—the "rest of the story." It sheds light on why we have pollution problems and why some proposed solutions won't work. Good economics, like good science, belongs in the classroom.

Part Two

CHAPTER FOUR

Will Billions Starve?

·····················

HERBERT LONDON, A PROFESSOR at New York University, tells how one evening his ten-year-old daughter sat down at the dinner table and announced that she and her family were eating too much. By overconsuming, they deprived starving Cambodians of food, she said. London's daughter had learned at school that "there is a finite world food supply," and that Americans' overeating means deprivation for others.[1]

All too often, American children learn that people are starving because:

🌰 The world's population is growing too fast.

🌰 The world can produce only so much food.

🌰 The people of the Western nations are consuming too much.

POPULATION GROWTH FOREVER?

The typical text begins its section on population by showing world population climbing at an alarming rate. It usually includes a graph like this:

INCREASE IN WORLD POPULATION

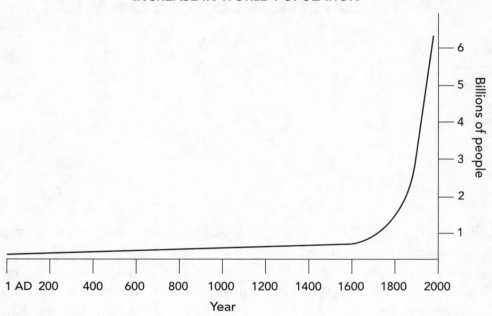

The graph usually ends at the year 2000, creating a frightening picture of unending growth. The writing supports this image.

One text says that in many countries the population doubles every twenty to thirty years, and food and other resources cannot keep up with population growth.[2] Another book actually makes up frightening figures. *Biological Science: An Ecological Approach* reports that the U.S. population in 1990 was 239 million. "If it doubles just twice, our population size also will be nearly 1 billion."[3] (No responsible demographer suggests that this will happen.)

What the textbooks fail to show is that the growth rate of the world's population peaked in the mid-1960s and is slowing in most nations. They also fail to point out that the world's food supply has grown even faster than population has grown.[4]

In the 1960s, world population was growing at slightly over 2 percent per year, an unprecedented rate, but by the late 1990s the rate had dropped to 1.33 percent. It is expected to drop below 1 percent growth in the 2020s.[5] The United Nations now estimates that population in the year 2050 will be between 7.3 and 10.7 billion.[6] Thus, although no one knows for sure, some demographers think that by about 2100 world population will level off at between 10 billion and 12 billion people.

A more realistic graph, which extends farther into the future, would look like this:

INCREASE IN WORLD POPULATION

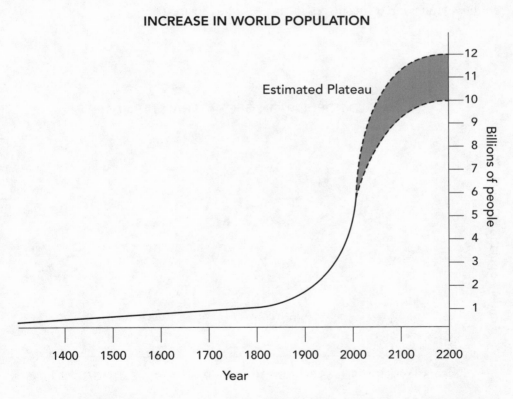

Demographers now think that the rapid growth of population during the twentieth century may be a one-time thing. Certainly, it reflects the dramatic decline in death rates in this century. Thanks to modern health care, sanitation, and better nutrition, fewer women and children die in childbirth, more children reach maturity, and more adults live to old age.

Population levels climbed so rapidly because, until recently, people continued to have as many children as they did in the past, when only a few children in any family were likely to survive. Lower birth rates have lagged behind the dramatic declines in death rates.

But now, birth rates are going down, too. According to United Nations figures, during the last 25 years the average number of children per couple went down from 6.6 to 5.1 in Africa, from 5.1 to 2.6 in Asia, and from 5 to 2.7 in Latin America and the Caribbean.[7] In several countries in Asia—Singapore, Malaysia, and Japan—birth rates fell so low that government leaders have considered incentives to increase birth rates![8]

WORLD POPULATION GROWTH RATE, 1950–1995

Source: United Nations, *World Population: The 1994 Revision* (New York: UN Department for Economic and Social Information and Policy Analysis, 1994), pp. 56–58, 62, 64. (Note: "medium variant" projections used for 1990/95).

IT STARTED WITH MALTHUS

Fears of overpopulation go back at least as far as Thomas Malthus, a clergyman and early British economist. In 1798, Malthus sounded the alarm in *An Essay on the Principle of Population*. He argued that population would grow faster than food supplies, and thousands would starve.

Malthus thought that resources, including land for producing crops, were fixed. While food supplies could increase, they could not increase enough to keep up with rising population. Each new birth would mean that the same resources must be divided into ever smaller portions. Thousands of new births would mean thousands of new mouths to feed with those same fixed resources. Starvation would result when the supply of farmland was exhausted but population continued to increase.

Malthus did not anticipate how machinery, fertilizers, pesticides, modern seed-breeding techniques, modern transportation, and many other factors would increase human beings' ability to produce food. Today, for example, American farmers are so productive that millions of acres of U.S. farmland are deliberately kept out of food production.[9]

Human ingenuity keeps coming up with new technology, from new food varieties to new ways to raise crops. Such technology is likely to continue, said the late economist Julian Simon. "Tractors and wheeled irrigation pipes, which are making enormous contributions today, seemed quite unrealistic a hundred or fifty years ago."[10]

A major study from the Food and Agriculture Organization of the United Nations (FAO) indicates that overall demand for food will grow at a slower rate in the future, reflecting slower population growth and the fact that many people now have adequate diets.[11] The FAO study predicts that global capacity to grow more food will "not be a major obstacle" in providing enough food for the world's population.[12] Some experts are worried less about population growth per se than that people are getting more wealthy. As incomes grow, demand for meat grows.[13] This will lead to major changes in agricultural production, but the changes reflect wealth, not hunger.

In spite of these findings, the authors of our children's textbooks still see the issue in Malthusian terms.

🌰 One text concedes that U.S. farmers produce a food surplus, but asks, will they "still be able to do so in the future, as more and more farmland is covered with cities, dams, highways, and other kinds of development?"[14]

🌰 Another says grimly, "Supporters of Malthus' ideas say that improvements in medical care and farming only put off the time when there will be far too many people for Earth to support."[15]

In later editions of his book, by the way, Malthus was somewhat more optimistic than in his early writing. But nearly two hundred years later that part of the message has not reached textbook writers.

IS CARRYING CAPACITY FIXED?

Echoing Malthus, the texts perpetuate the idea that there is a fixed "carrying capacity" of the Earth. Carrying capacity is a term used by biologists to describe how much land is necessary to support certain numbers of animals. Our textbooks indiscriminately apply it to people, too.

🌰 "No one knows the total carrying capacity of the earth," says the Globe text *Concepts and Challenges in Life Science*. "Some areas may be close to their carrying capacities now. As a result, [human] population growth is a serious problem facing the world today."[16]

🌰 The Prentice Hall text *Biology: The Study of Life* states, "At some point in the future, human population growth must stop because the earth will reach its carrying capacity and will not be able to support any more humans."[17]

But people, unlike animals, do not merely eat what food is available, and die if it isn't around.[18] People grow food and are capable of producing more of it if needed, so "carrying capacity" for humans is far different than for animals, if it has any meaning at all. Most scholars are confident that we have more than enough food to feed the world's growing population. (One expert claimed some years ago that the world could feed forty-seven billion people with a diet of the kind Americans were enjoying in the 1960s.)[19]

In the 1950s, scientists developed new varieties of wheat and rice that dramatically increased food production, especially in Asia. The increase in production became known as the Green Revolution. Today, the Green Revolution continues. While scientists don't expect any single "miracle" crop, the new varieties continue to proliferate. They range from high-protein corn to grains that thrive in acidic soils.[20]

Currently, world population is increasing at 1.33 percent, but production of wheat has been increasing at 2 percent and rice at 3.5 percent.[21] Furthermore, the world currently has idle cropland that could be put under cultivation. The United States has about 60 million acres of unplanted farmland. Argentina has about 90 million acres, now used for pastureland, that could be quickly cultivated.[22]

FEELING GUILTY

These optimistic messages are drowned in a sea of blame. Instead of recognizing the role of modern technology in improving the lives of people all over the world, textbooks criticize the industrialized countries for their use of resources.

🐝 A civics textbook, Glencoe's *Challenge of Freedom,* asks children to imagine the "global village." If the world were a village of one hundred people, it says, "seven or eight people would control half the village's resources and income."[23]

🐝 *The Kids' Environment Book* is more explicit: "We in the United States account for about 5 percent of all the people in the world, but we use a quarter of the planet's energy and goods. Think about that the next time you hop in the car to go to the store."[24]

These statements mislead our children. The United States doesn't just consume a quarter of the world's resources; it also produces a quarter of the world's output.[25] Whatever Americans obtain from other countries they purchase from willing sellers. They don't "take" things. They efficiently turn resources into output, much of which goes to foreign countries. Without U.S. technology and productivity, the poor nations of the world would be poorer still.

Does Population Growth Cause Poverty?

Many texts claim that a slower growth rate of population would reduce poverty. Slower growth "will put less strain on the limited resources" of poor nations, says the Holt text *World Geography Today.* "The nations with the highest growth rates are generally the poorest nations per capita."[26]

It is true that some nations with fast-growing populations are poor, but population growth is not the cause. Extreme poverty usually occurs because government policies prevent people from engaging in productive activities. In such nations rapid population growth can make life worse, but poverty is what makes population growth a problem.

High levels of population do not themselves cause poverty, as recent studies have made clear.

🐝 Evidence that population growth hurts economic development is "weak or nonexistent," reports Allen C. Kelley in a prominent economic journal, the *Journal of Economic Literature.*[27]

🐝 "Concern about the impact of rapid population growth on resource exhaustion has often been exaggerated,"[28] say the prestigious National Research Council (NRC) and the National Academy of Sciences (NAS).

Some of the richest countries in the world have high population densities and few natural resources. These include Hong Kong, Japan, and Singapore.

CHINA: ONE CHILD OR ELSE

The Chinese government's one-child policy has led to high levels of abortion, in some cases coerced abortions and sterilizations, and even to reported infanticide. One text is straightforward about the severity of these measures: "Parents who fail to heed the official limit face penalties ranging from heavy fines to loss of jobs to forced abortion and even sterilization."[29]

But others give tacit approval. "Although the situation in China may seem like a great restriction on the freedom of some individuals, further expansion of the Chinese population would lead to far worse consequences for the entire population,"[30] says the Kendall/Hunt text *Biological Science: An Ecological Approach.*

The Silver Burdett & Ginn text *World Geography: People in Time and Place* describes the Chinese one-child policy and then states that China's greatest problem is "going to be feeding its growing population."[31] The implication is that the policy is necessary.

In general, our children's texts approve of active government intervention to control population growth. The Glencoe text *World History: The Human Experience* explains that food production cannot keep up with population growth in many countries. It then points out that many of these countries are using population control measures and specifically cites Thailand, where over 70 percent of the families practice family planning aggressively pushed by the government.[32]

Experts are not really sure why birth rates are falling swiftly around the world. The dramatic declines in China's population growth rates started well before the "one-child" policy, which began in 1979. Some experts believe that the declines were due to major improvements in infant mortality (parents then had more confidence that their children would live to maturity) and to government campaigns recommending fewer children and later marriages.[33]

In Singapore, birth rates fell in the 1960s and 1970s. Thomas Poleman of Cornell University points to government programs there, especially the decision to make large families wait the longest for new government housing, as a major cause.[34]

The declines also reflect families' changing wishes about family size.[35] Among the reasons behind these changes are economic growth and the shift away from agriculture in many developing countries:

🌰 In countries where agriculture is the primary occupation, even very young children can be productive and families don't need to invest much in their education. (Before the mechanization of American agriculture, U.S. farm families were large and children helped work the fields.) Many children add to the family's labor supply and wealth.

🌰 In industrialized countries, children must be educated before they can be productive. They don't add to the family's wealth until many years after they are born, and investing in their education is expensive. In these countries, parents tend to have fewer children.[36]

WHY DO PEOPLE STARVE?

If there is enough food to go around, why do people starve? The primary answer is politics.

In recent years, famines have swept through parts of Africa, as they did in China and the Soviet Union earlier in this century. Droughts have been a factor, but war, political strife, and government policies are the central cause.

Many countries "have suffered or are still going through severe disruptions caused by war and political disturbances," explains the Food and Agriculture Organization of the United Nations."[37] In Ethiopia and Somalia, for example, warring parties have used food as a weapon to starve regions of the country. When the rest of the world tried to help by sending food, poor roads, lack of storage facilities, and conflict between troops made it difficult to get food to those who needed it.

Even when war is not going on, government policies can hurt food production. This has happened in many countries in the world, but these policies are particularly severe in the Sahel region south of the Sahara Desert. Many African governments there control the price of grain and keep the prices paid to farmers low.[38]

Despite all these problems, African food production has increased in Kenya, Zimbabwe, the Ivory Coast, and South Africa in recent years. Crop production in Africa could double with new technology.[39] In any case, says Dennis Avery of the Hudson Institute, "Africa is a vestige of the hunger problem which once faced all of the Third World—it is not a forerunner of impending famine for the Earth."[40]

QUESTIONS AND ANSWERS

With this background, you can readily answer questions that children may ask about food and population. For example:

Are There Too Many People?

No. The Earth's "carrying capacity" is enormous. Human ingenuity is more than equal to the challenge of meeting the demands of a growing population.

Does Population Growth Cause Starvation?

No. Food production has increased faster than world population, and this trend is likely to continue. Political strife and misguided governmental policies are the most important factors leading to starvation.

Are Americans Consuming Too Much?

This is a moral question that each family will answer for itself. The important point for environmental education is that Americans produce as much as they consume, and what they consume from other countries they purchase from people who sell it willingly. They don't "take" anything from anybody.

Should Governments Try to Control Population?

Again, this is a moral question that each family will answer for itself. It appears that government programs to control population have had some success but that economic growth will be more important over the long run.

ACTIVITIES

Here are some activities and discussions that can help develop a more accurate understanding of population and food problems.

Think about Earlier Generations

Many people these days are learning about their "roots" through genealogy. Helping children to think about earlier generations can quell worries about overpopulation, too.

Typically, past generations had a lot of children. Some of them died at early ages. Those that survived had to go to work when they were very young, and, for many, there was no such thing as retirement. People worked as long as they could—but they died earlier than they do today. The table on the next page shows change in family size, total population, and life expectancy.

Few families traveled far from home because there were no cars or planes. Families seldom took vacations because parents had to work most of the year. Home entertainment consisted of reading, playing the piano, or, later, listening to the radio. Food was less available, with far fewer varieties.

If they wish, let your children tell what they know about their family's history. Or, you might refer them to the fascinating chapter on life earlier this century that Dixy Lee Ray presented in her book *Trashing the Planet* (Harper 1992). American history can help children see that improvements in lifestyle from generation to generation occurred at the same time that the U.S. population increased. In economic systems characterized by private enterprise, more population does not reduce prosperity.

U.S. FAMILY SIZE AND LIFE EXPECTANCY

	U.S. Average Family Size (# of People)	Total U.S. Population (in Millions)	U.S. Life Expectancy (Years)
1900	4.76	76.0	47.3
1910	4.54	92.0	50.0
1920	4.34	105.7	54.1
1930	4.11	122.8	59.7
1940	3.76	131.7	62.9
1950	3.54	151.3	68.2
1960	3.67	179.3	69.7
1970	3.58	203.3	70.9
1980	3.29	226.5	73.7
1990	3.17	248.7	75.4

Sources: *Historical Statistics of the U.S., 1789–1945,* U.S. Department of Commerce, Bureau of the Census, 1949, pp. 29, 45. *Statistical Abstract of the U.S.,* U.S. Department of Commerce, Bureau of the Census, 1993, pp. 55, 85. *Historical Statistics of the U.S.: Colonial Times to 1970,* U.S. Department of Commerce, Bureau of the Census, 1975, pp. 41, 55.

A Trip to the Supermarket

Have students visit the supermarket and report back. Discuss the foods that weren't available when you were their age. Did you have as many frozen foods? Did you have as many fresh fruits and vegetables during the winter? What about new varieties such as kiwi, starfruit, and bok choy? Think of some foods that were available to you but not to your grandparents. Discuss the improvements in transportation and technology that have increased the quantity, variety, and quality of foods.

Compare the prices of chicken and lobster. Chickens are raised by farmers who must buy or grow the grain to feed them. Lobsters live in the ocean and people merely have to catch them. Yet lobsters cost more than chickens. Farmers can produce as many chickens as people are willing to buy, but lobsters are in limited supply.

During the Great Depression, one politician promised "a chicken in every pot"—that is, that someday every family would be able to afford to eat chicken. Today chicken is so inexpensive that it can be sold in fast-food restaurants.

Have children look at the produce section, where prices vary considerably from day to day. An early frost can kill citrus fruit; and floods have wiped out Arizona's lettuce crop. When such natural disasters occur, supply goes down and the price goes up. Some people buy apples instead of oranges, or use less lettuce. But the higher price also encourages producers to find or grow more oranges and lettuce, if they can. The result is that, while prices fluctuate, there is always a diversity of produce in most stores.

Plan a Garden

Help young people imagine that the only food that their family will eat will come from a garden. Looking at a calendar, they should plan when they will plant, how long certain crops will take to mature, and when the harvest will occur. At harvest time, what will they do with all the fresh food? How will they preserve it for the winter? How will the quality compare with that of fresh food?

Consider how many of our favorite foods would not be available if we had to depend upon just what this garden can grow. Point out how many foods come from other parts of the country or even other nations. Some apples come from Japan; some kiwis come from New Zealand; many vegetables come from Mexico.

Children will learn that there is more to the abundance of food on our tables than simply growing it. They will learn the importance of food preservation, processing, and distribution.

Natural Resources— On the Way Out?

·············

PERHAPS YOU REMEMBER, as we do, the energy crisis of the 1970s. Then-President Jimmy Carter appeared on television wearing a sweater, and he asked the American people to turn down the thermostat. "We could use up all of the proven reserves of oil in the entire world by the end of the next decade,"[1] he said at one point.

There is nothing wrong with turning the thermostat down, but former President Carter's worries were based on misinformation. Like many textbook authors, he thought that there weren't enough natural resources to go around, and that there would be even fewer as the population grew and people were wasteful.

> "At the present rate of use, it is estimated that coal reserves will last about 200 more years," says the Merrill text *Science Connections*. "Petroleum may run out in 20 to 30 years, and natural gas may last only another 70 years."[2]

> "You may face mineral shortages in your lifetime," says another.[3]

45

🌰 "At the current rate of consumption, some scientists estimate that the world's known supplies of oil, tin, copper, and aluminum will be used up within your lifetime,"[4] says a third.

These claims are not justified. World supplies of most natural resources are not running out. Fossil fuels and most minerals are more abundant than in the past—that is, they are more readily available and cheaper than they used to be. Most resources are so plentiful that they will last for centuries.

This news may come as a surprise, especially if you remember the high prices of fuel and the energy shortages in the late 1970s. How can we say with confidence that the world is not going to run out of its important non-renewable resources? We will explain the reasons in this chapter.

RUNNING ON EMPTY?

Fear of scarcity pervades the texts. Students learn that there is only so much tin or coal or iron or oil to go around and, once used, it will be gone forever. The drumbeat is steady:

🌰 "Once nonrenewable resources are used up, their supplies are gone,"[5] says Globe's *Concepts and Challenges in Earth Science*.

🌰 "Once they [minerals] have been used, they are gone forever,"[6] says the Silver Burdett & Ginn text *General Science*.

🌰 "Once these nonrenewable energy sources (coal, oil, and natural gas) are used, they are gone,"[7] says the D. C. Heath text *Earth Science: The Challenge of Discovery*.

One reason they will be gone, say the texts, is that the United States is using too much of these resources.

🐝 "The United States has about 5 percent of the world's population. However, it uses about 60 percent of the world's natural resources,"[8] says the Holt text *American Civics.*

🐝 "The average person in a developed nation uses 80 times as much energy as the average person in a developing nation, who lives without electricity or a car,"[9] says the Addison-Wesley text *Civics: Participating in Our Democracy.*

🐝 And another asks, "How long can they [Americans] continue to abuse their natural wealth?"[10]

Youngsters are bombarded with instructions to conserve energy. Most of these are harmless and a few are useful. After all, our children should turn off the lights when they leave a room. But many texts also urge political action to cope with the supposed crisis.

🐝 Readers of the D. C. Heath text *Earth Science: The Challenge of Discovery* are asked to "think of two ways the United States could use gasoline tax money to conserve energy." (The teacher's edition explains: "The need for an international energy policy becomes apparent as students consider the multiple factors involved in worldwide energy use."[11])

🐝 "The supply of fossil fuels is being used up at an alarming rate," says the Glencoe text *Biology, An Everyday Experience.* "Governments must help save our fossil fuel supply by passing laws limiting their use."[12]

WHY THEY ARE WRONG

It is true that resources are finite, but this is largely irrelevant to human experience. Specific natural resources are limited in quantity, but in most cases the services that they provide can be supplied by other resources as well.

Throughout history, people have feared the depletion of a vital resource only to find that when the price rose, they could switch to another resource and get the same service. During the Middle Ages in Europe, charcoal from wood was the primary source of energy. As wood became more scarce, the price rose and people began to search for a substitute. Eventually, they found it in a previously worthless rock—coal. In the mid-nineteenth century, whale oil was used for lamps. As it became more difficult to find whales in the oceans, whale oil prices began to rise, and people began to fear that whale oil would disappear. According to economist J. Clayburn LaForce, however, as the price rose, people began to look for substitutes and they found one in coal oil.[13]

> People don't really want copper wire, petroleum, and electricity. They want communication over long distances, warmth in winter, and transportation.

Indeed, the steady increase in the use of coal set people worrying, too. A prominent economist, W. Stanley Jevons, said in 1865 that he doubted England's prosperity could continue once its supplies of coal were exhausted.[14]

But as the most easily mined coal was used up, the price of coal began to rise and people began searching for additional sources of energy. (They also wanted one that burned more cleanly.) Farmers in western Pennsylvania had been cursed with a black liquid substance on their land that harmed their crops and pastures, driving down the value of their land. To a few entrepreneurs, this black liquid, known as "rock oil," looked promising, and in 1859 the Pennsylvania Rock Oil Company of Titusville, Pennsylvania, successfully dug for oil. The gooey substance took the pressure off coal, and today coal is plentiful, even in England.

WHAT PEOPLE REALLY WANT

Most textbooks miss the point about natural resources. The authors think that what is important is the resource and whether it is renewable or nonrenewable. But what we want is not the resource itself, but the service provided by using the resource.

People don't really want copper wire, petroleum, and electricity; they want communication over long distances, warmth in the winter, and transportation to their homes and offices. These services can be provided by many different resources, especially as technology advances.

Consider copper. Copper is a highly efficient conductor of electricity, so it is widely used for the wiring that supplies electricity to our homes and connects our telephones. Some people think that the world faces a serious copper shortage, and that this could stunt economic growth. But we don't rely on copper the way we used to, not because it is scarce but because other materials are proving more useful.

For telephone lines, we are beginning to use fiber optic cables instead of copper wire. These glass fibers, derived from ordinary sand, can carry many more messages at a time than copper wire can. Because fiber optic cables can replace copper today, there will be less need to use copper for communication. Communication satellites have also replaced copper wire. There is little reason to doubt that we will have ample supplies of copper for generations to come.

PRICES MAKE A DIFFERENCE

People shift from one resource to another in response to changes in prices. As natural resources become scarce, their prices increase. As prices increase, several things happen.

Consumers begin to conserve. In recent history the price of oil has twice gone up dramatically. The first hike occurred after the outbreak of the Middle East War in 1973 and an oil embargo by oil-producing countries; the second occurred in the late 1970s after the overthrow of the shah of Iran. (Both events were the result of political actions, not natural shortages.)

In both cases, the higher prices caused consumers to use less energy. They turned down their thermostats in winter, turned off the air conditioning in the summer, drove less, and tuned up their cars so they would run on less fuel. As time went on, they bought more fuel-efficient automobiles and increased the insulation in their houses. These measures didn't happen all at once, but they gradually reduced the demand for oil. Consumers also shifted to substitutes. People can substitute warmer clothes for home heating, as Jimmy Carter recommended, and can replace air conditioning with fans or

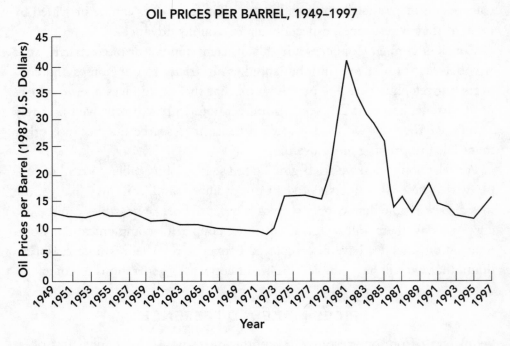

OIL PRICES PER BARREL, 1949–1997

Source: Energy Information Administration, *Annual Energy Review 1993* (Washington, D.C.: U.S. Department of Energy, 1994), Table 5.17.

fewer clothes. They can use other fuels such as coal and natural gas. In the 1970s and 1980s, people took just such steps.

The price rise also increased the incentive of producers to supply more oil. Before the embargo, the price of oil was so low that it did not encourage exploration for new oil reserves. When prices surged upward, oil exploration did, too.

In addition, price increases stimulated producers to increase supply by figuring out how to get oil from fields that had been considered dry. New techniques like slant drilling, water extraction, and deeper drilling could pay off when the price was higher.

These changes caused the price of oil to stop climbing. In fact, in the mid-1980s, to the surprise of many people, the price of oil collapsed. The average price in 1981 had reached nearly $32, but it fell to $12.51 in 1986.

(Expressed in 1998 dollars, the price fell from $57.38 in 1981 to $18.61 in 1986.)[15] During the 1990s the price fluctuated, falling below $10 in late 1998 and then rising rapidly in the first half of 1999. Even so, oil is readily available and relatively inexpensive—in spite of taxes that have been added to the price.

ANOTHER MISTAKEN IDEA: "KNOWN" RESERVES

Most of the predictions in our children's textbooks are based on a simple calculation that is used inappropriately. The textbooks report the "known" or "proven" reserves of important minerals or sources of energy. They divide this figure by the consumption per year to predict how soon we will run out.

As every geologist knows, "proven" or "known" reserves is a very limited concept. It is not meant to describe all the reserves on the planet, but those that can be recovered economically at present prices.[16] If oil costs $25 a barrel, oil that can't be extracted for less than $25 isn't counted as a reserve because no one is willing to extract it. So "known" reserves at $25 per barrel exclude a lot of oil that we know about. It would be extracted at $30 or $40 a barrel, but not at $25.

Most predictions about known reserves in our children's textbooks are based on a simple calculation that is used inappropriately.

If we began to deplete the "known reserves," prices would go up, at least temporarily. Petroleum companies would seek out additional sources, and "known" reserves would increase.

The U.S. Geological Survey (USGS) has developed estimates that reflect this fact. In addition to "known" reserves, the USGS estimates "ultimate recoverable" resources, which are 0.01 percent of the material in the top kilometer (six-tenths of a mile) of the earth's crust. It even includes the amount estimated to be in the entire Earth's crust. As the graphs indicate, when these estimates are used, the number of years until depletion of a resource goes up dramatically.[17]

For example, "known reserves" of copper are expected to last about 45 years but "ultimate recoverable" reserves would last about 340 years, and the amount in the Earth's crust represents 242,000,000 years.[18] These figures are largely ignored in the textbooks.

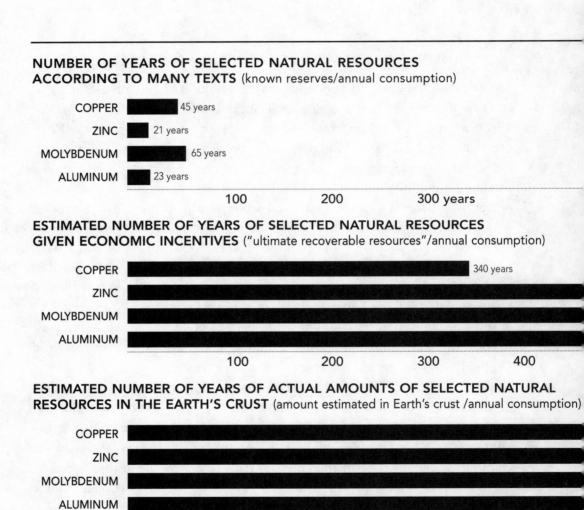

NUMBER OF YEARS OF SELECTED NATURAL RESOURCES ACCORDING TO MANY TEXTS (known reserves/annual consumption)

COPPER — 45 years
ZINC — 21 years
MOLYBDENUM — 65 years
ALUMINUM — 23 years

100   200   300 years

ESTIMATED NUMBER OF YEARS OF SELECTED NATURAL RESOURCES GIVEN ECONOMIC INCENTIVES ("ultimate recoverable resources"/annual consumption)

COPPER — 340 years
ZINC
MOLYBDENUM
ALUMINUM

100   200   300   400

ESTIMATED NUMBER OF YEARS OF ACTUAL AMOUNTS OF SELECTED NATURAL RESOURCES IN THE EARTH'S CRUST (amount estimated in Earth's crust /annual consumption)

COPPER
ZINC
MOLYBDENUM
ALUMINUM

100   200

QUESTIONS AND ANSWERS

The most important point students should understand about natural resources is that they change over time. Natural resources aren't useful until human beings figure out how to use them, and human ingenuity is constantly finding how to use new resources or old resources in new ways.[19]

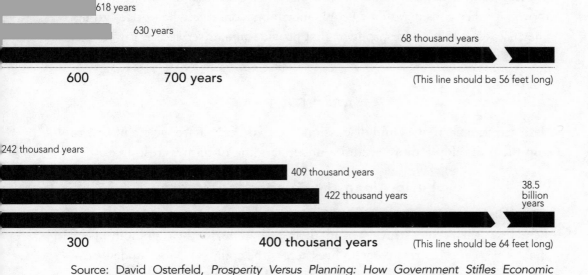

618 years

630 years

68 thousand years

600   700 years   (This line should be 56 feet long)

242 thousand years

409 thousand years

422 thousand years

38.5 billion years

300   400 thousand years   (This line should be 64 feet long)

Source: David Osterfeld, *Prosperity Versus Planning: How Government Stifles Economic Growth.* New York: Oxford University Press, 1992, 95, Table 4-5, citing William Nordhaus's data.

As long as the human mind is free to be creative and ingenious, we should not worry about depleting our natural resources.

Now you can answer some questions that young people may ask.

Are We Running Out of Natural Resources?

No. Most natural resources are plentiful. While some may become more scarce over time, price changes will cause people to find substitutes. The resources that we use will change over time. Materials that were previously unknown or neglected will provide the services we want.

How Much Oil Is Left in the Ground?

No one knows for sure. The textbooks claim that we may run out of reserves of oil and other raw materials in a specified number of years. But these estimates reflect only the reserves that can be obtained at current prices. If prices go up, "known" reserves will increase.

Should We Conserve Natural Resources?

Conservation of natural resources is a good idea but it should not be placed above all other considerations. People inevitably conserve when prices go up. They use less and look for products that provide similar services at lower cost. There is a natural tendency to conserve when something becomes scarce.

ACTIVITIES

Here are some activities and discussions that you can share with children to help them develop a more accurate understanding of natural resources.

A Trip Along the Telephone Wires

Ask students to take an imaginary trip along the telephone wires. Discuss with them how their voice travels from their telephone to their grandmother's phone (or to another relative who lives across the country). Most students can understand that the voice is converted into a fluctuating electrical current that travels along copper wires and through switching stations. Tell them that the telephone network was originally like this but it has changed.

As the number of phones, fax machines, and computers increased in recent years, more and more phone lines were needed. The price of copper wire began to be a problem for the phone companies. Phone companies wanted to find a cheaper way to send the multitude of signals. So now that same call may travel from a child's house to a satellite station, where it is converted into microwaves and transmitted to a satellite in space and then transmitted back to earth near grandmother's house, where it is converted back to electrical impulses and travels by copper wire to her telephone. Or the phone call may leave the house and be put on a fiber optic cable made of glass (which originally came from ordinary sand) and travel with thousands of other calls to a distant location.

> **Throughout history, people have feared the depletion of a vital resource only to find that when the price rose, they could switch to another resource and get the same service.**

Another way to illustrate these concepts is for young people to visit an electronics store and have the manager show them all the products that can be linked by telephone (computers, fax machines, etc.). Or they can go to the phone company and have an engineer explain how the phone network in the country works. You can also point out the various advertisements on television (AT&T, MCI, Sprint, etc.), which show how extensive our communication network is. Human ingenuity responding to higher prices has constructed a communications system that is less dependent on copper than in the past.

"Betting the Planet"

Young people may enjoy the story "Betting the Planet," which appeared in *The New York Times* in 1990.[20] Ten years earlier, at the crest of a wave of public alarm over the rising price of oil and other commodities, economist Julian Simon offered to make a wager. He challenged anyone to select a commodity and name a future date. On that date, he said, the commodity would be cheaper than it was when the bet was made (assuming that general inflation was taken into account).

If the material turned out to be more expensive, Simon would pay an agreed-upon amount. If it was cheaper, the other person would pay Simon.

Paul Ehrlich, the well-known advocate of population control, took up the challenge. He selected five metals—copper, chrome, nickel, tin, and tungsten—that he was sure would cost more in ten years because we would start running out of them. Simon bet that the prices would be lower.

By 1990, the five metals had fallen in real (that is, in inflation-adjusted) terms. Julian Simon easily won the bet.

Simon wasn't simply lucky. He knew that the prices of all major commodities have fallen over time and saw no reason to expect that process to change. When materials appear to be scarce, prices go up, but these price hikes are usually temporary. Higher prices lead consumers to look for substitutes and spur producers to seek out new sources of supply. Over time, more supply and less demand cause prices to fall.

Another Way to Look at Materials

A policy analyst, Stephen Moore, has compiled an index that illustrates how cheap some metals are today. (See the next page.) His index is based on how long it would take for a person to earn enough money to buy a pound of the metal. Instead of using the actual dollar amount, he used 100 as the figure for 1990, and based all the other numbers on the 1990 figure.

In 1980, the figure for copper was 125. That means that a person had to work 25 percent more time to earn enough money to buy a pound of copper than he or she would in 1990. (If it took 100 minutes of work for the average worker in 1990 to buy a specific amount of copper in 1990, it would have taken 125 minutes in 1980.) The table indicates that the cost of copper in terms of hours worked went down dramatically during the past century.

Sit down with children and a piece of graph paper. Using the numbers provided below, ask them to draw a graph (it could be one graph or as many as three) showing how prices, measured this way, have changed for these metals.

Discuss with these students why the price has decreased. There may be a

	Copper	Lead	Mercury
1890	928	683	1496
1900	944	651	1238
1910	568	513	1025
1920	278	324	619
1930	217	236	923
1940	158	184	1184
1950	135	215	248
1960	129	123	409
1970	155	109	532
1980	125	136	235
1990	100	100	100

Source: Stephen Moore, *Doomsday Delayed: America's Surprisingly Bright Natural Resource Future,* p. 30.

number of reasons. Demand for copper, as we have seen, fell because substitutes were cheaper. Lead is known to be dangerous, so people have been looking for alternatives to use in paint and gasoline. Also, there may have been an increase in supply of these metals. In any case, producers have more than kept pace with the demand for these metals. We can expect that progress to continue with these and with all major natural resources.

CHAPTER SIX

Are Our Forests Dying?

....

WHEN MICHAEL LIVED IN Flagstaff, Arizona, he would take his sons hiking, camping, and fishing in the forest around the city. (Most people think of Arizona as all desert, but Flagstaff is in the middle of a large green forest of ponderosa pine.) During these expeditions they sometimes passed the local lumber mill or saw logging trucks on the roads. Michael told his boys that while the forest provided recreation, it also supplied lumber for homes and jobs for loggers and mill workers.

Now the sawmill is closed, and the logging trucks are permanently parked. The men and women who worked in the forest products industry have found other work or have left town.

The mills shut down because of pressure from environmentalists. Some environmental activists believe that logging itself is bad. Textbooks, influenced by such views, often give our children a one-sided picture of logging and a completely distorted view of what our forests are like.

> Our schools, influenced by environmental activists who believe that logging is bad, give our children a one-sided picture of logging and a distorted view of what our forests are like.

NO TREES LEFT?

Our children learn that our forests are largely gone. They were cut down by greedy commercial interests, and they will never be the same again.

🐝 "Virtually all of the United States east of the Mississippi River used to be tree covered…," writes Anne Pedersen in *The Kids' Environment Book*. "We've cut most of those trees down in order to clear land for agriculture and development and to use the trees for lumber and other wood products."[1]

🐝 "Commercial interests in the United States took an especially narrow view of the forests until after World War II, seeking monetary gain with little concern for the future,"[2] says *Environmental Science: A Framework for Decision Making*.

🐝 "Large areas of forests also have been wasted," says the Merrill text *Biology: Living Systems*. "At one time, forests covered most of the eastern and western United States. These forests were cleared for farmland and much of the timber was burned or used for other purposes. By the early 1900s, it was evident that too much of this natural resource had been removed."[3]

🐝 "Americans had often been careless and very wasteful with their natural resources,"[4] says the Glencoe history text *Two Centuries of Progress*.

🐝 "What if the forests that are cut down for paper are not replanted?" asks the Merrill text *Biology: The Dynamics of Life*. "Eventually wood would become a limited resource." (Just in case students miss the point, the text shows a picture of a clearcut forest.)[5]

But was clearing land for farms and using the wood to build homes "wasteful?" After all, in the nineteenth century, people wanted farms and homes more than they wanted pristine forests full of dangerous animals. And what is the current state of our forests? The texts avoid these questions.

ARE WE RUNNING OUT OF TREES?

The premise that the nation is running out of trees is simply untrue. Every year more wood is grown in the United States than is being cut, and the number of acres planted with trees goes up nearly every year.[6] Forested land is about the same as it was in 1920, but far more timber is growing on it than at that time.[7] And in parts of the country, especially New England and the Southeast, the regeneration of forests has been dramatic.

Roger Sedjo, an economist with Resources for the Future, a respected environmental research organization, reviewed the state of American forests a few years ago. "By most criteria, U.S. forests are in excellent condition…," he wrote. "[T]here can be little doubt that the forests at the end of the 1980s were in much better condition than they were in 1920."[8]

From 1952 to 1992 annual timber harvests increased in size substantially, from 10.8 to 16.3 billion cubic feet. But in spite of these harvests, the amount of growing timber stock (that is, live trees per acre) steadily expanded. In 1992, timber volume per acre was one-third larger than it was in 1952.[9]

Regrowth has occurred in every region of the country except the West, where much of the forest is government-owned. In the East, South, and the Great Lakes states, forest expansion has been dramatic. In New Hampshire, forest cover has increased over the last one hundred years from 50 percent of the land area in the 1880s to 86 percent in the 1980s! Massachusetts, Connecticut, and Rhode Island experienced a combined increase from 35 percent to 59 percent.[10] The story of forest regeneration is a remarkable success story. Bill McKibben, a prominent environmental writer, described the regrowth in the eastern United States in a 1995 article in the *Atlantic Monthly,* "An Explosion of Green."[11] He exulted in this "mostly unnoticed renewal of the rural and mountainous East," calling it the "great environmental story of the United States, and in some ways of the whole world." Unfortunately, children are not learning about it in school.

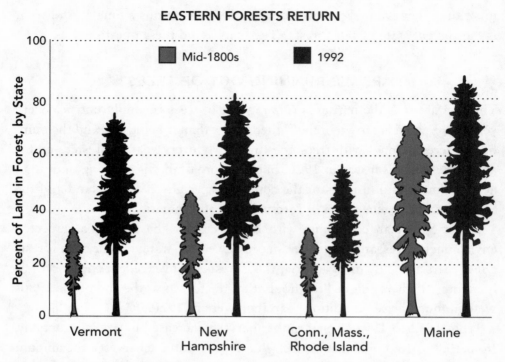

EASTERN FORESTS RETURN

Source: D. S. Powell, D. R. Darr, Z. Zhu, and D. W. MacCleery, *Forest Resources of the U.S., 1992.* General Technical Report RM-234 (USDA/Forest Service, September 1993), p. 6.

WHY SO MUCH LOGGING?

In American history texts, our young people learn that greedy lumber companies exploited America's forests by overcutting timber and that government saved the forests by establishing national parks and forests. The fact that the private sector was largely responsible for the recovery of forests after 1920 is left out.

It is true that many forests were heavily logged from colonial times to the end of the nineteenth century, but this logging should be put into perspective. When the first colonists arrived in the early 1600s, about half the continental United States was forest.[12] There was so much land and so many trees that settlers viewed forests as impediments. They cut down trees to make way for farms, towns, and cities. With trees so abundant, settlers never envisioned that there could be a shortage of wood—and, in fact, there never was.

When the country began to industrialize after 1850, wood became a valuable resource. Wood was used for fuel in early factories, for railroad ties and bridges, and for construction of houses, farms, and manufacturing centers. Logging changed. Instead of individuals clearing trees for private use, logging became an important part of the nation's industrial economy.

Some logging companies bought land and harvested its timber. But because timber was so plentiful they could not make any money from replanting. They left the land to regenerate naturally or to be used for agriculture. This created the image of greedy "cut and run" logging that is found in our children's textbooks. Yet there was not any economic reward for replanting trees for future harvest. Even Gifford Pinchot, who became the first director of the Forest Service, could not make a profit when he tried to manage timber in North Carolina.[13] The price of timber was too low to cover the full cost of replanting.

Harvesting timber from public land was extremely difficult to do legally. Most laws that allowed public land to be sold or distributed to the private sector were designed for agriculture, and sales were limited to 160 acres per person. Some logging companies unscrupulously stripped public land of trees.[14]

By 1920, the portion of U.S. land area that was forested had fallen from 40 or 50 percent of the total land area[15] to 32 percent,[16] still a large portion of our nation. Since 1920, as we have seen, large areas in the Northeast and South have returned to forest. Experts are still trying to decide whether forested area overall has increased. Clearly, however, many more trees are grown per acre and these trees produce more timber per acre.

The extensive logging of the late nineteenth century led many people to fear that all the nation's wood would someday disappear. In 1905, President Teddy Roosevelt predicted a "timber famine." Gifford Pinchot said in 1910 that the nation might have only thirty years of timber harvests left.[17]

Ironically, just as calls were being made to set aside forests to make sure that the nation didn't run out of wood, the demand for wood was beginning to abate. Total wood consumption in the United States peaked in 1907; this level of usage was not reached again for seventy years.[18]

The price of wood had begun to go up, so people starting looking for substitutes. Steel and concrete began to replace wood for building bridges. Oil and coal replaced wood as a fuel in industrial furnaces and locomotives. Railroad ties were treated to make them last longer. Market forces slowed down wood consumption.

DID THE GOVERNMENT RESCUE OUR FORESTS?

An underlying theme of textbook discussions of the forests is that the commercial sector exploited them and the government saved them.

- President Theodore Roosevelt "backed efforts to save the nation's forests by preventing short-sighted lumbering companies from overcutting," says the Glencoe text *American Odyssey: The United States in the Twentieth Century.*[19] Roosevelt felt that the nation's natural resources "must be protected from greedy private developers, eager to make a quick dollar."

- "The federal government manages and supervises the use of America's natural resources,"[20] says the Merrill text *American Government: Principles and Practices.*

As we have seen, this image oversimplifies the story of America's forests. The Forest Service was created because influential people like President Roosevelt feared that the private sector would use up all the trees and believed that only the government could manage them with a view to the future. They were mistaken about this, just as many others have mistakenly predicted the disappearance of natural resources such as minerals, coal, and oil (as we saw in chapter 5). The mistake is understandable. It came about because they didn't take into account the shifts that would occur as natural resources, including wood, became more expensive.

The Forest Service did bring management expertise to the forests that it supervised. Indeed, it was supposed to manage government timberland scientifically without influence from either politics or short-term commercial interests. But achieving this goal of "scientific," totally nonpolitical, management has been quite difficult, in fact, impossible.[21] Today the Forest Service is regularly embroiled in political controversies. Environmentalists lobby to reduce the amount of logging on national forests, while the timber industry lobbies to increase it.

Americans are not really sure what they want their Forest Service to do. Should its purpose be, as originally envisioned, "multiple use," producing timber where appropriate and also allowing recreation and human use? Or should the Forest Service curtail logging to preserve large stands of "old-growth" or "ancient" forest? These questions are the subject of frequent debate, and Forest Service policies have swung from extensive logging to extensive preservation as political forces have changed.

The impression that the government is a smoothly running machine that corrects the flaws of the private sector is not a realistic one. The Forest Service manages 140 million acres of forested land, about 19 percent of the nation's total, for a variety of uses and objectives.[22] About 90 million national forest acres have been withdrawn from timber production, either for wilderness or for some other reason.[23]

With so much acreage out of production, timber growth greatly exceeds harvest rates.[24] Superficially, this situation may seem environmentally sound, but, in fact, it is contributing to unhealthy conditions. The buildup of old trees has increased the number of catastrophic wildfires, especially in the West.[25] In addition, the cutbacks in logging shift the burden of timber production to Canada and to private forests in the eastern United States. As a result, some privately owned forests are being overcut to meet the demand.[26]

RESTORATION—A SUCCESS STORY

In the decades following 1920, America's forests regenerated dramatically. Contributing to this regeneration were the reversion of farmland to forests, a concentrated effort to fight fires, and the management of private forests as tree farms or plantations.[27]

Declines in Farming

During the 1920s and 1930s, dramatic changes occurred in farming. The Midwest and the Great Plains became the nation's breadbasket, and farming was abandoned in parts of the East and South. Forests began to replace crop-land. Between 1920 and the early 1950s, cropland in the East declined by thirty-one million acres (an area larger than the state of Pennsylvania). In the South, pines reclaimed land that had produced tobacco or cotton. In some cases the farmland was used to create tree plantations; in others, the land naturally regenerated into forest.

Fire Fighting

Fire was a serious deterrent to forest management. Until the 1940s, fires reg-ularly consumed between twenty million and fifty million acres of forest each year.[28] Wildfires could start almost anywhere in the nation's forests and spread over thousands of acres, devastating public and private land. As long

MILLIONS OF ACRES OF FOREST LOST THROUGH FIRE, 1930–1989

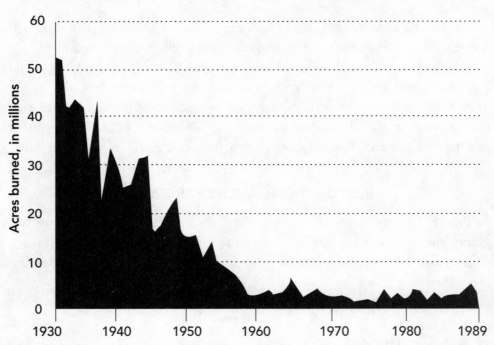

Source: D. S. Powell, D. R. Darr, Z. Zhu, and D. W. MacCleery, *Forest Resources of the U.S., 1992*. General Technical Report RM-234 (USDA/Forest Service, September 1993), p. 19.

as fires were frequent and largely uncontrolled, landowners were unlikely to plant trees for future harvest. Fire could destroy an investment overnight.

The Clark-McNary Act, passed by Congress in 1924, provided funds for fighting fires and established a system of coordinated federal and state efforts to fight fires. By the early 1960s, fire damage had generally fallen to under ten million acres per year.[29] This lower risk of fire made forest management more attractive.

Planting Trees for the Future

While forests regenerate naturally if left alone, planting speeds up the process. Planting genetically superior species can increase the quality and quantity of wood.

Beginning around 1920, foresters began to plant trees for future harvest. By the mid-1980s, foresters were planting about 2.5 million acres per year.[30] More than 80 percent of all the trees planted in America each year are planted by private companies and private timber growers.[31] Although textbooks blame the private sector for exploitation of forests in the 1800s, it is given no credit for forest restoration in the 1900s.

PRIVATE VS. PUBLIC TREE PLANTING IN THE UNITED STATES, 1950–1990

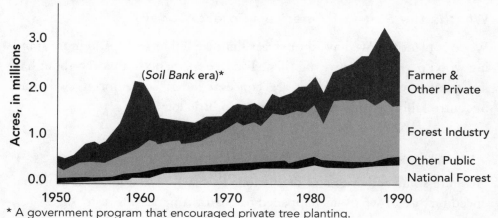

* A government program that encouraged private tree planting.

Source: D. S. Powell, D. R. Darr, Z. Zhu, and D. W. MacCleery, *Forest Resources of the U.S., 1992.* General Technical Report RM-234 (USDA/Forest Service, September 1993), p. 20.

QUESTIONS AND ANSWERS

The story of American forests is a fascinating one. It is a story of settlers arriving in a heavily forested country where there were so many trees that they were an impediment to settlement. These pioneers cleared the land and used the wood. Gradually, as wood became more scarce, prices rose. People began to look for substitutes, and the timber industry began to manage forests for the long term. Forests regenerated.

Now you are ready to answer some questions that young people may ask.

Is America Running Out of Trees?

No. The amount of wood grown increases every year, and every year more wood grows than is harvested.

Why Were So Many Trees Cut Down?

When the settlers arrived there were so many trees that it was difficult even to farm until some of them were cut. Later, wood was so widely available that it was used to build houses; for fuel in factories, ships, and railroads; and for railroad ties and commercial buildings. As long as wood was cheap and plentiful, people did not bother to replant the trees.

What Is the State of America's Forests Today?

Wood is plentiful. We have more trees than we did in 1920, and more standing wood per acre than we did then. Today, experts do not worry about having enough wood, but many are concerned that some forests will burn uncontrollably because there has been too little logging.

ACTIVITIES

Here are some activities and discussions that will give students a more balanced picture of what has happened to North America's forests.

Is "Old Growth" Better Than "New Growth"?

"Old-growth" forests are forests whose trees have not been cut or burned for a long time, perhaps several hundred years. New or "second-growth" forests have grown up after being logged or cleared by forest fires. The forests in New England that have replaced farmland are new growth, for example.

Some textbooks suggest that ancient or "old-growth" forests are better than new or "second-growth" forests. If you live near forestland, perhaps students can see for themselves if this is the case. They should find out if the forest they visit is "old-growth" or "new-growth." They should ask a park or forest ranger to discuss the differences. Some animals such as the northern spotted owl, which nests in the cavities of old trees, thrive in old-growth forests, although these owls have also been found in younger forests. Small mammals and most large game animals such as deer and moose, however, are more plentiful in younger forests. These forests usually have a greater variety of trees and plant life because the forest floor gets more sunlight than in old-growth forests.

Perhaps you have both kinds of forest in your region. If not, children can learn more about the differences through library research.

Keep in mind that forests that were never logged are not necessarily composed of old trees. Forests change. Before settlers came to the United States, forest fires were frequent. In fact, Native Americans often encouraged fires to make the land more attractive to game. So, even if the settlers had never cut down any trees, we would have forests with trees of many different ages, not simply "old-growth."

Visit a Lumberyard

Take your children to the local lumberyard to learn how consumers and suppliers respond to changing prices of wood. As prices go up, people conserve wood. By buying less wood, they leave more for others. When wood prices go down, the opposite happens. People want to use more wood, and they conserve competing materials such as plastic and steel. Because people respond to changing prices, we are not likely ever to run out of wood.

At the lumberyard:

🌲 Ask the manager how the price of lumber has changed recently. Has it gone up or down? Why?

🌲 Ask the manager to show the children the wide variety of wood products, such as plywood, hardwood veneers, particleboard, pressure-treated wood, wood pellets for wood stoves, bark for landscaping, and so on. When wood becomes expensive, suppliers develop products that make a limited amount of wood go farther. Particleboard, for example, uses small bits of cheap wood but is as strong as more expensive lumber. Hardwood veneers—thin layers of wood that are glued on top of less-expensive plywood—make attractive furniture cheaper than it would be if solid hardwood lumber were used throughout.

🌲 Ask the manager to point out nonwood products that also extend the life of wood or enable people to use less wood. Paints and preservatives protect wood outside. Steel strapping and holders strengthen wood construction. Drywall replaces wood paneling inside homes. Steel studs are used in the walls of homes and office buildings.

Timber Growth and Cutting in the United States

Ask young people to study the following graph and then ask them a few questions. The graph should reassure them that the United States is growing more timber than it is cutting. The United States is not running out of trees.

1. Was more timber grown or logged in 1920?

More timber was logged.

2. What would happen if the 1920 trend had continued until 1986?

The United States would begin to run out of timber.

U.S. TIMBER GROWTH AND REMOVALS, 1920–1991

☐ Net Growth   ■ Removals

Source: D. S. Powell, D. R. Darr, Z. Zhu, and D. W. MacCleery, *Forest Resources of the U.S., 1992*. General Technical Report RM-234 (USDA/Forest Service, September 1993), p. 16.

3. In 1952, was more timber grown or cut?

More timber was grown than cut.

4. What trend was established for the amount of timber cut and grown between 1952 and 1991?

For every year given on the graph, more timber was grown than cut.

5. If this trend continues, what will be the result in the future?

The United States will continue to have a supply of timber into the future.

CHAPTER SEVEN

The Rain Forest— One Hundred Acres a Minute?

·····························

AROUND THE GLOBE AT the equator lies a hot, humid, tropical belt of land, much of it covered by canopies of leafy trees. The understory teems with rich vegetation, exotic birds, a myriad of small mammals, and a multitude of insects.

This is the rain forest. And just about every schoolchild learns that it is in danger.

- An area the "size of the state of Nebraska is stripped of trees every year,"[1] says the Silver Burdett & Ginn text *World Geography: People in Time and Place*.

- One hundred acres of rain forest are destroyed every minute, says *50 Simple Things Kids Can Do to Save the Earth*. This is "enough to fill 50 football fields."[2]

- "Some experts predict that if present practices continue, one-third of the world's tropical forests will vanish by the year 2000," says Scott

Foresman's *History and Life*. "Other experts believe that all of the world's tropical rain forests could be gone by the turn of the century unless the deforestation is halted."[3]

It isn't just that forests are being converted to cropland, these books say. The soil is soon exhausted since its nutrients have been absorbed by the trees and other vegetation. "Thus, within a few years, land once covered by awe-inspiring forest is reduced to useless wasteland," sums up Prentice Hall's *World Geography*.[4]

North Americans are partly responsible for this devastation, the books say.

- "You can help save rain forests by not buying rain-forest woods such as teak and mahogany," says *Environmental Science*.[5]

- Cattle ranches are replacing the rain forest, says *The Kids' Environment Book*. "Remember, the next Big Mac you eat may have started life as a cow in Brazil,"[6] it says.

- "Do you think a boycott of fast-food companies would halt the destruction of rain forests?" asks *Focus on Life Science*. "Would you be willing to participate in such a boycott?"[7]

A MORE OBJECTIVE LOOK

Deforestation usually refers to the complete conversion of forest to cropland or other uses. Sometimes the wood from the forest is logged; at other times, trees are burned to clear the land.

Deforestation is a legitimate concern. However, the problem should be viewed objectively, not sensationally. One textbook, *Environmental Science: A Framework for Decision Making,* indicates that there are differences of opinion about the severity of the problem[8] and includes an essay arguing that the extent of deforestation is exaggerated. But most textbooks tell only the scary part of the story.

Some conversion of the rain forest is not a bad thing. As we saw in chapter 8, the United States experienced extensive forest clearing in the late nineteenth century. Many prominent people, including President Theodore Roosevelt, feared a "timber famine." They thought that the nation would run out of wood. But the "timber famine" never materialized. As prices rose, demand for wood declined, and supply increased. In addition, public and private efforts combined to encourage better forest management.

Deforestation is a legitimate concern. However, the problem should be viewed objectively, not sensationally.

"It is clear," wrote resource economists Roger A. Sedjo and Marion Clawson in an important review of the state of forests, "that dynamic growing societies will generate pressures on and changes in the forest resource base."[9] The widespread clearing of tropical forests is likely to be temporary.

The textbooks are somewhat misleading about the estimates of rain forest clearing. Sedjo and Clawson, relying on numbers provided by the Food and Agriculture Organization of the United Nations, report that during the 1980s about 59,459 square miles of forest were cleared per year.[10] This is about 0.8 percent of the tropical forest, and is in line with the many textbook estimates.

But these figures include all types of forests and vegetation in tropical areas, not just tropical rain forests. Children aren't told that tropical areas have six vegetation zones: tropical rain forests, moist deciduous forests, dry deciduous forests, very dry forests, desert zones, and hill and low-mountain zones.[11] As the table on the next page indicates, tropical rain forests are less than half the total forest in every area except Asia.

- So when books claim that "100 acres a minute" of rain forests are being destroyed, the actual figure is more like 21 acres a minute.

- When they say that rain forests the size of Nebraska are being destroyed every year, the actual number is about one-fourth that area or less than the combined areas of Vermont and New Hampshire.

Texts also mislead students by an almost complete failure to discuss the planting of new trees. In Asia, 10 percent of the total forest area is in forest plantations, and one acre of trees is planted for every two that are cut.[12] In Latin America, even though tree plantations represent less than 1 percent of total forest area, about one-third of Latin America's output of wood for industrial use comes from them.[13] The table below gives a more complete picture.

WORLD TROPICAL FOREST DATA

	Tropical Forests (all forest types)		Rain Forests			Tree Planting (all forest types)	
	Total Forest as % of Land Area	Deforesta-tion (annual)	Rain forest as % of Total Forest	Rain forest Deforesta-tion (annual)	Ratio of Total Forest /Rain Forest Deforesta-tion* (in acres)	Tree Plant-ing as % of Total For-est	Ratio of Deforesta-tion/Tree Planting ** (in acres)
Africa	24%	0.7%	16%	0.54%	184/1	.57%	32/1
Asia & Pacific	35%	1.2%	57%	1.2%	82/1	10.0%	2/1
Latin America & Caribbean	56%	0.8%	49%	0.42%	234/1	.94%	12/1
Total	37%	0.8%	41%	0.63%	158/1	2.5%	6/1

Source: United Nations, *Forest Resources Assessment 1990, Tropical Countries #112,* Food and Agriculture Organization of the United Nations, Tables 3, 4, 7, 8.

*For example, in Africa, for every 184 acres of rain forest, 1 acre was cut.

** For example, in Africa, for every 32 acres cut, one acre of new trees was planted.

WHAT CAUSES DEFORESTATION?

Textbooks identify many causes of deforestation. "The three main causes of tropical deforestation are subsistence agriculture, commercial logging, and cattle ranching," says the textbook *Environment.*[14] Others emphasize overpopulation and poverty, especially in Brazil,[15] and, as we have seen, overconsumption, especially of beef, by the developed world.

It seems to be easier to blame the Western world than to concede that governments of some countries are bringing on the problems themselves. Yet Robert Repetto, an analyst with the World Resources Institute, an environmental think tank, points out a number of policies that are contributing to deforestation:[16]

- In Malaysia, the Philippines, and the Brazilian Amazon, sometimes the only way to obtain ownership of land is to clear it and cultivate it.[17]

- In Indonesia, the government gave companies generous tax concessions to encourage logging.[18]

- Often "migration to forested regions has been seen as a means of relieving overcrowding and landlessness in settled agricultural regions. . . ."[19]

In 1989, Dennis J. Mahar, an economic adviser for the World Bank, reported on policies of the Brazilian government that encouraged deforestation:[20]

- Beginning in the 1960s, the government took major steps to open up the Amazon region to keep out immigrants from neighboring Peru and Venezuela.[21]

- The government started massive road-building programs (with the help of the World Bank).

- The government subsidized settlers who would clear land for agriculture. [22]

- The government subsidized loans for farming and created special tax breaks for cattle-raising.[23] (In spite of these extensive tax credits, few of the cattle ranches are actually profitable, says Mahar. In fact, says John O. Browder of Tulane University, without government subsidies, "producing rain forest beef would be a financial impossibility."[24])

Such policies far outweigh the impact of Americans eating hamburgers or using too much wood.

SOME GOOD NEWS

Some positive developments have occurred that should make children feel better about the future of rain forests around the world. They include:

- Timber volume in the temperate climates (that is, not the tropics) is increasing rapidly, including in the former Soviet Union and Canada.[25] In the United States, more timber is grown each year than is cut.[26] The world is not running out of wood or trees.

- Wood production in Latin America is undergoing a major transition, say Sedjo and Clawson. Trees are being grown as crops in tree farms or plantations, where trees that are cut are continually replaced by new plantings.[27]

- Detrimental policies of governments and the World Bank are beginning to change, and private conservation organizations around the world are taking action to protect the rain forest. For example, they have worked with the governments of countries that have rain forests to create "debt-for-nature" swaps.

"DEBT-FOR-NATURE" SWAPS

"Debt-for-nature" swaps are ways that private individuals around the world can help protect the rain forest or other areas of environmental concern. They emerged some years ago to give governments an incentive to protect resources.

Many countries in the tropics engaged in heavy borrowing, especially during the 1970s, and are having trouble paying back these debts. Private environmental organizations like the Nature Conservancy and the World

Wildlife Fund raise funds and then offer to pay a portion of a country's debts to other governments or banks.

If they pay off a bond owed by the government, for example, they receive in return the right to the interest that the government pays on the bond. This interest can be used to protect an environmental resource. Twenty-one debt-for-nature swaps had been made by the end of 1991, most of them in Costa Rica and Ecuador.

"Debt for nature" swaps are ways that private individuals around the world can help protect the rain forest or other areas of environmental concern.

No one knows how significant swaps will be. Economists Robert T. Deacon and Paul Murphy point out that they represent a small amount of money (about $100 million) compared to the total debt of these countries. Also, there is no way to make governments carry out their part of the agreement if they don't wish to. But such swaps do provide an avenue for protection of the rain forest that wasn't there before.[28] One swap between the World Wildlife Fund and Ecuador created a conservation fund that was twice as large as the government's budget for parks.[29]

In the years ahead, we may see other innovative ideas as concerned people around the world offer funds for protection of special places. If preserving the rain forest is important to people in the rest of the world, it seems fair for them to help do it.

"LUNGS OF THE EARTH?"

When forests are cleared by burning, the fires release huge quantities of carbon dioxide into the air. Textbooks claim that this will increase global warming. And once the trees are cut down, they can no longer produce oxygen and absorb carbon dioxide through photosynthesis.

 "Destruction of vegetation reduces photosynthesis, and carbon dioxide levels in the atmosphere may increase," says *Biology Today*. "Some scientists predict this may contribute to a greenhouse effect—a global warming of the Earth's surface."[30]

🌰 The Scott Foresman text *History and Life* says that the rain forests "currently produce about 40 percent of all the oxygen that we breathe." If they are destroyed, carbon dioxide will build up in the atmosphere.[32]

🌰 The *Kids' Environment Book: What's Awry and Why* states that between 1 billion and 2.5 billion tons of carbon dioxide are added to the air every year as a result of deforestation. This is between one-fourth and one-half of all carbon dioxide released annually worldwide.[33]

It is true that burning trees adds carbon dioxide to the atmosphere. Burning releases carbon from the trees, which then combines with oxygen to form carbon dioxide. In 1989 Richard A. Houghton and George M. Woodwell estimated that deforestation could add between 0.4 and 2.5 billion tons of carbon each year (in the form of carbon dioxide) to the air. But these are guesses with a wide range of uncertainty, and they pale in comparison to the 100 billion tons that Houghton and Woodwell say are emitted by plants and soil through a process called respiration.[34]

Are Americans exploiting the forest by eating too much meat? No.

Calling rain forests the "lungs of the earth," as curriculum material published by Zaner-Bloser does,[35] or saying that the rain forests produce 40 percent of the world's oxygen implies that clearing the forests will affect our ability to breathe. And children take this message literally. Children have been known to make gasping sounds when they see paper littering the road—they have the idea that paper, which comes from trees, is taking oxygen out of the air.

Trees do contribute oxygen to the atmosphere through photosynthesis, but their contribution represents only a small part of the total amount of oxygen in the air. (Oxygen represents slightly more than 20 percent of our atmosphere.)

And while burning does add carbon dioxide, logging itself does not. (Some carbon dioxide is released from the soil after logging, however.) When trees are made into wood and used for construction of houses, their carbon is retained as long as the logs remain. The textbooks do not make this point.

SPECIES—EXTINCT BEFORE THEY ARE COUNTED?

Children are told that thousands of plant and animal species will become extinct due to the loss of the rain forests.

- "Scientists estimate that no fewer than one out of every two species on our planet dwells in the rain forest," says Prentice Hall's *World Geography.* "Many of these species have yet to be discovered. It is also estimated that one species of plant or animal life becomes extinct every day due to the cutting and burning."[36]

- "Scientists estimate that over 100 species of plants in these forests are becoming extinct each day," reports Merrill's *Biology: An Everyday Experience.*[37]

- Life-saving medicines will be lost. Linda Schwartz's book *Earth Book for Kids: Activities to Help Heal the Environment* says that the rain forests have plants that are used in 25 percent of all drugs and 70 percent of drugs used in cancer treatments.[38]

It is true that many medicines, perhaps one-fourth of all prescription drugs,[39] are derived from rain forest plants. But once the drugs have been identified, they can usually be made synthetically.

It is possible that some important genetic material could be lost if species disappear with the rain forest. Some steps are being taken to protect these resources. Drug companies recognize that the tropics may contain the raw material for future drugs.

In 1991, Merck & Co. arranged to pay $1 million to the Instituto Nacional de Biodiversidad (INBio), a conservation and science group in Costa Rica that is trying to identify and catalog the country's plants, insects, and microorganisms. In return, Merck received exclusive rights to review samples from INBio for possible commercial applications for two years.[40]

In spite of many claims, no one actually knows how many species are being lost in the rain forests or elsewhere in the world. This complicated issue is the subject of chapter 9.

QUESTIONS AND ANSWERS

You are now ready to talk with your students about the rain forest. You will find it easier now to answer some of their questions. For example:

Will the Rain Forest Disappear?

No, although it is currently under pressure. Some tropical countries are experiencing what the United States experienced about one hundred years ago—widespread logging and conversion of forest to other uses. But that was a temporary phase for us, and it should be temporary for the rain forest, too.

Are Americans Exploiting the Rain Forest by Eating Too Much Meat?

No. Cattle can be raised in many different places, not just a former rain forest. Many cattle ranches in Brazil were created largely through government subsidies. These subsidies have more impact on deforestation than whether Americans eat hamburger or not.

Is Deforestation Destroying the Oxygen We Need to Breathe?

No. Vegetation does produce oxygen through photosynthesis, but its contribution is a small part of the total oxygen in the atmosphere.

Does Deforestation Contribute to Global Warming?

Deforestation by burning does contribute some carbon dioxide to the atmosphere, and some people think the increases in carbon dioxide are causing warmer temperatures. No one knows how much carbon dioxide deforestation adds, however, and we're not sure that increases in carbon dioxide will cause significant global warming. (We'll discuss that in chapter 11.)

ACTIVITIES

Here are some activities and discussions that you might like to share with young people.

What a Map Can Tell Us

The map on the following page can help children better envision the size of the Brazilian rain forest.

The round shape of the world sometimes causes maps to convey an inaccurate impression of size. Areas near the poles sometimes look larger than areas near the Equator. We have drawn two maps to the same scale and superimposed the map of the United States on a map of South America. This should help children see just how big Brazil is. Destruction of the rain forest is a serious concern, but students should have an accurate view of this problem.

Living in a Poor Country

The textbooks sometimes cite subsistence farming or "slash-and-burn" agriculture as a cause of deforestation. But they don't really explain why such agriculture causes deforestation.

Ask young people to imagine that they live in a country where the only way to obtain farmland is to clear it. Their family clears a section of forest by cutting it and then burning it. The fires put the nutrients that were in the trees back into the soil, which helps crops to grow.

After a few years, some of the major nutrients are used up. It would be possible to restore some nutrients through the use of fertilizer and modern farming techniques.[41] But the family could travel a few miles to another area and clear that land, too. Which will the family do?

It may be easier to move away and clear more land than to nurture the soil in land that has already been cleared. In some places, lack of private ownership contributes to deforestation. If no one owns the land, no one will take care to replenish the soil.

SIZE OF THE UNITED STATES RELATIVE TO BRAZIL

Visit a Hardwood Lumberyard

Most cities have lumberyards that specialize in hardwoods such as oak, mahogany, and teak. These woods are valued for their strength, durability, or beauty, and are used for furniture and decoration. Some of these woods come from the rain forest.

Visit such a lumberyard (look under "Hardwoods" in the Yellow Pages) and ask the owner or manager to show your children the different kinds of wood and tell them where they come from. If they come from Latin America or Asia, ask the manager to explain why the wood comes from so far away. Is the manager concerned that deforestation may lead to the disappearance of the wood? The manager, of course, is not an expert on tropical deforestation, but his or her perspective will help young people look more realistically at the issue of using too much wood from the rain forest.

CHAPTER EIGHT

American Wildlife— On the Edge?

....

EIGHT-YEAR-OLD HUNTER ALLEN was fascinated by bats. One day he learned that bats had been found in the attic of a community center near his home in Huntington, Massachusetts. The people restoring the building wanted the bats to move out.

Hunter worried that the bats might be killed or have a hard time finding a place to live. But he had read in the National Wildlife Federation's magazine *Ranger Rick* that it is possible to make homes for bats. So Hunter wrote for instructions, got a few other Cub Scouts to help him, and asked a lumber company to donate some wood. They made "bat boxes" and, with the help of Hunter's mother, nailed five boxes on the side of the community center for the bats.[1]

Practical suggestions for helping animals, such as this one, are rare in our schools. The textbooks create an image of a world about to lose large numbers of species. They make the job of saving species or helping wild animals seem overwhelming and a task that only the government can handle.

Textbooks paint a grim picture of wildlife in the United States.

🐝 Wildlife "has decreased sharply as the human population has grown,"[2] says the Holt text *Biology Today*.

🐝 The Merrill text *Focus on Life Science* notes that "in recent years, many wildlife populations have been decreasing, largely due to changes in environment."[3]

🐝 "[T]he growth of cities and suburbs has led to the destruction of the natural habitats of many types of plants and animals,"[4] says the Prentice Hall text *Biology: The Study of Life*.

🐝 "[H]unters have devastated many species,"[5] states the Prentice Hall text *World Geography*. (Often children are left with the impression that all hunting is bad and should be stopped.)

EXTINCTION—MOSTLY OUT OF DATE IN THE UNITED STATES

Much of what our children learn is out of date. It is true that during the nineteenth century in North America, wildlife numbers declined. Some species, such as the passenger pigeon and the heath hen, disappeared entirely, and others, such as the grizzly bear, remain reduced in numbers. But the rebound of many species has been dramatic and largely unreported:

🐝 The beaver, which once ranged over the entire continental United States, almost disappeared except for places in the Rocky Mountains and Pacific Northwest. Now the beaver is found in all states except Hawaii.[6]

🐝 The population of pronghorn antelopes dropped from thirty million or forty million to reach a mere thirteen thousand in 1930, but it has recovered to over one million today.[7]

🐝 Wild turkeys, found in only a few southern states in the 1930s, are now found in forty-three states.[8]

In sum, says Winston Harrington, writing for the research organization Resources for the Future, many game species are "more numerous today than 80 to 100 years ago"[9] and migratory birds such as the trumpeter swan, the whooping crane, and the peregrine falcon have made dramatic recoveries.[10]

> While the California condor and the black-footed ferret are close to extinction, the grizzly bear and the wolf are not, although some populations may be endangered.

A few animals, including the California condor and the black-footed ferret, are still close to extinction. In most cases, however, the animals we hear so much about—the grizzly bear and the wolf, for example—are not in danger of extinction. Rather, populations are endangered in certain places.

The federal government has designated grizzly bears as a threatened species in the lower forty-eight states, but the population is healthy in Alaska and much of Canada.

Wolves, which were exterminated earlier in this century in Yellowstone National Park,[11] were recently reintroduced there. But viable populations of wolves also exist in Canada and elsewhere in the northern United States.

Along the Columbia River and its tributaries in the northwestern United States, salmon populations are at risk due to dams on the rivers and overfishing in the ocean. But Alaska has experienced record-high runs of wild salmon in recent years.[12]

DEPLETION AND RESTORATION

The history of wildlife in North America is a lot like the history of its forests. It is a story of abundance followed by depletion, and depletion followed by restoration.

The texts recognize that loss of habitat and overhunting led to the decline and extinction of animals in the 1800s. But they ignore the more funda-mental reason: the absence of incentives to maintain wildlife populations. Early on, supplies of wild game seemed virtually inexhaustible, and no one thought it was important to restrict access to wildlife through laws or regu-lations. In fact, such restrictions reminded Americans of the Old World class structure that had discriminated against peasant hunters.

Early on, supplies of wild game seemed inexhaustible. Restricting access to wildlife was unthinkable.

In the early days of our country, wild animals were viewed as free for the taking. They represented a common pool of animals that could be taken at will. By and large, the only limit on hunting and trapping was the ability of the hunter or trapper to kill game.

Unlike livestock, game animals were not fenced in and may have migrated over large territories. Property rights existed only for dead animals. Thus, settlers and hunters had no incentive—or ability—to conserve live animals. If they did, someone else could kill any animals they left. Thus, hunters had an incentive to kill as much game as possible.

As the U.S. population moved westward, settlers cleared the forests for farms, and the habitat for wildlife changed. Animals that require large areas in which to roam had a more difficult time. Grizzly bear territories extend for thirty miles, for example, and salmon use entire rivers. Settlers also hunted and trapped animals, and commercial hunters killed game to sell as food. Over time, this hunting reduced the numbers of many animal species, including the beaver, bison, passenger pigeon, wood duck, heath hen, and others. The common pool of wildlife became seriously depleted. Wildlife experienced the "tragedy of the commons" (discussed in chapter 3).

Only a few animal species actually became extinct. Charles Mann and Mark Plummer say that five birds disappeared as a result of commercial hunting and forest clearing east of the Mississippi and around the Great Lakes. They were the ivory-billed woodpecker, the passenger pigeon, the Carolina parakeet, the heath hen, and the Bachman's warbler.[13]

Still, many populations were severely reduced in numbers. The stories of the passenger pigeon and the bison are particularly striking.

Passenger Pigeon

The passenger pigeon was so common in the early 1800s that no one thought it could ever die out. In 1810, naturalist Alexander Wilson saw a flock in Kentucky that he claimed contained more than 2 billion birds. (He estimated the flock to be a mile wide and 240 miles long.)[14] The flocks darkened the sky as they passed over.

Since the birds required so much food and space, the advance of settlements undoubtedly affected their numbers by reducing their habitat. But commercial hunting was a big factor, too. Hunters shot pigeons and shipped them east for sale, much as farmers ship chickens around the country today. During a forty-day period in 1869 three rail cars full of pigeons were shipped to market daily from Hartford, Michigan. Nearly twelve million birds were shipped during that time. And over a two-year period nearly sixteen million birds were shipped from another Michigan town.[15]

By 1890, the passenger pigeon was rare. The last one died at the Cincinnati Zoo in 1914.[16]

Hunters shot pigeons and shipped them east for sale, much as farmers ship chickens around the country today.

Bison (or Buffalo)

Great herds of bison (also known as the American buffalo) roamed the Great Plains during the early nineteenth century. Like the passenger pigeon, they were a common pool of animals that anyone could kill. With no one to protect them, they almost disappeared.

When bison became extremely rare in the mid-1880s, a few people took steps to save them. One was a naturalist, Ernest Harold Baynes, who formed the American Bison Society in 1905. This organization helped establish the National Bison Range in Montana.[17]

There are at least 130,000 bison in the United States today, on both public and private lands. While national parks such as Yellowstone protect bison herds, one reason the bison numbers are growing is that people want to eat bison meat, which is leaner than beef. Because the herds are owned, markets lead to their growth in numbers, not their destruction.

ALARM AT THE TURN OF THE CENTURY

During the late 1800s, many people became alarmed at the disappearance of wildlife. Bison were rescued, as we have seen. The National Audubon Society was formed to protect birds, especially egrets, whose plumes often decorated women's fancy hats. The Audubon movement advocated legislation to protect birds and conducted campaigns to educate the public, trying to arouse moral indignation against the plume trade. Audubon also created a system of private wardens who protected wildlife in key areas and it established a network of private wildlife refuges.[18]

When bison became extremely rare in the mid-1880s, a few people took steps to save them. They formed the American Bison Society in 1905. Today there are at least 130,000 bison in the U.S., on both public and private lands.

In response to the changing public mood, state and federal governments also took action. By 1880, game and fish departments, supported by hunting and fishing license fees, were established in every state then in the Union. The federal precursor to the Fish and Wildlife Service was formed in 1885.[19] These agencies did many things to protect wildlife. They established hunting seasons, set hunting limits, outlawed commercial hunting, established game and wildlife refuges, and began restoring animals to their original ranges. Stricter enforcement of trespass laws also reduced hunting.

As time went on, more federal laws were passed to protect wildlife. For example, the Pittman-Robertson Act, enacted by Congress in 1937, taxed the sale of guns and ammunition and gave the funds to the states for wildlife restoration. It also set professional standards for state wildlife personnel.

Indeed, today fees for hunting licenses support most state fish and game departments. Federal excise taxes on hunting guns and ammunition and fees for duck licenses have been used to acquire millions of acres of federal wildlife refuge lands.

ESA—FRIEND OR FOE?

Children's textbooks often cite the Endangered Species Act (ESA) as an effective way to protect endangered species. While some texts point out that the act has aroused controversy, they consider it at least a step in the right direction.

- The act "embodies an encouraging attitude toward nature that has now become public policy," says one text.[20]

- The "power and controversy" of the act is illustrated by the story of the Tellico Dam, says another. (In 1978, discovery of the snail darter, a small fish that appeared to be endangered, halted construction of a dam in Tennessee. Congress passed a law allowing the dam to be built, anyway.)

- "The Fish and Wildlife Service has found that the the most effective way to save most species is to protect their habitats,"[21] says another. Protecting endangered species "may mean restricting human use of some areas," it continues.[22]

Some textbooks recognize that the Endangered Species Act has been controversial, since it has prevented government agencies and private individuals from activities such as building and farming in certain areas.

What the books don't say is that the act may be harming the species it seeks to protect.

Suppose a homeowner discovers a painting by Rembrandt in his attic. Most people would be thrilled to find such a treasure and would protect it. But suppose the owner was required to convert his or her home into a museum and display the painting for the benefit of the public, while paying all the costs. Most of us would consider this unfair. And the homeowner might be tempted to burn the painting before anyone found out about it.[23]

Now consider what happens if a landowner finds an endangered animal species on his or her property—something the owner might view as valuable, like an Old Master painting. The landowner will have to protect the species—following strict rules of the Fish and Wildlife Service—without compensation.

These restrictions could lead some people to destroy such an animal before anyone finds out about it. (This practice has been described as "shoot, shovel, and shut-up.") Or perhaps the landowner would do something to the land to make it unattractive for the species. While such action is deplorable, we should at least understand it. It helps explain why the Endangered Species Act has not been very successful in accomplishing its objectives.

THE SPOTTED OWL: HOW THREATENED?

Many people assume that the spotted owl—which has been in the news for some years—is headed for extinction unless we make heroic efforts to protect it. But this is unlikely. For one thing, the northern spotted owl—the subject of controversy in the Pacific Northwest—is a subspecies. There are two other spotted owl subspecies, the California and the Mexican.

Second, the northern spotted owl may be more adaptable than we think. The northern spotted owl (like its relatives) nests in the cavities of old trees. People fear that if old trees are cut down, there may not be enough places for the owl to nest. But Lowell Diller, a zoologist for the Simpson Timber Co., has found high densities of spotted owls on redwood forests owned by Simpson, even though less than 2 percent of these forests are old-growth.[1]

The "Thomas Committee," which advised the Fish and Wildlife Service on the owl, also had some optimistic information about the owl. The committee (headed by Jack Ward Thomas, who later became head of the Forest Service) concluded that the northern spotted owl would not disappear completely in the Northwest even if no action were taken. Its numbers would fall to 739 pairs of owls. But if it were listed as threatened (and then given protection by restrictions on logging), its numbers could reach 1,820 pairs.[2]

For some people what is really important is not the owl, but old-growth

Only twenty-seven species, out of about fourteen hundred U.S. species listed, had been delisted by early 1995. Of these, only eight could be described as "success stories." (Some of the delistings were for errors in the original listing.)[24] At best, the act has led to a greater awareness of endangered species and has helped a few high-profile species, such as the whooping crane, but this kind of record cannot be called a rousing success.

trees. In a now-famous statement, Andy Stahl of the Sierra Club Legal Defense Fund said in 1988: "Thank goodness the spotted owl evolved in the Pacific Northwest, for if it hadn't, we'd have to genetically engineer it."[3] Stahl was joking, but his comment reveals that the spotted owl is a tool for protecting old-growth forest.

President Clinton approved a plan that will preserve large areas of old-growth forest for the owl. Most of this is public land, but private landowners, too, must restrict logging.

Will this achieve the goal of protecting spotted owls? Perhaps. But environmental writer Robert J. Smith is not so sure.

"Who would attempt to aid the recovery or expansion of the spotted owl?" he asks. "To do anything to make one's lands attractive to a threatened or endangered species would subject the owner to the strong likelihood of having the use of his property restricted and its economic value reduced." A much fairer approach, he says, would be for the government to buy land that it considers necessary for the spotted owl.[4]

1. Donald R. Leal, "Unlocking the Logjam Over Jobs and Endangered Animals," *San Diego Union-Tribune*, April 18, 1993, G-4.
2. Robert H. Nelson, "Rethinking Federal Forest Management," Working Paper 90-34, Political Economy Research Center, Bozeman, Montana, January 1991, 9.
3. Quoted in Randy Fitzgerald, "The Great Spotted Owl War," *Reader's Digest*, November 1992, 92.
4. Robert J. Smith, "The Endangered Species Act: Saving Species or Stopping Growth?" *Regulation*, Winter 1992, 85.

WHO IS SAVING SPECIES?

The somewhat grim facts about the ESA do not mean that species cannot recover. Some species have rebounded through public and private conservation efforts. Your children may not know about the following:

Peregrine Falcons

The peregrine falcon was close to extinction in the 1970s when Dr. Thomas Cade of Cornell University and his associates began captive breeding. Some environmentalists and government officials objected to their decision to raise falcons rather than try to let them breed in the wild, but they persisted.

Through his efforts—and, most scientists believe, through the elimination of DDT use in the United States—the peregrine has rebounded. Peregrines nest on skyscrapers and under major bridges.[25] The bird was taken off the endangered species list in 1999.

Bluebirds

Bluebirds nest in holes in old trees and fence posts. Bluebird numbers were declining in the 1970s because older trees had been cut down and because sparrows and starlings were competing for the spaces. In recent years, members of the North American Bluebird Society have put up thousands of bluebird nest boxes, and bluebird populations are recovering.[26]

Ducks

Many organizations, some of them supported by hunters, protect and restore habitat for ducks. Although taxes paid by hunters enable state and federal conservation agencies to acquire duck habitat, private organizations are a significant force in habitat protection:

 Since 1937, Ducks Unlimited has preserved or restored six million acres of wetlands in the United States and Canada. This organization, which has 550,000 members, works with private landowners to develop duck nesting areas and preserve wetlands.[27]

🦋 The Delta Waterfowl Foundation (headquartered in Deerfield, Illinois) protects ducks with its "Adopt a Pothole" program. It pays farmers in the United States and central Canada to maintain the shallow depressions or "potholes" in farmland that provide nesting places for waterfowl.[28]

🦋 The Delta Wildlife Foundation (headquartered in Stoneville, Mississippi) works with farmers to maintain wetland areas. It sponsors and places boxes for wood ducks and helps restock Canada geese. It encourages other environmental actions, too, from planting food plots for deer to building and distributing bluebird nest boxes.

Deer and Elk

Deseret Land and Livestock is a 200,000-acre ranch in Utah that welcomes deer and elk while also raising domestic livestock. The ranch has dramatically increased its wild deer and elk herds. It receives fees from hunters who are willing to pay to hunt because they can be sure of success. The ranch has supplied elk to public hunting lands owned by the Utah state government.[29] And the Rocky Mountain Elk Foundation, headquartered in Missoula, Montana, helps acquire habitat for elk.

Hawks

In the 1930s, the government of Pennsylvania paid bounties for killing certain kinds of hawks that were considered a nuisance. Hawk Mountain in eastern Pennsylvania was a major flyway for hawks and a favorite spot for hunters to gather and shoot them. Concerned about the killing, Rosalie Edge raised the funds to buy 1,400 acres of the mountain. She closed the land to hunters and created Hawk Mountain Sanctuary. It exists today as an educational and conservation center specializing in birds of prey.[30] Located between Allentown and Harrisburg, the sanctuary is well worth visiting (telephone: 610-756-6961).

Salmon

Environmentalists in the Northwest are finding new ways to protect wild salmon. In hot summers, streams where salmon spawn can dry up due to lack of rain and to farmers and ranchers who divert water from the stream for irrigation. To keep the water flowing, environmentalists have begun buying the rights to the water and leaving the water in the stream. The farmers are compensated for the loss of their crops, and the water continues to protect and nurture fish. One group that does this is the Oregon Water Trust in Portland, Oregon.

QUESTIONS AND ANSWERS

The state of wildlife in American is much better than the textbooks imply. Despite the growth of cities and towns, an enormous amount of land has been converted from farmland to wildlife habitat, as we discussed in chapter 8, and many people are devoting their lives to protecting wildlife. The outlook for wildlife preservation in the United States is more promising than our children are led to believe.

Now you are ready to answer some questions young people may ask.

Are We Losing Species in the United States?

Yes, we have lost some and we may lose a few more. Some species, such as the California condor, may not be able to recover, despite enormous effort. However, many animals are recovering. Others, such as wolves and grizzly bears, are endangered in some areas but are doing well in others.

Why Did the Passenger Pigeon Become Extinct?

The passenger pigeon was once so abundant that no one thought protecting it was necessary. But much of the pigeon's forest habitat was cleared, and because the pigeon was part of the common pool of wildlife, the "tragedy of the commons" contributed to its demise. (See chapter 3 for a discussion of the "tragedy of the commons.") Anyone who held back from killing it for food could not preserve it for the future because someone else could kill it. With no owners to protect the pigeons, hunters killed them in great numbers. In addition, the pigeon's habitat shrank as settlers turned wild land to farmland.

Does the Endangered Species Act Save Species?

At best, it has saved only a few species, but it has probably saved some populations. One reason for its poor record is that it penalizes people who find endangered species on their property. These penalties may make people try to keep such species away. Thus, the act sometimes makes an enemy of the species it is designed to help.

ACTIVITIES

Fortunately, there is plenty of good news. Many wild animals are increasing in number, and many people are helping restore wildlife populations. The following activities will give your children a more optimistic outlook.

Watching Wild Birds

Even small towns now often have a store that specializes in wild birds. You can buy bird feeders and seed there. The store personnel will tell you what kinds of seeds attract local birds and where the feeder should be placed to attract birds. Let students know that, according to a recent survey, sixty-three million people feed birds each year. This is one way in which people voluntarily help protect birds.

If children become interested in birds, they may want to buy or build nest boxes. For instructions on building bluebird boxes, they can contact the North American Bluebird Society, Dept. B, P.O. Box 74, Darlington, WI 53530. For information about purple martins, they can contact the Purple Martin Conservation Assocation, Edinboro University of Pennsylvania, Edinboro, PA 16444. For general information about birdwatching, they can subscribe to *Birdwatcher's Digest*, P.O. Box 110, Marietta, OH 45750. Introducing your children to birds may start them on a lifelong hobby.

Hunting and Fishing

Millions of Americans love to hunt and fish. Because hunters and anglers want to make sure that wild game and fish have a place to live and breed their young, they support organizations, public and private, that protect wildlife habitat. Ducks Unlimited and Trout Unlimited often have local chapters that could send a representative to speak to a class. You may wish to contact their national headquarters by writing to: Ducks Unlimited, One Waterfowl Way, Memphis, TN 38120-2351 or Trout Unlimited, 1500 Wilson Boulevard, Suite 310, Arlington, VA 22209-2310.

One Glass, Two Straws

Children might like to do this exercise, but you may prefer simply to describe it to them. They will quickly get the idea.

Imagine two very thirsty children, each with a straw in a single glass of Coke. How long will it take them to finish the Coke? Not very long. If one slows down, the other one will get most of the Coke. This is an illustration of the "tragedy of the commons." When you are taking something that you want from a common pool, you are likely to take it as fast as you can. If you don't, someone else probably will!

Now suppose that each child has a separate glass, each half-filled with Coke. In this case, the children are not under pressure to drink the Coke so fast. One child might wait awhile before drinking it, perhaps putting it in the refrigerator for later. As long as the child is assured that he or she has a right to that half-glass, he or she won't feel pressured to drink it now. In effect, each child "owns" the Coke in the glass. Each child now has private property.

Parents might put a number of soft drink cans in the refrigerator (twelve cans for both children) and see how fast this "common property" disappears. Later, put in a sixpack for each child, with each sixpack marked with the child's name. Now, the soft drinks will probably disappear more slowly. The children will feel secure that their "property" will be there when they want it.

CHAPTER NINE

Where Have All the Species Gone?

....

JANE'S SON DAVID WAS JUST learning to write. He was too young to read environmental textbooks. But he knew that elephants in Africa were being *"pocht"* (that is, killed by poachers).

The message starts in preschool or kindergarten, and it doesn't stop. "Just imagine what it will be like for you and your children to live in a world without elephants, giraffes, tigers, or monkeys,"[1] says a biology text.

The truth is, we don't know how many species are disappearing.

The idea that all these animals will completely disappear is an extreme exaggeration. But by exploiting our children's natural sympathy for animals, these books build up an impression that the world will soon be devoid of most of the animals that our children love.

The Kids' Environment Book: What's Awry and Why tells the story this way: For six hundred million years, animals and plants became extinct at the rate of one species per year. By the 1970s it was one per day, and in the 1990s it may be one per hour. "If we keep up this pace, 20 to 50 percent of all known species that exist this minute will have died out by the year 2000,"[2] the book reports.

The Kids' Environment Book is not a textbook, but the texts march to the same drumbeat:

- "It has been estimated that 25 percent or more of the species now on Earth may become extinct within the next 50 years," states the Merrill text *Science Connections*.[3]

- "Although estimates vary considerably, some biologists have predicted that one million of the species that are alive today could be extinct by the year 2000," says *Introduction to Environmental Studies*. "This amounts to the loss of 100 species per day for the remainder of this century."[4]

Who is supposedly responsible for this destruction? People, of course. People crowd out species, destroying their habitat.

- "People are largely responsible for causing the extinction of nearly 10,000 species each year,"[5] says Prentice Hall's *Life Science*. The reason: More and more land is needed for humans to live and grow food on.

- "As the number of people on the earth increases, people use up more and more space," says the Globe text *Concepts and Challenges in Earth Science*. "Land that was once covered with forest is now used for cities, farms, roads, and industries."[6]

Many other animals disappeared because of hunting.

- The black rhinoceros is hunted for its horn, which is ground up and used as a potion.

- The African elephant is pursued for its ivory tusks, which are used for jewelry.

🐝 "Daggers made from rhino horns, jewelry fashioned from sea turtle shells, and fur coats made from jaguar skins are just a few of the wildlife products illegally sold each year," says Ranger Rick's *NatureScope*.[7]

While the texts are correct about the dangers to these animals, they offer no explanation of why these animals are hunted to the point of near extinction or how to protect them.

LOOKING AT THE NUMBERS

When children think about endangered species, they think about elephants, giraffes, and other appealing creatures. Yet the sweeping claims about extinction also include very small, often microscopic, animals and plants—insects and fungi, for example. While these beings are also important for ecosystems, children should know that they account for the major part of these high numbers. And, as we will see, the high numbers are based on a somewhat controversial theory.

The truth is, we don't know how many species are disappearing. We don't even know the number of species that exist.

Scholars have identified and named 1.4 million species.[8] In 1980, the *Global 2000* report published by the president's Council on Environmental Quality estimated that there are between three and ten million species.[9] But in 1991, Paul R. Ehrlich and Edward O. Wilson said that there may be one hundred million species![10]

The numbers have grown because there may be many more insect and other arthropod species than previously thought. But as Dennis Murphy, director of the Center for Conservation Biology at Stanford University, admits, "Nobody knows how many species there are."[11]

Since scientists are uncertain about how many species there are, they are also unsure about how many species are disappearing.

In 1980, the *Global 2000* report predicted that "at least 500,000 to 600,000 species" would become extinct in the next twenty years.[12] In 1993, Julian Simon and Aaron Wildavsky reviewed the source of these figures.[13]

🐝 They found that the *Global 2000* report based its predictions on estimates by Norman Myers in his 1979 book, *The Sinking Ark*. But Myers did not provide any basis for this estimate.

🐝 They concluded that "pure guesswork" is the basis of a figure—one hundred species a day—that many people have treated as a "scientific statement."[14]

Scientists have been trying to figure out if there is a reliable way to predict how many species will be lost when habitat disappears. A famous series of studies actually attempted to measure how many species were lost when habitat was destroyed. And these were some studies! (Frankly, it was difficult for the two of us, Michael and Jane, to believe the descriptions of this process. Yet these studies have been described in several books, most notably *Noah's Choice,* by Charles C. Mann and Mark L. Plummer.)

In the 1960s, several biologists, including Edward O. Wilson, decided to test out the relationship between species loss and habitat loss by actually destroying the habitat on some small islands. Before and after, they would count the number of species that had disappeared. So they hired exterminators to destroy living things on small mangrove islands (little islands usually smaller than a house) off the southern coast of Florida. The exterminators built scaffolding around the islands, draped them with nylon, and pelted them with methyl bromide and tear gas.[15] After they had done their deed, scientists did their counting.

Based on these studies (and some others in which the researchers actually destroyed portions of little islands),[16] the scientists began to estimate what percentage of species will disappear in an area if a certain percentage of habitat is lost. E. O. Wilson presents this "rule of thumb": If 90 percent of a habitat is destroyed, 50 percent of the species are lost.[17]

But the results of all these studies are so variable that it is not clear that this rule of thumb is valid even for islands. And it may not apply at all to forests and other places that aren't cut off by water. Professor Lawrence Slobodkin, writing in the journal *Nature,* concluded that the many studies have shown that the theory is "useless for explaining or predicting actual cases."[18] Others defend the theory, but predicting future extinctions on the basis of this evidence is scientifically risky.

A BRIGHTER PICTURE

When it comes to actual extinctions that we know about, the picture is brighter. It is true that some species and subspecies have disappeared during the past few centuries, from the dodo bird in the seventeenth century to the Bali tiger in the twentieth, and many bird species on the Hawaiian Islands have become extinct. But for the most part the recorded losses have not been on the massive scale claimed in our children's texts.

🐝 Puerto Rico was almost completely stripped of its forest at the turn of the century. "Yet it did not suffer massive extinctions," writes Charles Mann. Only seven of the island's sixty species of birds disappeared. Ariel Lugo, a scientist who has studied Puerto Rico for a decade, explains that crops provided cover for the birds and the forest regrew rapidly.[19]

🐝 During the nineteenth century, forests were extensively logged east of the Mississippi and around the Great Lakes. Only five birds became extinct, say Charles C. Mann and Mark L. Plummer in their book *Noah's Choice*. They were: the ivory-billed woodpecker, the passenger pigeon, the Carolina parakeet, the heath hen, and Bachman's warbler.[20]

🐝 A recent book prepared by the World Conservation Union, *Tropical Deforestation and Species Extinction*, also supports the idea that the rate of extinctions is low. "Despite extensive inquiries we have been unable to obtain conclusive evidence to support the suggestion that massive extinctions have taken place in recent times as Myers and others have suggested," the authors write.[21]

SAVING ELEPHANTS AND TIGERS

When it comes to the exotic animals that children and young people really do care about, such as elephants, tigers, and rhinos, textbooks usually blame hunting. Yes, this is the immediate cause, but not the full story.

Consider the African elephant. Late in the 1980s, many people became worried about these giant, lumbering creatures. In several African countries, governments had created national parks but could not keep away poachers, who wanted the elephant's ivory tusks. Since elephants can cause enormous damage (they can tear down trees and destroy a year's crop of corn in a night), many people living near elephants were letting poachers kill them, especially if the poachers gave rewards.

International conservation groups such as the World Wildlife Fund pushed for an international ban on trade in ivory. That ban was adopted in 1989, but elephant numbers continued to fall in some countries. In others, including Zimbabwe, Botswana, Namibia, and South Africa, elephant populations were increasing, not falling. But international conservation groups ignored this fact.

Elephant populations were going up in these countries for a number of reasons, including effective law enforcement. In addition, in parts of Zimbabwe, elephants were being protected because local villagers had a sort of ownership of the nearby elephants.

They received the benefits when elephants were legally hunted, and do so today. Villagers receive meat from the elephant plus proceeds from the sale of elephant hides and from hunters' payments for tusks, as well as from other hunter fees. Even though elephants can be very destructive, villagers who profit from the elephants will protect them from poachers. (This "ownership" does *not* mean that wild animals must be domesticated like cattle and sheep in order to save them.) The success of these programs led, in 1997, to a partial lifting of the ban on ivory trading.

In Kenya, in contrast, where many elephants are kept in large national parks, the poaching goes on—in spite of the ban on most ivory trading. The chief reason is that no one benefits directly from the herd through the kind of "ownership" found in parts of Zimbabwe. Thus, the people who live near elephants are not eager to help park rangers protect the herds for the future.[22]

So, too, with the tiger in Asia. Many Asians want tiger pelts and tiger bones (which they make into potions), and are willing to pay handsomely for them. Governments, under pressure from environmentalists, are attempting to protect the tigers by setting up reserves and trying to keep out poachers. But they have been unsuccessful.[23] If villagers received benefits when the tigers were legally hunted, tigers would more likely be protected.

Today, as things stand, the only way to derive income from the tigers is to kill them illegally. Legal hunting and selling are not the problem, despite what the textbooks say. The problem is that no one has a personal incentive to protect the tigers, so poaching occurs.

Wildlife preservation is a complex issue, involving the loss of habitat, the effects of introduced species, and other problems. Protecting wildlife today sometimes requires active human intervention. Without such management, wild animals can sometimes destroy their own environment. What is missing in our children's texts is the recognition that people must have incentives to protect animals if they are to be saved from extinction.

WHAT PEOPLE ARE DOING TO HELP

Overall, however, there is good news about endangered species. As human population grows, so does the ability of people to develop ways to protect wild animals and plants. Around the world, individuals, environmental organizations, and governments are trying to save endangered species.

- The Nature Conservancy and the World Wildlife Fund have sponsored the debt-for-nature swaps discussed in chapter 7. These reduce countries' debts in return for protection of animal or plant habitat.

- The Nature Conservancy purchases land all over the world in order to protect endangered species.[24]

As we saw in chapter 7, pharmaceutical companies have begun to work with organizations in tropical countries to identify and preserve plants that may become the basis for medicines.

Many zoos and animal centers are trying to save species in danger of extinction through captive breeding. For example, the Exotic Wildlife Association, an international organization of game ranchers, owns nineteen thousand animals that belong to species that are threatened or endangered in the wild.[25]

QUESTIONS AND ANSWERS

Now you can answer questions about endangered species.

How Many Species are Becoming Extinct?

No one knows. The very high numbers (ten thousand a year, for example) are based on guesses about how many species there are and how many are disappearing. These numbers include not only familiar animals like rhinos and tigers but also countless species of insects, spiders, and fungi. These are important to ecosystems but children are probably most concerned about larger animals. Some of these, like rhinos and some kinds of tigers, could become extinct in the wild.

What Are People Doing to Protect Endangered Species?

Around the world many people and organizations are protecting endangered wildlife. Governments have set aside parks, and groups like the Nature Conservancy purchase land that has endangered species on it. Zoos and universities conduct captive breeding programs to ensure the continuation of some endangered animal species.

Will the African Elephant and the Black Rhinoceros Disappear?

They will probably not become extinct, as long as there are organizations and zoos that will protect some of them. But they may become extinct in the wild unless some way is found for people who live near these animals to benefit from protecting them.

ACTIVITIES

Here are some activities to inform young people about programs that help save animals all over the world. Perhaps a class will want to get involved in one.

Visit a Zoo

Take your children to a zoo and ask the zookeeper to tell them about its programs to breed endangered animals and reintroduce them into the wild. Perhaps the zookeeper can explain some of the difficulties in reintroducing animals into the wild. If this zoo doesn't have such programs, he or she can undoubtedly tell them about places that do.

Ask the zookeeper how young people might get involved by volunteering their time to help animals.

The African Elephant

Children are rarely told that elephants are thriving in Zimbabwe and nearby countries. As this chapter indicates, elephants in these countries thrive because villagers have a stake in taking care of the herds. They do not actually own or domesticate the elephants, but they act like owners because they benefit by making sure that elephants continue to survive.

Talk to children about how people might act differently toward the elephant if they received the meat and hide from an elephant that is killed—and sometimes cash as well. Would they allow poachers to wipe out the elephant? Probably not.

You could also discuss ownership of other animals such as cows and chickens. Why, you can ask, don't we worry about the possible extinction of cows and chickens the way we worry about the possible extinction of elephants and tigers? After all, millions of people use these animals for food every day.

The answer, of course, is that animals become extinct when they have no owners with a stake in their future. While it would be difficult for wild animals to have "owners," they will be protected if people living near them have a stake in their future.

You may wish to share the story of successful wildlife conservation programs in Africa by introducing older children to *The Myth of Wild Africa* by Jonathan S. Adams and Thomas O. McShane (W. W. Norton, 1992).

Noah and the Ark

The Biblical story of Noah and the Ark (Genesis: 6-9) makes interesting reading. It illustrates how one good man and his family saved animals from catastrophe, making sure that the offspring of the animals would continue to populate the earth.

Talk with your children about modern-day "Arks" created by people who take on the responsibility of stewardship. These include zoos, nature centers, wildlife refuges, and ranches that specialize in game. They include organizations such as the Nature Conservancy, which protects endangered species by creating preserves; the World Center for Birds of Prey in Idaho, which uses captive breeding when necessary to save falcons and other raptors; and the Fossil Rim Wildlife Center in Texas, which preserves endangered animals from around the world. These groups do not always protect animals in the wild, but they make an important contribution to their survival.

Part Three

CHAPTER TEN

The Air We Breathe

....

YOU PROBABLY REMEMBER SEEING a scene from a Sherlock Holmes play or movie that was eerily wrapped in London fog. We know today that the thick, grey smoke that swirled ominously around the lampposts in the nineteenth century wasn't just fog. It was air pollution at its worst. Black smoke hung over London, created by dust from the low-grade coal used for heating in the crowded residential districts.

The "fog" eventually disappeared. Over time Londoners used cleaner coal and then replaced coal with oil, electricity, and gas. London's last famous "killer fog" took place in 1962.[1]

But widely used textbooks would make you think that those days are still with us:

🐝 "In the last forty years, thousands of people have become ill or died from unusually heavy levels of air pollution," says the text *Health for Life*.[2]

🐝 "Each year the United States dumps about 130 million metric tons of pollutants into the air. That amount is more than half a metric ton for every person in the country,"[3] says the D. C. Heath text *Earth Science: The Challenge of Discovery*. (The text does not mention that there are an estimated one million metric tons of atmosphere for every person on the earth.)[4]

🐝 Air pollution "may well pose the greatest danger of all.... There is the growing fear worldwide that unless the harm is stopped, we may eventually destroy all life on our planet,"[5] says Edward F. Dolan in his book *Our Poisoned Sky*.

According to many children's books, the chief culprit in producing air pollution is the automobile.

🐝 "Over half our air pollution is caused by automobiles," says the civics text *Exploring American Citizenship*.[6]

🐝 "Our cars emit many toxic substances, including large amounts of carbon monoxide, which interfere with the blood's ability to absorb oxygen, which in turn may threaten the growth and mental development of unborn babies," says *This Planet Is Mine: Teaching Environmental Awareness and Appreciation to Children*.[7]

BUT THE AIR IS CLEANER

Air pollution used to be a serious problem in urban United States. Today, although a few cities such as Los Angeles and Denver still have serious smog, most Americans live in a pleasant atmosphere where smog is a rare occurrence. Air quality has improved dramatically. Automakers have reduced emissions of pollutants; our homes mostly use natural gas and electricity, not coal; and industries have reduced the particulates from their smokestacks.

The Council on Environmental Quality reported on the change in airborne levels of pollutants between 1975 and 1989. As the following table indicates, lead went down by 93 percent, carbon monoxide by 47 percent,

AIR POLLUTION IS DECREASING NATIONALLY
REDUCTIONS BETWEEN 1975 AND 1989

Pollutant	Percent Reduction
Lead	-93
Carbon Monoxide	-47
Ozone	-14
Particulates	-20
Nitrogen Oxide	-17
Sulfur Dioxide	-46

Source: Council on Environmental Quality, *22nd Annual Report* (Washington, D.C.: Superintendent of Documents, U.S. Government Printing Office, March 1992), p. 10.

ozone by 14 percent, particulates by 20 percent, nitrogen oxide by 17 percent, and sulfur dioxide by 46 percent.[8]

More recent figures confirm that the trend continues. For example, the Environmental Protection Agency (EPA) reported in 1995 that emissions of sulfur dioxide fell by 7 percent between 1989 and 1994, and carbon monoxide emissions fell by 5 percent during the same period, even though the U.S. economy grew by 9 percent.[9]

Even in the Los Angeles basin, there has been significant improvement. Between 1955 and 1992 the peak level of airborne ozone in Los Angeles fell from 680 parts per billion to 300 parts per billion. This drop occurred even though the number of motor vehicles in the area rose from 2.3 million to 10.6 million.[10]

It is true that many cities technically do not meet the EPA's standard for ozone, which is a principal component of smog. (High in the stratosphere, ozone protects the Earth from harmful ultraviolet radiation, as we will see in chapter 12. But close to the ground, ozone is a pollutant.)

In fact, in 1990 about half the U.S. population lived in areas that had not achieved the EPA's standards for ozone.[11] Fortunately, except for southern California, "non-attainment" of the EPA ozone standard usually occurs just a few days a year.[12] A December 1991 National Academy of Sciences report on ozone reveals that most of the variation in ozone comes from "natural fluctuations in the weather," not from "year-to-year changes in emissions."[13]

The improvement we see in air quality continues the progress that has been going on for decades, thanks to better technology and competitive market forces. Economist Robert Crandall of the Brookings Institution reviewed statistics for airborne sulfur dioxide and particulates and concluded that these pollutants declined faster before the Clean Air Act was passed in 1970 than after.[14] (The following graph shows significant declines in New York air pollution during the 1960s.)

CHANGES IN SULFUR DIOXIDE LEVELS IN NEW YORK, 1963-1972

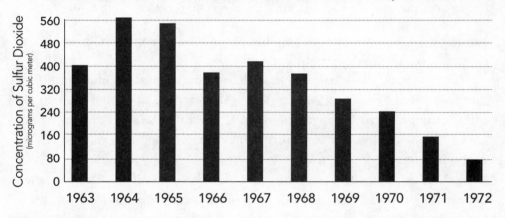

Source: H. Schimmel and T.J. Murawski. "SO₂—Harmful Pollutant or Air Quality Indicator?" *Journal of the Air Pollution Control Association* 25 (1995): 739–40.

AIR POLLUTION—HOW DANGEROUS?

Does this mean that there is no air pollution problem? No. There can be real effects on human health, especially on people who are already sick.

 In 1993, *Scientific American* cited two studies of Californians showing that people living in polluted areas have higher levels of chronic diseases, including bronchitis and asthma.[15]

❀ Researchers from the Harvard School of Public Health found that in several cities increases in very small particles in the air may be linked to an increase in the number of deaths over the next few days. This correlation was found even though the total particulates (that is, the portion of the air comprised of particles) were well within federal standards.[16]

Given these facts, it is important to keep improving air quality. But textbooks are not very helpful about how to do it.

AUTOMOBILES: THE ENEMY

The textbooks treat the automobile as the enemy in the war against pollution. They urge children to ride bikes, join car pools, or use mass transit. We, the authors of this book, have seen the results.

Devin (Michael's son who was eight years old at the time) was riding with his father one day. He noticed that many cars had only one person. By using cars so wastefully, he said, people were making pollution much worse.

Then a bus stopped nearby. Michael asked Devin to count the number of people in the bus. It was just a handful. As he finished counting, the bus suddenly took off in a cloud of black smoke. Devin had to agree that cars may well be causing less pollution per person than buses.

Such a reality check is not found in the books our children are reading. The best-selling book *50 Simple Things Kids Can Do to Save the Earth* is especially pointed about cars:

❀ "There are more cars in America than anywhere else in the world— 140 million of them!"

❀ "Every year American cars drive a trillion miles."

❀ "When these millions of cars burn up gas, they produce something called 'exhaust.' It's one of the worst things for the Earth."

🐝 "Bicycles don't make exhaust—they don't pollute. So if you already ride a bike, you're already saving the Earth."[17]

Certainly riding bikes and car pooling are good ideas. But children should learn that:

🐝 Today's new cars emit 96 percent fewer hydrocarbon tailpipe emissions (that is, pollutants) than models of the early 1970s.[18]

🐝 Most automobile pollution is caused by a very small fraction of cars. Fewer than 10 percent of all cars are responsible for more than 50 percent of total automobile pollution.[19]

🐝 The private automobile provides enormous benefits. It enables millions of people to go where they want to go, when they want to go, and it moves them from door to door—benefits that are especially important for parents with young children.

To address air pollution effectively, it is necessary to focus on real pollution sources. Probably the biggest is poorly tuned vehicles.

Luckily, the technology for such an approach already exists. Donald Stedman, a University of Denver chemistry professor, has developed a device that uses an infrared beam of light to measure pollutant emissions from vehicles as they drive by on the road or highway.[20]

Is the air getting cleaner? Yes. The Federal Council on Environmental Quality reported in 1992 that the major air pollutants had all declined since 1975. That progress has continued.

The device can be fitted with a camera to record license plates. Stedman's invention, which is being used experimentally in about thirty places around the world, could identify the real polluters at considerably less cost than mandatory emissions programs and other regulatory schemes.

So far, this idea has been ignored in the textbooks.

QUESTIONS AND ANSWERS

Air pollution is a serious issue. For hundreds of years, air pollution has been recognized as aesthetically unpleasant and dangerous to health. But air pollution has been declining over the decades. In most parts of the country, the air is clean most of the time. Children should be taught this side of the story, too.

Now you can answer their questions.

Do We Need Tougher Laws?

We need better laws more than we need "tougher" ones. The last major law addressing air pollution was passed in 1990. It required auto manufacturers who sell cars in California, the area with the most pollution, to build cars that burn cleaner fuels. But the law did not target the cars that were really doing the polluting.

Is the Air Getting Cleaner?

Yes. The Federal Council on Environmental Quality reported in 1992 that the major air pollutants had all declined since 1975. That progress has continued.

Is Air Pollution Dangerous?

Yes, it can be. Severe air pollution is harmful to people's health, especially those with asthma or other lung diseases. But the air today is much cleaner than it used to be.

ACTIVITIES

The following activities will help put today's air pollution problems into perspective.

Remembering the Good Old Days

Most of us have a nostalgic view of the past. We imagine the nineteenth century as resembling the Currier and Ives prints that show a horse-drawn sleigh traversing a snow-covered country road. But life before the automobile was anything but pristine.

Ask your children if they would rather live in a world with "clean, nonpolluting" horses instead of polluting cars. Most will jump at the chance.

Then ask them to add to their current list of household chores feeding the horse twice a day and cleaning the stall or corral. (Few children realize that horses can create twenty pounds of manure per day and that this "pollution" must be disposed of.)

Imagine every car in the school parking lot replaced by a horse. What would the streets be like? How would they smell?

Or, visit a local stable. Have the owner or manager show children the stalls and what it means to "muck out a stall." Ask the owner to tell them how much waste is produced by the horses and how the people who work at the stable get rid of it. Then ask the children to imagine every car in the school parking lot replaced by a horse. What would the streets be like? How would they smell?

A Tale of Two Cities

Show children the following photographs of Pittsburgh, Pennsylvania.

These photographs, which appear in the book *Pittsburgh: Then and Now,* were taken from the same location eighty-one years apart. The caption reads in part: "At the turn of the century, many workers lived in close proximity to the mills.... To say that darkness reigned at noon in these valleys was not an exaggeration on many days."

Ask the children which city they would like to live in. Most will pick the picture of the clean Pittsburgh. Ask them if the people who lived in the dirty Pittsburgh liked living there. If not, ask them why they think people lived there.

The reason, of course, was that jobs were available, and back then people needed jobs more than clean air. But gradually, changes took place in Pittsburgh's industrial and business economy. Today, the people of Pittsburgh have clean air and good jobs as well.

PITTSBURGH 1906

PITTSBURGH 1987

Source: Arthur G. Smith, *Pittsburgh: Then and Now* (Pittsburgh: University of Pittsburgh Press, 1990), p. 114-5. Reprinted by permission of Karen E. Smith.

A Matter of Prosperity

While many factors contributed to Pittsburgh's cleaner air in 1987, one important factor that is often forgotten is the increase in the wealth of its citizens. The following chart shows income per person in 1906 and 1987 (adjusted for inflation). The average income was nearly four times as high as in 1987 as it was in 1906. Progress has continued, and in 1997, the average income was $30,088.

U.S. PER CAPITA INCOME*

1906	1987
$6,983	$27,351

* Per Capita GNP in constant 1997 dollars.

Source: *The Statistical History of the United States from Colonial Times to the Present.* (New York, NY: Basic Books, Inc., 1976) p. 224. *Statistical Abstract of the United States, 1998.* (Washington, DC: U.S. Department of Commerce, Bureau of the Census), p. 456. Consumer Price Index:ftp://ftp.bls.gov/pub/special.requests/cpi/cpiai.txt. 7 June 1999.

In the early part of this century the United States was much poorer than it is today. People were more concerned with making a living than having a clean environment. But today, because we have greater wealth than we had then, we are better able to clean the environment.

Many Third World cities are polluted today. As they become wealthier, they, too, will take additional steps to protect their environment. As people become more affluent, they will insist on less pollution, and they will be willing to spend money, sometimes through their taxes, to help clean the air.

CHAPTER ELEVEN

A Hotter Planet?

·····················

IT IS THE YEAR 2040, and it is very hot. Tourists are visiting an unnamed city—by boat. The entire city, except for the tops of the highest skyscrapers, is under water. "Up ahead is Ruth Stadium," says the guide, "where our local baseball team won the World Series of 2018. You could play water polo in it today, if you wanted to."[1]

One of the tourists mops sweat from his brow. Yes, it is always warm these days, even in January. The continual heat melted the Arctic ice caps and sea levels rose by twenty-five feet. "Is this scene only fantasy?" ask the authors of the science text in which it appears. "Perhaps. But it may someday be fact. Your great-grandchild might be that man riding on the sightseeing boat."

Welcome to global warming.

Consider this radio broadcast from the year 2050, found in a civics text:

Good morning for December 12, 2050. It looks like another hot day with temperatures reaching about 95 degrees. Meanwhile Hurricane Lou is dumping up to 12 inches of rain on parts of the South and Southwest. And it looks like no part of the nation will have a white Christmas this year—our long-range forecast says the temperature will be in the 90s right up through New Year's Day.[2]

And then there is the illustration of the New York City skyline—with the Statue of Liberty and its skyscrapers covered by water, except for the tops of the World Trade Center towers and a few other tall buildings.[3]

IS THE EARTH GETTING WARMER?

Despite these frightening depictions, global warming should not keep young people awake at night.

It is true that over the past one hundred years, the Earth became slightly warmer, but only about half a degree Celsius, or 1 degree Fahrenheit. The Intergovernmental Panel on Climate Change (IPCC), a group of climate specialists organized by the United Nations and the World Metereological Organization to assess information about climate change, estimates that the increase was between three- and six-tenths of a degree Celsius, or one-half to 1 degree Fahrenheit.[4] But most of the warming occurred before most of the greenhouse gases were put in the atmosphere by human actions.

As for the future, scientists do not know if the Earth will continue to get warmer. If it does, the increase may be so slight as to be hardly noticeable.

Clearly, apocalyptic claims such as a twenty-five-foot rise in sea level are no longer taken seriously—by anyone except perhaps textbook writers. Recent studies have predicted a possible rise in sea level of six to forty inches, not feet.[5] And one reputable study suggests that warming would lower sea levels. (Warming would lead to more snow in the Arctic, which would increase the size of the northern ice-sheets.)[6]

As for temperature predictions, they, too, have moderated. In 1989, some scientists were predicting an increase in global temperatures of between 3.5 and 5 degrees Celsius (6.3 to 9 degrees Fahrenheit) perhaps as early as the middle of the twenty-first century.[7] In 1990, an intergovernmental panel of scientists projected an increase of 3 degrees Celsius (5.4 degrees Fahrenheit) by the year 2100.[8] But the latest estimate is that temperatures may increase by between 1 and 3 degrees Celsius (between 1.8 and 5.4 degrees Fahrenheit) by the year 2100.[9]

Global warming first captured public attention because of some very hot summers in the 1980s, especially one in 1988. On a hot day James Hansen, who heads NASA's Goddard Institute, told a congressional committee that he thought that human actions were beginning to raise the world's temperatures—that global warming had arrived.

By some measurements, we have, indeed, been in a period of warm weather. However, measurements of temperature taken by satellite (rather than measurements close to the ground) showed no warming trend between 1979 and mid-1996.[10] In fact, there was a slight cooling trend, which may be explained by the 1991 eruption of the Mt. Pinatubo volcano in the Philippines. (Volcanic dust kept out sunlight, cooling the Earth.) Recently, a new analysis questioned the reliability of these satellite-based temperature figures, and they were recalculated. According to one of the scientists monitoring these temperatures, they still show no distinct warming until 1998, when the weather pattern called El Niño apparently raised temperatures. Balloon-based temperature readings have been similar to satellite data, he says.[11]

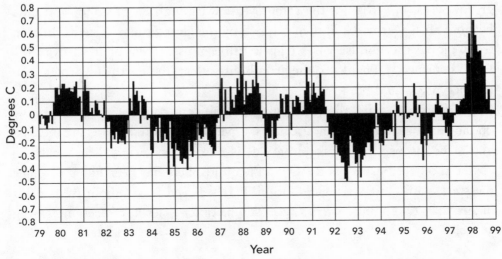

CHANGES IN EARTH'S TEMPERATURE AS MEASURED BY SATELLITE, SHOWING NO SIGNIFICANT WARMING TREND

Source: John R. Christy, Earth System Science Laboratory, University of Alabama in Huntsville.

WHAT SCIENTISTS KNOW

Let's look at what scientists do know. They agree that average world temperatures have gone up slightly since good record-keeping began about one hundred years ago, probably about half a degree Celsius, or about 1 degree Fahrenheit.[12] That increase, which is pretty small, may reflect natural variation in temperature. Also, it appears that the world has been getting warmer since the "Little Ice Age" ended naturally about 250 years ago.[13]

And temperatures haven't been going up steadily. There was a significant decline in temperatures between 1938 and 1970. That decline led scientists in the 1970s to worry about a coming Ice Age. In fact, Stephen Schneider, a scientist now predicting severe global warming, urged in 1976 that people consider "massive world-wide actions" to hedge against the possibility of a new Ice Age.[14]

When people talk about global warming, they usually mean that temperatures will rise due to the "greenhouse effect." There is nothing sinister about the greenhouse effect. A number of gases, including water vapor, CO_2, methane, and others, keep the earth warm by trapping infrared rays that would otherwise be lost to space. (Infrared rays are invisible rays of heat that are emitted by all objects.)

This warming process is something like the buildup of heat that occurs in greenhouses, but it is not the same. Most warming in a greenhouse occurs because air is warmed and then trapped by the glass or plastic walls. In contrast, global greenhouse gases trap invisible rays of heat emitted from the Earth's surface.[15] Thanks to the greenhouse effect, the Earth is warmer than it otherwise would be.

Scientists who think the earth will get significantly warmer base their view on the fact that some greenhouse gases, especially carbon dioxide, are increasing in the atmosphere. Carbon dioxide is released when fossil fuels such as coal and oil are burned; and CO_2 in the atmosphere has been going up since the start of the Industrial Revolution. It is believed to be about 32 percent higher than two hundred years ago.[16] Some other gases have been increasing as well.

Keep in mind that carbon dioxide, while extremely important, represents a very small part of the total atmosphere—about 0.0365 percent or 365 parts per million. (In contrast, oxygen represents about 20 percent of the atmosphere or about 200,000 parts per million!)

THE COMPUTER DID IT

One reason why global warming has received so much attention is that computer models predict it. Climate models are simplified descriptions of the world's climate, written in mathematical formulas on computer programs. Actual climate data (temperatures, wind patterns, cloud cover, etc.) are also fed into the computers. By changing the formulas, scientists can change the description of the climate.

Some years ago, scientists decided to see what would happen if they assumed that CO_2 had doubled, as they thought it would by the middle of the twenty-first century. The result: significantly higher temperatures, higher by between 2 and 6 degrees Celsius. The projections looked scientific. But scientists know that these computer models are just one scientific tool with both strengths and weaknesses. Robert Jastrow, founder of NASA's Goddard Institute, and two colleagues point out that the models give such a rough picture of the Earth's climate that they miss entirely the effect of mountains such as the Sierra Nevadas and the Cascades. According to these models, the climate of heavily forested Oregon and the climate of the Nevada desert would be about the same.[17]

Another problem is that scientists are really guessing about how different aspects of the climate affect one another. For example:

🦟 Water vapor is far more effective than carbon dioxide in trapping heat. Carbon dioxide will increase temperatures significantly only if water vapor increases significantly. But will it?

🦟 Clouds (composed of water vapor that has condensed into droplets) may increase if carbon dioxide goes up. Some clouds increase the warming effect, and others decrease it by reflecting sunlight back into space.[18]

✾ Oceans and vegetation absorb CO_2, but how much, how fast, and for how long? No one knows.

If some of the early computer projections are correct, we should already have seen significant warming—an increase over the past one hundred years of 1.7 degrees Celsius (3 degrees F), says climatologist Patrick Michaels.[19] But, as we have seen, the actual increase is only about half a degree Celsius. Recently, scientists have proposed that air pollutants such as sulfur dioxide may have slowed down the warming that would otherwise occur.[20]

Another problem is that the pattern of warming does not follow the rise in CO_2.

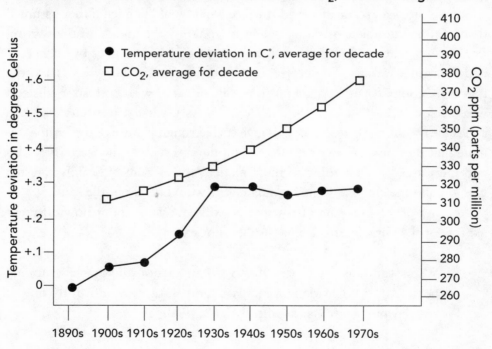

CHANGES IN TEMPERATURE AND LEVELS OF CO_2, 1890s through 1970s

Source: Arizona State University, Climatology Labratory 2/23/94. Data averaged for 10 year periods.

If CO_2 and other greenhouse gases caused the Earth to warm, temperatures should have risen roughly in tandem with the increase in greenhouse gases. However, as the accompanying graph shows, global temperatures show an erratic pattern. They rose in the first half of the century, but flattened out between the 1930s and 1970s, only to rise again after that.[21]

And temperatures in the Arctic, which should be getting significantly warmer if the computer projections are right, have been going down. Over the past forty years, they declined by 1.5 degrees Celsius (2.7 degrees F).[22]

A WARMER WORLD—SOME BENEFITS?

Children's textbooks, reflecting the popular view, discuss only the negative impacts of warming. But some scientists note that if the world gets warmer, that would not be all bad.

- "In fact," says Andrew Solow, a scientist at Woods Hole Oceanographic Institute, "there is some irony in the description of global warming as problematic, since it is not unreasonable to view human history as a struggle to stay warm."[23]

- Thomas Gale Moore, a prominent economist at the Hoover Institution, has even concluded that higher temperatures similar to those predicted by the Intergovernmental Panel on Climate Change would reduce deaths.[24] Cold temperatures lead to death more often than hot ones, he found.

- More carbon dioxide in the air will benefit many plants. It causes more luxuriant growth, larger flowers, and greater crop yield.[25] Some scientists think that rising levels of CO_2 in the air have already contributed to the Green Revolution (that is, the remarkable increases in food production of the past few decades).[26]

QUESTIONS AND ANSWERS

It is little wonder that children are frightened. You may be, too. But now you can give children a more balanced picture.

Is the World Going to Get Hotter?

No one really knows. Carbon dioxide keeps heat from being emitted into space. Because carbon dioxide is increasing in the atmosphere, temperatures may get warmer. However, the warming may be so small that it will cause little or no harm.

Are Human Activities Causing Global Warming?

Perhaps. By burning fossil fuels, humans add carbon dioxide to the atmosphere, and more carbon dioxide should keep more heat in the Earth's atmosphere. But the increase in warmth may be very small since many, many factors affect climate. Until recently, some scientists were more worried about a coming Ice Age than too much warming.

Has the World Been Getting Hotter?

Yes, a little. Scientists think that the Earth's average temperatures have increased by between three- and six-tenths of a degree Celsius, or between one-half and one degree Fahrenheit over the past one hundred years. But the increase has been irregular, not steady, and it may simply reflect natural variation in temperatures over time.

Is Carbon Dioxide Itself Harmful?

No. In fact, it is a beneficial part of the atmosphere. It provides food for plants. More carbon dioxide in the atmosphere should increase plant growth. More plant growth means more production of oxygen through photosynthesis.

ACTIVITIES

The following activities should help reassure students that the world is not "out of control" even if a modest amount of warming should occur.

Carbon Dioxide and Dinosaurs

The school or city library undoubtedly has books with illustrations of dinosaurs and their world. (We have provided a couple of suggestions below.) Show the illustrations to students and ask them to describe the trees and other vegetation that surround the dinosaurs. Then ask them if this world was warmer or cooler than the one we currently live in.

Now tell them that the Earth had an atmosphere that contained carbon dioxide levels that were five to ten times greater than now. The high CO_2 levels contributed to the rich vegetation. The earth was warmer and wetter, not burning up or drying out. (At other times, however, high carbon dioxide levels coexisted with cold temperatures.) The point is that the image of global warming that many people hold may be unnecessarily grim.

Suggested Reading

Kate Brasch, *Prehistoric Monsters* (Salem House, 1980).

Jane Werner Watson, *Dinosaurs and Other Prehistoric Reptiles* (Golden Press, 1970).

Take a Trip to a Greenhouse

What better way to learn about the "greenhouse effect" than to visit a commercial greenhouse? (Look under "Greenhouses" in the Yellow Pages.) Keep in mind that the "greenhouse effect" is a misnomer. The warming in a greenhouse occurs differently, as we discussed earlier in this chapter. But greenhouses create a warm, moist environment that encourages rapid plant growth. In addition, many greenhouses increase the CO_2 level. As students learn in basic science, plants use CO_2 to make food through photosynthesis. With high CO_2 levels, the plants have more of what they need to grow vigorously.

Ask the greenhouse manager to explain how conditions in the greenhouse are controlled to help plants grow. Does this greenhouse add carbon dioxide? Why or why not?

A New Ice Age?

Doomsday predictions of climate change are nothing new. Young people may not be aware that in the mid-1970s many people worried about the coming Ice Age.

At the library, children should look up the following articles and book:

Nigel Calder, "In the Grip of the New Ice Age," *International Wildlife*, July 1975.

Douglass Colligan, "Brace Yourself for Another Ice Age," *Science Digest*, February 1975.

"Are We Headed for a New Ice Age?" *Current*, May/June 1976.

The Cooling, by Lowell Ponte (Prentice Hall, 1976).

Indeed, in the early 1990s, after parts of the United States experienced heavy snows and severe cold, a new interest in an Ice Age reemerged. Have children look this one up, too: Michael D. Lemonick, "The Ice Age Cometh?" *Time*, January 31, 1994.

CHAPTER TWELVE

Sorting Out Ozone

·····················

ONE EVENING BEFORE BEDTIME, Russell began to cry. He was worried about the ozone layer that surrounds and protects the earth. His father had told him that the air conditioner in the family car had chemicals that "eat" the ozone when they evaporate. Russell, a second-grader in Forest Hills, New York, felt hopeless.[1] But his father urged him to do something about it. And he did.

Russell started an environmental club at his school. His group, Kids Save the Ozone Project (Kids STOP), lobbied the mayor and city council in New York City to pass a law requiring CFCs in auto air conditioners to be recycled. The group even lobbied the president to urge him to support a worldwide ban on CFCs.

Russell became concerned about the ozone layer because it troubled his father, but many children learn in school that the thin layer of ozone in the stratosphere is being "eaten away" by man-made chemicals, primarily chlorofluorocarbons (CFCs). Without ozone to protect us, students are told, the sun's ultraviolet (UV) rays will damage crops, cause skin cancer, and injure our eyes. One children's book shows little PacMan-like creatures eating the ozone molecules.[2]

Concern about ozone depletion has a basis in science. It probably has more scientific support than global warming or widespread species extinction. But, fear of ozone loss is exaggerated. There is no ozone crisis.

OZONE—THE SIMPLE VERSION

Ozone depletion is a complicated scientific issue. But in textbooks and other children's books, the message is simple.

🐝 *Earth Science: The Challenge of Discovery* says that "ozone loss will cause millions of people to get skin cancer."[3]

🐝 "Direct exposure to this harmful solar radiation would probably kill much life on Earth,"[4] says *We the People*, a civics text.

🐝 "[T]he loss of atmospheric ozone can increase the chances of skin cancer and birth defects in people and slow the growth of some food crops,"[5] says the Glencoe text *World Geography: A Physical and Cultural Approach*.

🐝 Too much UV radiation increases "skin cancer, eye ailments, and other disease in humans, disrupts the growing cycles of crops, damages fish populations in the oceans and affects the earth's weather in ways that are not yet understood,"[6] says a book for children.

To understand this issue, we should start with oxygen. The normal oxygen that we breathe is composed of two atoms of oxygen (O_2). Ozone is a molecule composed of three atoms of oxygen (O_3). It is found in extremely small quantities high above the earth, most of it in the stratosphere, the atmospheric layer between ten and thirty miles up.

Because most ozone is found there, the stratosphere is sometimes called the "ozone layer." But the amount of ozone is so small that if all the bits of ozone in a column of space in the stratosphere were compressed together, the ozone would be about one-eighth of an inch thick.[7]

This thinly scattered ozone absorbs some of the sun's ultraviolet (UV) rays, preventing them from reaching the atmosphere close to the Earth. These rays are invisible components of sunlight. Ozone absorbs only very short rays, which scientists call UV-B radiation.

The major worry is not stratospheric ozone itself but, rather, the radiation that is normally blocked by ozone. If ozone declines, more UV-B rays will reach the earth on a clear day. Too much of this radiation can cause sunburn, irritation of the eye's cornea, and skin cancer.

OZONE—TWO COMPLEX ISSUES

There are two ozone depletion issues. (And we're only talking about the ozone that exists many miles up in the stratosphere! Ozone close to ground is part of smog.)

First, scientists have been trying to figure out if the worldwide layer of stratospheric ozone is thinning. And, second, they have been trying to figure out what causes the so-called "ozone hole" above Antarctica. These are separate questions, although the textbooks tend to mix them up, creating confusion.

🌲 "Today this ozone layer is thinning," says *Save the Earth: An Action Handbook for Kids,* referring to the worldwide layer of ozone.

🌲 It continues: "Vast continent-sized 'holes' or areas where ozone loss is 50 percent or more, have been discovered over Antarctica in the last decade. . . ,"[8] referring to the ozone "hole."

The Global Ozone Issue

Let us begin with the question of the worldwide thinning. Ozone is an unstable molecule. It can break apart, forming oxygen and a free-floating oxygen atom. This is what "ozone depletion" means. Natural forces that break ozone apart include trace gases such as hydrogen oxides, nitrogen oxides, and chlorine.

But ozone is also constantly created. Sunlight reacts with oxygen, breaking the oxygen molecule (O_2) into free-floating oxygen atoms. When a loose oxygen atom joins an oxygen molecule, O_3 is formed again. Creation and destruction of ozone go on all the time. The ozone layer is not a solid that is "eaten away" by chemicals. It is not a fabric that is being "torn."

Natural fluctuations of ozone are very large. Over a few months, the amount of ozone can vary by 50 percent over parts of the United States.[9] From day to day, the amount of ozone can vary by 25 percent.[10] Because these changes occur naturally, they arouse little concern. And because these fluctuations are so large, it is difficult for scientists to know whether the ozone layer is thinning over time or, if it is, what is causing the thinning.

The Antarctic Ozone "Hole"

In 1985, British scientists reported that during the period between August and October of 1984, the amount of ozone over Antarctica had dropped dramatically—more than 40 percent below what it had been some years before. This loss extended over an area broader than the entire Antarctic continent. This reduction in stratospheric ozone became known as the "ozone hole."

In children's books, it is pretty scary. "In 1984, about 30 percent of the ozone was gone; in 1985, 50 percent; in 1987, 60 percent," says *The Kids' Environment Book.* "On October 5, 1987, scientists recorded a level that was barely one-third of normal. By then the hole was bigger than the continental United States and as deep as Mount Everest is high."[11]

Our children are rarely, if ever, told that this thinning of the ozone layer over Antarctica is temporary—that is, it lasts for only a short period of time each year—or that it probably reflects conditions unique to the South Pole. Over the North Pole, there has been a small amount of thinning of ozone late in the winter.[12]

CFCS—CAUSE OF IT ALL?

Now, enter the supposed villains: CFCs (chlorofluorocarbons). Many scientists believe that these chemicals are both thinning ozone and directly contributing to the ozone "hole." Let's see why they think this.

CFCs contain chlorine. In addition, they have an unusual property. They are inert. That is, they don't react easily with other chemicals. This makes them nontoxic and nonflammable.

Because they are so safe, they have been widely used, especially for cooling in refrigerators and air conditioners, but in other ways as well. They were found in aerosol propellants at one time, but their use in the United States of America was banned in 1978 after concerns about ozone loss first surfaced. They were also used in the production of some plastic foam products such as Styrofoam cups, plates, and fast-food containers, a point that some books still emphasize.

Ozone depletion is a complicated issue. But in our children's textbooks the message is simple. One book shows little PacMan-like creatures eating the ozone molecules.

Because these chemicals don't break apart easily, they stay in the atmosphere a very long time. Gradually over many years, they float up to the stratosphere. There they are finally broken apart by sunlight, and their chlorine atoms are released.

These chlorine atoms, through complex chemistry, can change two ozone molecules (O_3) into three oxygen molecules (O_2). Scientists theorize that a single chlorine atom can break apart up to 100,000 ozone molecules.[13] In the atmosphere, however, other chemical reactions interfere, slowing but not stopping the process.

Are CFCs causing ozone to thin around the globe? And are they causing the ozone "hole"? Let us look at each ozone issue again.

The Global Ozone Issue

Scientists aren't sure how much the ozone layer is thinning. A panel of scientists convened by the National Aeronautics and Space Administration (NASA), the Ozone Trends Panel, reported in 1988 that ozone levels above the Northern Hemisphere had declined by between 1 and 3 percent per decade.[14] These figures were later refined, updated, and published by a group headed by NASA scientist Richard Stolarski.[15]

In 1991, the Environmental Protection Agency went further—it announced that the ozone layer above the United States had decreased by 4 percent to 5 percent between 1979 and 1990. However, this statement was based on an oversimplified analysis of satellite data. For one thing, there was an upturn after 1986. Second, the eleven and a half years of records may not be enough to distinguish human-caused decline from the variation caused by the natural sunspot cycle, says S. Fred Singer, the scientist who designed the instrument used on satellites to measure ozone.[16]

The amount of ozone in the stratosphere changes due to the sun's ultraviolet radiation are associated with the eleven-year sunspot cycle. When the sun is at its strongest, there is more UV radiation in the stratosphere to break apart oxygen molecules, and more ozone is formed. When the sun is at its weakest, less oxygen is broken apart and less ozone created. One study concluded that "73 percent of the global O_3 declines between 1979 and 1985 are due to natural effects related to solar variability. . . ."[17]

Sorting out the "natural effects" is an enormous challenge. While chlorine from CFCs appears to be combining with ozone molecules to deplete ozone, the impact of natural forces on the increase and decrease of stratospheric ozone is also tremendously important. The most recent studies, taking into account chlorine, solar cycles, and volcanoes, can still only explain part of the loss of ozone that has been calculated for the period between 1979 and 1994.[18]

The Ozone "Hole"

Scientists have figured out that the Antarctic ozone hole occurs this way: The polar vortex, a circular wind pattern around Antarctica, keeps warmer air from the tropics out during the winter, a time when the air temperature above Antarctica falls to minus 80 degrees Celsius (–112 degrees F) or lower. It is so cold that ice clouds can form in the stratosphere (which, during the winter, is completely dark).

When the sun becomes visible above Antarctica in early spring (remember, in the Southern Hemisphere spring starts in September), the sun can trigger chemical reactions involving the ice crystals, ozone, and chlorine. The source of most of the stratospheric chlorine is CFCs, although there are some natural sources of chlorine, too.

Chemicals that have been "holding" this chlorine release it. The chlorine reacts with ozone, depleting it. As the season progresses, however, the vortex breaks up and the ozone layer is replenished with a fresh supply of ozone-rich air from the tropics.[19]

So, it appears that the direct cause of the ozone "hole" is chlorine in the stratosphere. But natural conditions play an important part, too.

The Big Fear: Cancer

If the ozone layer is thinning, will more UV radiation reach the Earth? And, if so, will it increase skin cancers?

In theory, the answer to both questions is yes. But, as we have seen, we aren't sure how much depletion there is. More important, there is little evidence that UV radiation is increasing.

In fact, some scientists have measured just the opposite. The major study of UV radiation reaching the United States showed a slight decrease in UV radiation between 1974 and 1985. While this was a limited study, it shows the opposite of what one would expect if the ozone layer were thinning.[20] A more recent study showed an increase in UV radiation at a station in Toronto, Canada, but the study was based on only four years of measurements, and for two of those years there were problems with the information.[21]

A NOAA (National Oceanic and Atmospheric Administration) scientist reports that UV rays have decreased—by between 5 and 18 percent during this century (possibly due to increased clouds and haze).[22] These studies suggest that the danger from ultraviolet radiation, at least in the United States, may be lessening rather than increasing.

Skin cancer rates have been increasing since World War II, probably due to changes in lifestyle. Just fifty years ago, people still wore bathing suits that covered much of their bodies. Dr. Frederick Urbach, a Temple University dermatologist, says that recent increases in skin cancer rates "are due to people spending more time outside, not more UV."[23]

Fortunately, this type of skin cancer is easily treated. The death rate from nonmelanoma skin cancer is less than 1 percent.

As for melanoma, a very dangerous cancer of the skin, its relationship to sun exposure isn't clear.[24] A study by Richard B. Setlow of Brookhaven National Laboratory and his colleagues concluded that the effect of sunlight on melanoma was almost entirely through either visible light or the UV-A part of the light spectrum, not the very short UV-B wavelengths that are blocked by ozone. In other words, ozone and melanoma appear to have little to do with each other.[25]

UV RADIATION—IN PERSPECTIVE

The most important fact that the textbooks fail to mention is that ozone depletion, if it is occurring, is similar to increasing one's exposure to UV light by moving closer to the Equator or higher up a mountain. Nearer the Equator, the angle of the sun is more direct and people are exposed to more UV light. As one ascends a mountain, the thinner air blocks less of the UV radiation.

- If the ozone level above the United States has decreased by 4 or 5 percent, as the Environmental Protection Agency estimated (but rather carelessly) in 1991, the effect would be about the same as moving sixty miles south, say from Seattle to Tacoma.[26] Moving south increases one's exposure to UV radiation about the same amount as a 4 or 5 percent decrease in ozone.

- A scientific paper pointed out that a person who moves from Oslo, Norway, to San Francisco experiences an increase in UV exposure of 100 percent and increases his or her risk of skin cancer by 250 percent.[27]

What about Crops?

Another worry is that plants could receive too much UV radiation. But Alan Teramura, a leading expert on the effects of UV radiation on plants, points out that plants are remarkably adapted to withstand changes in UV exposure. Even if ozone declined by 20 percent, he says, we "wouldn't see plants wilting or fruits dropping unripened from their vines."[28] Although some plants could be damaged, others would be unaffected or produce greater crop yields.

What about Algae?

When there is an ozone "hole" over Antarctica, the amount of UV radiation does increase significantly there. Some textbooks suggest that plankton, the tiny algae in the water around Antarctica, may not be able to cope with so much radiation. Since other animals feed on these algae, their loss could affect the entire food chain.

Osmund Holm-Hansen, director of polar research at the Scripps Institute of Oceanography, studied these algae. He and his colleagues concluded that the ozone hole would decrease their growth by less than 4 percent while the hole was overhead, and would reduce annual growth by only 0.2 per cent (two-tenths of a percent) at most.[29]

What about Birds?

Keep in mind that when the ozone "hole" occurs in the spring, levels of UV radiation rise to about what they are in the Antarctic summer. This is the level of UV radiation that most migratory animals experience, anyway. Summer is the time that most migratory animals are there.

BAN CFCS, RAISE RISKS

Textbooks insist that drastic measures were needed to avoid further loss of ozone, and they applaud the Montreal Protocol, the 1987 international agreement to phase out CFCs. In the United States, CFCs were outlawed as of January 1, 1996.

The costs and risks of eliminating CFCs are rarely mentioned.[30] Most texts imply that the task will be easy and will have no harmful effects. They omit some important facts:

- CFCs are nontoxic chemicals that have saved lives and improved our standard of living. They keep our food safe and our homes, cars, and factories comfortable.

- Substitutes are less efficient. Refrigerators and auto air conditioners must use more energy to produce the same amount of cooling. This means burning more fossil fuels and more pollution. Hardly an ideal solution for the environment!

- Rapid adoption of substitutes makes the chance of serious problems more likely. One substitute known as HCFC 123 caused tumors in rats. The tumors were not cancerous, but it led one producer of industrial refrigeration systems to hold off on using it until it had been tested further.[31] Several substitutes produce a substance, TFA, that is toxic to plants, and some scientists worry that it could accumulate in wetlands.[32]

- Because substitutes cost more and don't work as well, there is now a multimillion-dollar black market in Freon (the best-known CFC). Freon is being smuggled into the country, says *The New York Times*.[33]

- Maintaining auto air conditioners will be costly, because they will have to be retrofitted to use the substitutes.

The United States and other industrial countries may be able to cope with more expensive refrigerators and troublesome car air conditioners. But developing countries, which are supposed to phase out CFCs early in the next decade, will experience more severe problems.

🐝 Lack of refrigeration is already a serious health problem in many countries. If refrigeration becomes more costly, more people may unknowingly eat contaminated food. Some will become sick. And more people will go hungry because food cannot be safely preserved.

🐝 The most difficult problem in providing children with life-saving vaccines is keeping them cold. Lack of CFCs makes the job even harder.[34] Many countries still use kerosene fuel for portable refrigerators.[35] It will be more difficult to replace such dangerous refrigerators with cheap, safe ones.

🐝 Old methods of food preservation, such as salting and smoking meats and fish, add potentially cancer-causing substances. These could put people at risk for cancers more dangerous than the skin cancer cited in the textbooks as a risk from ozone depletion.[36]

QUESTIONS AND ANSWERS

Responsible scientists still have more questions than answers about ozone. But we do know some things about it. Here are some questions that you can answer now.

Is the Ozone Layer Disappearing?

No, it is not disappearing. Scientists think that there may be a decline in ozone caused by some chemicals, but this decline is so small that it is hard to distinguish from natural changes.

What Happens If the Ozone Layer Thins?

A thinner ozone layer means that more UV radiation will reach the Earth on a clear day. However, a significant increase in UV radiation hasn't been measured, except temporarily over Antarctica due to the ozone "hole."

And keep in mind that people increase their exposure to the sun's UV rays voluntarily by moving closer to the Equator and moving to higher altitudes.

These changes are often much greater than any increase in exposure that may have been caused by ozone loss.

What Is the Ozone Hole?

The ozone hole is a large thinning of ozone above the Antarctic. It occurs each year in the Southern Hemisphere's spring (that is, autumn in the Northern Hemisphere), when the winds of the polar vortex keep out ozone-rich air. As the season progresses, and the vortex dissipates, the "hole" closes up again. It is not permanent. When it occurs, more UV radiation reaches the South Pole and the surrounding area.

What are CFCs?

CFCs, or chlorofluorocarbons, are chemicals that have an unusual property. They are inert, which makes them very safe. However, it also means that they don't break apart easily. Scientists have found that gradually over time they float up into the stratosphere, where sunlight breaks them apart, releasing chlorine. Scientists believe that the chlorine reacts with stratospheric ozone, depleting it.

ACTIVITIES

As you can see, ozone issues are complicated. Here are some activities that will help children understand these issues better.

Changes in Exposure

People make far greater changes in their exposure to UV rays than any change that may be caused by ozone depletion. Exposure to UV radiation changes as people move from north to south (in the Northern Hemisphere) and as they move to higher elevations.

Students can compute the changes in UV radiation exposure.

For every sixty miles traveled south, UV exposure increases by 5 percent. If a person travels from Washington, D.C., to Richmond, Virginia, a distance of 180 miles, how much will UV exposure increase? *UV exposure will increase by 15 percent. No one thinks that human exposure to UV radiation exposure has gone up anywhere near this much as a result of ozone loss.*

For every 150 feet of elevation, UV exposure increases 1 percent. If a person travels from Philadelphia, Pennsylvania, which is at sea level, to Denver, Colorado, which is at an elevation of 5,280 feet, how much will his or her UV exposure increase? *Exposure will increase by more than 35 percent. Again, this is far more than any estimate of increased exposure to humans that may have occurred through ozone loss.*

A Summer Vacation

Ask your children whether they would be willing to give up a vacation trip to the mountains or to the beach because of the danger of increased UV exposure. This could lead to a discussion of trade-offs and choices.

If they aren't worried about increased UV radiation exposure by traveling, how much should they worry about the current state of the ozone? There is no definite answer here. The point is to think about choices we make.

Children should be aware that regardless of the state of the ozone, basking in too much sunlight is not a good a thing. Physicians say that children should avoid sunburns by sunbathing less and by wearing sunscreen lotion whenever they are in the sun.

Alternatives to CFCs

Discuss the pros and cons of spending huge sums of money to convert to CFC substitutes. Air conditioners and refrigerators will become more expensive. This might not bother Americans too much, but what about people in poorer nations? Should their ability to have refrigeration and air conditioning be restricted? Would your children be willing to give up those things?

CHAPTER THIRTEEN

Acid Rain

....

SIXTEEN-YEAR-OLD DAN Shuman of Dover, Pennsylvania, noticed that the trees in his backyard were dying. And when he fished, he caught fewer trout and bass in the lakes and streams near his home. He suspected that acid rain was to blame.

He read in a fishing magazine that Dickinson College provided acid rain monitoring kits. So Dan recruited fifteen energetic Boy Scouts and raised money from several sports clubs. (The testing kits were $20 each.)

With his volunteers and kits, Dan set out to monitor twenty-two streams in the area. After a year of testing streams, Dan sent the information to Dickinson College for analysis. The college reported that the water was contaminated by acid rain.[1]

Yes, Dan and his crew of Scouts may have found acid contamination, but they did not find proof that acid rain was killing fish. The likelihood that his trees were dying from acid rain is slight. As we shall see, while acid rain does exist, it doesn't have the widespread effects that are claimed for it.

DEAD FISH, DYING TREES

"High in the Adirondack Mountains of northern New York State, a crystal blue lake shimmers in the sun," begins one account in a science text. "Cradled by green slopes, the lake once held huge trout, which drew anglers from all over the country. But now the lake has no fish. Why? For years the lake has been pelted by polluted rain that is almost as acid as vinegar. Unable to survive the high acid content of the water, the fish died."[2]

Other texts may not be so dramatic, but they convey the same message:

- "Acid rain that falls into lakes and streams kills fish," says the Globe text *Concepts and Challenges in Earth Science*. "Acid rain also causes brick, stone, and metal structures to weather, or break apart."[3]

- "Acid rain that falls into lakes can destroy both plant and animal life," says the eighth-grade text *Life Science*.[4]

- "Trees all across the Northeast are dying [from acid rain],"[5] says the D. C. Heath text *Earth Science: The Challenge of Discovery*.

- "Many believe that it [acid rain] is the main reason why whole forests are dying in Europe and Canada,"[6] says the Addison-Wesley text *Civics: Participating in Our Democracy*.

- "Today, about one-third of the trees in [Germany's] Black Forest have been affected by acid rain,"[7] says Prentice Hall's *World Geography*.

Children learn that air pollution from cars and coal-burning power plants in the Midwest are carried by winds to the northeastern states and Canada. There, acid rain and snow pollute lakes, streams, and the ground. Forests, fish, and crops are dying, and buildings and statues are crumbling. Rarely do textbooks indicate that there is any question about the cause-and-effect relationship between acid rain and dying forests and lakes.

Textbooks and other materials suggest experiments to dramatize the perils of acid rain.

🐝 *Pollution: Problems and Solutions,* one of the titles in the National Wildlife Federation's Ranger Rick *NatureScope* series, instructs students to attempt to grow seeds with a mixture of water and vinegar. Not surprisingly, the seeds watered with the vinegar mixture don't grow.[8]

🐝 Other textbooks suggest making a heavily acidic solution and spraying it on living plants. After several weeks, children observe that the plants wither and die.

🐝 A book for children called *Ecology* instructs children to use a fish tank to create a closed system that has fish that produce carbon dioxide and grass that produces oxygen. The child experimenter sends sulfur dioxide gas into the air in the tank through a tube. Soon, the grass and fish die due to the acid rain that has been created in the mini-environment.[9]

These lab experiments are not accurate representations of the complex cause-and-effect relationships that surround acid rain.

🐝 In the Ranger Rick *NatureScope* experiment, students are using acidic water at a pH level of 3. Acid rain in the United States typically has a pH of 4.6. This means that the water used in the experiment is about forty times more acidic than the average acid rainfall.

🐝 In the other projects, students are not told how to calculate or control the pH level of the acidic water.

WHAT, EXACTLY, IS IT?

The term "acid rain" sounds ominous. It makes us think of rain so contaminated that it resembles car battery acid. But, in fact, the term simply means rain that has a higher concentration of hydrogen ions than natural rain. It occurs when clouds or raindrops pick up substances from vehicle exhaust and coal-burning power plants that form acids when dissolved in water. This moisture can be transported over some distance before it falls as "acid rain."

Most natural rainfall is slightly acidic because of natural carbon dioxide and nitrogen oxides in the air.[10] But pollutants can, indeed, make rain more acidic. Electrical power plants and automobiles emit sulfur dioxide and nitrogen oxides into the air when they burn coal and gasoline. These chemicals combine with water vapor to produce dilute sulfuric and nitric acids in rain.

Scientists measure acidity on a scale from 1 to 14. This scale, known as the pH scale, measures the concentration of hydrogen ions. A value below 7 indicates that the liquid is acidic; a value above 7 indicates that it is basic or alkaline. This scale is logarithmic; that means that one number represents a value ten times more acidic than the number just above it. For example, 4 represents a value ten times more acidic than 5 (or 100 times more acidic than 6).

pH SCALE

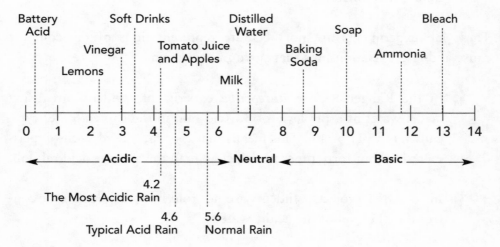

Normal rain has a pH of about 5.6. Acid rain typically has a pH of 4.6, and the most acidic rain in the United States (found in western Pennsylvania and nearby areas) has an average pH of 4.2.[11] That is similar to the acidity of tomato or apple juice.

WHAT SCIENTISTS SAY

In the late 1970s, many people became alarmed about acid rain. Small lakes, especially in Adirondack Park in upper New York State, were found to be acidic. Fish couldn't live in them, yet people remembered a time when some of these lakes did have fish. What had happened?

About the same time, people also began to see forests with many dead and dying trees, especially in Europe. They suspected, incorrectly, that the cause was acid rain resulting from sulfur dioxide emissions from European power plants.

The fear aroused at that time entered the textbooks. Unfortunately, the more complete story that has emerged from scientific studies has not replaced it.

Rarely do textbooks indicate there is any question about the cause-and-effect relationship between acid rain and dying forests and lakes.

Rarely do any books even hint that there is a large body of evidence that counters the apocalyptic claims about acid rain. Yet this evidence exists. It was collected by the U.S. government.

This ten-year study, called the National Acid Precipitation Assessment Program (NAPAP), cost more than $500 million and involved hundreds of scientists and technicians and resulted in hundreds of reports. Congress authorized the program in 1980 to find out what harm acid rain may be causing. A final report was issued in 1990, and its conclusions countered many of the previous assumptions about acid rain.

The scientists found that while acid rain may be harming some lakes and some trees, it is a much smaller problem than most people believed.[12] In fact, it may be beneficial for some agricultural crops and trees. The "Assessment Highlights" of the report came to these conclusions:

🌰 In its nationwide survey of waters, less than 5 percent of the lakes and 10 percent of the streams were found to be "chronically acidic." And this acidity was not necessarily caused by acid rain.

🐝 Florida, which receives minimal acid rain, not the Northeast, has the highest percentage of acid lakes (23 percent). These lakes appear to be acidic due entirely to natural processes—the lakes are surrounded by highly acidic soils, for example.

🐝 A special study of the Adirondack Lakes, where high acidity had aroused great concern, found that up to 30 percent of the small (two-to ten-acre) lakes in the region are acidic. But many of the lakes have natural organic acids, which can make the water acidic regardless of the acidity of the rain.

🐝 "There is currently no widespread forest or crop damage in the United States related to [acid rain]," said the report. "Some areas may benefit through nutrient enrichment by nitrogen and sulfur deposition."

🐝 Scientists discovered some harm to high-elevation red spruce trees in the Appalachians when acid rain was present with other factors such as stress from extremely cold winters. These forests account for only a small fraction of 1 percent of eastern woodlands.

The NAPAP study also found:

🐝 While acid rain contributes to corrosion of building materials, the magnitude "has been difficult to assess."

🐝 Sulfate particles in the air, which lead to acid rain, reduce visibility in some places by causing haze.

A subsequent report from NAPAP looked at the problems of European forests.

🌰 The effects of air pollutants "are small compared with other stresses affecting tree condition," the report said. (These include abnormal weather conditions and insect damage.)

🌰 Overall forest productivity has increased in Europe since the nineteenth century.[13]

Unfortunately, most students, and most adults, never hear about NAPAP's findings.

THOSE ADIRONDACK LAKES

Acid rain does not always make lakes acidic. Often, rain falls onto nearby ground and slowly moves through the soil before it enters the lake. If that soil is alkaline—that is, if it has many pieces of limestone in it—the limestone will neutralize the acid.[14]

So while the NAPAP study found that some Adirondack Lakes are acidic and can't support fish, one important reason is that they don't have the neutralizing or buffering capacity of alkaline soil. If acid rain falls on the streams that feed into these lakes, they gradually become acidic because the surrounding soil does not reduce the acidity.

NAPAP researchers also found evidence (by studying fossils of algae) that some of these Adirondack Lakes were acidic in preindustrial times. These lakes temporarily lost some of their natural acidity during the late 1800s.[15] (The fact that the Iroquois word "Adirondack" means "bark-eater" also suggests that fish were not plentiful in the past.)

The researchers also found that some Adirondack lakes lost fish for other reasons than acid rain. Changes in water levels (caused by beaver-made dams or human-made dams) and the introduction of predators explained some losses, for example. Researchers found that out of the 409 Adirondack lakes that contained brook trout in the past, 282 (about two-thirds) still contain brook trout. Of the 127 that no longer support brook trout, only 44 (about one-third) apparently lost the trout because of acid rain.[16]

One of the studies prepared for NAPAP said that the acid lakes in the Adirondacks could be neutralized by adding lime to the lakes. This would cost $170,000 per year or a total of $500,000 per year for the entire Northeast.[17] This would have corrected the biggest problem caused by acid rain. But Congress didn't seriously consider this alternative.

CONTROLLING ACID RAIN

Curriculum materials recommend stronger laws to control acid rain but seldom consider whether the costs are worth the benefits.

> *Pollution: Problems and Solutions* (a Ranger Rick's *NatureScope* title) warns that these laws may meet opposition from lobbyists who ask for more proof. But it cautions that "many researchers feel that coming up with such proof may take too long or may not be possible at all."[18]

> A science text discusses who should pay the cost of the necessary smokestack scrubbers—industry or the taxpayers.[19]

In 1990, Congress did, in fact, pass laws to control acid rain. Amendments to the Clean Air Act required all major electric utilities to reduce their sulfur dioxide emissions by 50 percent by about the year 2000. These regulations have been phased in gradually, but they will still speed up the reductions that would have occurred as old power plants were retired.[20] The regulations, it seemed at the time, would cost companies and electricity consumers about $4 billion per year.[21]

But Congress also instituted an innovative program that allows utilities to reduce the costs of adding scrubbers. Although all major utilities must cut back on their emissions, those that can control emissions cheaply can put on extra controls and obtain payment from utilities that can't reduce emissions so cheaply. This "trading" has made the regulations less costly than they would have been, while still achieving the same overall goals.

QUESTIONS AND ANSWERS

Fortunately, acid rain is much less troubling than most people think. With the background in this chapter, you can answer students' questions.

What is Acid Rain?

Acid rain is rain that has picked up substances from vehicle exhaust and coal-burning power plants that create acids when they are wet. It has a higher concentration of hydrogen ions than normal rain.

Can Acid Rain Kill Fish?

Yes, in relatively rare circumstances where the soils around the streams and lakes do not neutralize the excess acid. Such lakes can become too acidic for fish to survive. A number of small lakes in the Adirondacks are too acidic to support fish, and the cause may be acid rain. The acidity of lakes or streams is not a serious problem in most of the United States.

What Causes Acid Rain?

Acid rain is caused primarily by coal-burning electric power plants and vehicles that burn fuels producing sulfur oxides and nitrogen oxides. However, natural causes (specifically, carbon dioxide and nitrogen oxides in the air) make most rain slightly acid.

What Should Be Done about Acid Rain?

In 1990, Congress passed amendments to the Clean Air Act that required electrical utilities to reduce their emissions of sulfur dioxide. This may slightly reduce the number of acidic lakes. It will not restore most of the acidic Adirondack Lakes, but may have some other beneficial effects, such as improving visibility in some places, reducing the acid in some soils, and slowing the degradation of metal and stone on the exteriors of buildings.

ACTIVITIES

The experiments that follow are closer to real-world conditions than the experiments recommended in the texts we reviewed.

Learning About the pH Scale

To understand the debate over acid rain, students should understand the concepts of acid and base. These are measured on a scale called the pH scale, which runs from 0 to 14, with 7 representing substances that are neutral.

You can illustrate the concept, by using pH paper. It can be obtained from a "laboratory chemicals" company (look under "Chemicals" in the Yellow Pages). Or call VWR Scientific Products at 800-932-5000. Ask for pH indicator strips with a pH range of 0-14. (A box of 100 strips will cost $10 to $20.) Michael and his son Devin tried these experiments. *But we emphasize that these experiments require adult supervision!*

Understanding Acid and Base

(1) Materials needed: distilled water (not spring water), a clean glass, a straw, and pH paper.

Put about half a cup of distilled water in a clean glass. (Do not shake the water before the test.) Test the water using the pH paper. It should measure 7 on the pH scale (neither acidic nor basic).

Using the straw, ask the children to blow gently in the water for three or four minutes. Test the water again with the pH paper. This time it should measure slightly acidic. The reason is that our breath has carbon dioxide in it. The carbon dioxide reacts with water to make carbonic acid. Normal rain water is slightly acidic because the rain reacts with carbon dioxide in the air, forming carbonic acid.

(2) Materials needed: pH paper, small amounts of materials such as lemon juice, vinegar, ammonia, apple juice, cola, or baking soda.

Students should draw a line on a piece of paper with equal divisions from 0 to 14. Ask them to test the common household items above and record the pH readings on their scale.

From Acid to Base

Ask the children to take about one tablespoon of vinegar and mix it with a half cup of distilled water. Have them test this solution. It should measure about 3 on the pH scale. Now ask them to collect about two tablespoons of very fine ash from the barbecue or fireplace. Mix the ash with the vinegar solution. When it is dissolved, test the solution. The pH level should increase.

Explain that the ash is basic, and it has neutralized some of the acid.

Visit a Garden Center

Visit a local garden center or nursery. Ask the owner or manager to discuss differences in soils and how plants react to them. Ask this person to point out plants that thrive in acidic soil, and those that will die in such soil. Then have the manager show the different products available to treat soil so that it will be the right pH for specific plants.

CHAPTER FOURTEEN

Not a Drop to Drink

....

PIGEON CREEK WAS SO polluted that salmon stopped using it to breed. It was a dumping ground for used tires, trash, and litter. The children at the elementary school near the creek in Everett, Washington, wanted to do something about it.

They organized cleanup crews to remove tons of debris from the creek. They met with homeowners and businesses that were polluting the creek. They hatched salmon eggs, raised the young fish, and then released them in the creek. After a year or two, the fish returned to the newly cleaned creek to breed. The children had restored the creek to a place where salmon could live and breed.[1]

Their success is testimony to the power of individuals working together to protect the environment.

A FLOOD OF CRISES

Some educational materials encourage positive action like the children's stream cleanup project. For example, Ranger Rick's *NatureScope* suggests that children contact the Adopt-A-Stream Foundation[2] to find out how they can restore a polluted waterway.

All too often, however, the texts treat water pollution as crises, not as a manageable problem. They fail to teach why we have water pollution.

The first "crisis": We are running out of water.

Many textbooks observe that while three-fourths of the earth is covered with water, most of this water can't be used because 97 percent is salt water in the oceans and seas. Of the 3 percent that is fresh water, 2 percent is locked in the polar ice caps. This leaves only 1 percent available for use by plants, animals, and man.[3] The impression is that it is not enough.

🐝 The Earth "has a short supply of water suitable for drinking,"[4] says a D. C. Heath science text. And, it warns, "as the population grows, and as people buy more manufactured goods, the demand for fresh water increases."[5]

🐝 Groundwater is being used up faster than it is being replenished by natural processes. "As a result," the Prentice Hall text *Life Science* notes, "the level of groundwater drops and eventually streams and lakes may dry up."[6] Some texts show houses teetering at the edge of sinkholes caused by too many wells.

The second "crisis": Our drinking water is contaminated by chemicals.

🐝 "Pesticides, industrial waste, sewage, gasoline leaking from underground storage tanks, and contaminated water leaking from landfills all find their way into groundwater...," writes D. C. Heath's *Earth Science: The Challenge of Discovery*. "One service-station storage tank leaking only one gallon of fuel per day can ruin a volume of water that would supply 50,000 people."[7]

🐝 "Some industries bury their wastes in barrels, or drums, in the ground. If the drums rust and break apart, the wastes can leak into the groundwater. Industries also dump chemical wastes directly into water. . . ," says the Globe text *Concepts and Challenges in Earth Science.*[8]

The third "crisis": Oil spills.

🐝 The Exxon Valdez spill in Prince William Sound, Alaska, "covered an area larger than Rhode Island," says the D. C. Heath text *Earth Science: The Challenge of Discovery.* "Even with massive clean-up efforts, the effects of the oil on the bay's environment will last for decades."[9]

🐝 "Chemicals and metals from industrial wastes, oil leaks, and accidental oil spills, along with mine drainage and wastes from mining operations, account for the millions of tons of toxic substances dumped into our waterways each year,"[10] says the Glencoe text *Health: A Guide to Wellness.*

AN EMPTY FAUCET?

For most Americans, water is cheap and abundant. But usually after a series of dry years, some towns and cities impose regulations limiting the use of water—banning car washing and limiting the hours for watering lawns. The 1999 drought in the eastern United States led to such restrictions, as did a series of drought years in California in the late 1980s.

Such restrictions reinforce the impression that we are running out of water. In fact, they usually stem from governmental decisions that set the price of water too low.

The amount of water in the Earth's ecosystem is always the same; it is constantly being recycled through evaporation and precipitation. The Earth "has more than enough water to meet human demands," says Terry L. Anderson of Montana State University. The problem, he explains, is that "water is often found in the wrong place at the wrong time."[11]

Frequently, water is in the "wrong place" because it is cheaper than it should be, and this causes people to overuse it. Textbooks urge water conservation but they don't explain that low prices discourage conservation.

In the western United States, between 80 and 90 percent of all water is used for agriculture. The federal government sells water to farmers and ranchers at prices far below the cost of supplying it through dams and canals and other projects.

Typically, the farmer's price is less than $20 per acre-foot. (An acre-foot is the amount of water it takes to cover one acre of land with one foot of water, or 326,000 gallons). In contrast, towns and cities pay between $300 and $500 for each acre-foot.[12]

If farmers were paying the full cost of the water, they would use it more carefully. They might invest in drip irrigation systems, for example, which uses less water than the more common flood irrigation.[13] They would have an incentive to conserve.

Often cities are willing to pay more for the water, but state laws make it difficult for farmers to sell water to the cities. Some states and counties prohibit transfers of water beyond the local area. Cities have to find their own sources, often paying hundreds of dollars per acre-foot when they do.

Remnants of old water rules under state law also discourage conservation. For example, if water is not used, one's right to it disappears. (This is called the "use it or lose it" rule.) Until recently, western states required water users to divert their water from the stream or else they would lose the right to it. Leaving water in the stream to protect fish, for example, was not considered an acceptable or "beneficial" use.

Realistic pricing and laws allowing trades would change this situation. When water does become more expensive, people usually respond by using less of it. Industries can produce the same products with vastly different amounts of water:

 Some electric utilities use 170 gallons to produce one kilowatt-hour of electricity.

🐝 But it's possible to produce the same amount of electricity with less than two gallons![14]

Similarly, farming can use either a great deal of water or just a little. Higher prices would encourage farmers to conserve and perhaps to change the crops they grow. They could decrease their production of alfalfa and increase production of safflower, for example.[15] Wiser policies could make more water available for everyone, rather than having water restrictions year after year.

THE SINKING AQUIFER

Some books for children discuss the vast Ogallala aquifer that lies beneath parts of eight states, from Texas to South Dakota.[16] An aquifer is an underground pool of water, usually mixed with sand, and the Ogallala is one of the biggest. Farmers and ranchers draw up the water through their wells to irrigate millions of acres of cropland, which produce $20 billion worth of food and fiber each year.

Drawing water from a well can suck up water from the parts of the aquifer that lie under other people's land. The situation is a little like two children sipping Coke through straws in a single cup.

For some decades, more water has been taken out of the Ogallala than naturally seeps back in ("recharges") through rainfall or other sources. The impression given by the books is that nothing is being done about this.

True, years ago, the farmers living above the Ogallala aquifer had little knowledge of how to manage this resource. After all, it had always been there for the taking. Gradually, however, they became aware that the level of the water was sinking.

More people began to explore ways to solve or avoid overdrawing the aquifer. Better management practices and new irrigation technologies have started to work. Since 1980, the rate of decline has slowed in many areas, stopped in some, and, in a few, the water table is actually rising.[17]

In California, where there are smaller aquifers, people have worked out ways to divide up the rights to the water in the aquifer. If everyone knows how much he or she has a right to use, each person is more likely to conserve.

TICKING TIME BOMBS?

Landfills containing chemicals are pictured as ticking time bombs that will eventually pollute groundwater and surface water by seeping out.

> "Long-buried toxic chemicals—like those at Love Canal—have quietly seeped into the groundwater, poisoning private wells and city and town water supplies," says the Prentice Hall text *Your Health*. "Sadly, chemical wastes that are harmful to health often are only discovered after illness, birth defects, and cancer occur."[18] (In fact, while chemical wastes can enter groundwater and poison water supplies, long-term hazards from the most famous waste sites, including Love Canal in New York State, have not been scientifically confirmed by epidemiological studies.)[19]

> "In many parts of the United States, wells have been shut down and people are using bottled water," says the Merrill text *Biology: Living Systems*.[20] (The text does not report where in the United States this is occurring or whether it is for a very short time or a long period.)

Chemical wastes can pollute our water. But pollution problems are more complex than simply "bad guys" dumping chemicals.

Some texts attempt to spread the blame. "We all contribute to polluting Earth's waters," says one, citing the pollution caused by flushing toilets, washing hands, brushing teeth, and watering lawns.[21] The downside of this approach is that it instills guilt in children for everyday activities.

A better way to look at water pollution is to recognize why it occurs. Streams, rivers, and groundwater are essentially a common pool. Just as people tend to litter in public spaces, people allow waste to enter a commonly owned waterway.

If water weren't entirely a common pool, the picture would be different. In England and Scotland, it is possible to own rights to fish in streams and rivers. If fish are killed by pollution, fishermen can sue the polluter in court. In fact, the Anglers' Cooperative Association in England has obtained damages or injunctions for its members in hundreds of cases.[22] Ranchers in the western United States who have private trout streams flowing entirely within their property are careful to prevent pollution. However, private protection of other streams is rare, since fishing rights are not owned in the United States.

The Clean Water Act of 1972 was enacted to stop people from polluting. Since its passage, the Environmental Protection Agency (EPA) has been telling industries and municipal sewage plants how much they can emit into streams. The focus is on inputs—what goes into the stream—not on the outcomes—the quality of the water.

Over the years, it appears that there has been improvement in the cleanliness of our waterways. In 1990, an expert from Resources for the Future reviewed most of the available studies of water quality. He concluded that there had been "some improvement," although it "has not been dramatic." However, he also noted "local success stories of substantial cleanup."[23] (Another review noted significant reductions in chemicals such as DDT and PCBs in the Great Lakes since 1970.[24])

It is hard to know how much has been accomplished since there was little information about water quality conditions when the act was passed, and thus no basis for judging later progress.[25]

Nearly everyone agrees that most "point sources"—identifiable places where pollution enters a stream or river—have been controlled. But water that runs off fields, homes, buildings, parks, and farms, picking up natural and synthetic substances, still pollutes streams and rivers. This "non-point" source pollution is much harder to control.

SLICKS AND SPILLS

Oil spills can cause immediate—and very serious—harm to the environment, especially to fish, birds, and animals, like otters, that live in or near the ocean. But textbooks don't tell the full story of these spills.

Texts like the D. C. Heath *Earth Science* imply that the beaches may never be clean again.[26] Yet a 1990 government study of six highly publicized oil spills around the world concluded that water and beaches recover fairly quickly after even big spills.[27] The Congressional Research Service (CRS, an arm of Congress) found, for example, the following:

🐝 When the Argo Merchant, an oil tanker, was grounded off the shore of Massachusetts in 1976, the EPA administrator at the time called it "the biggest oil spill disaster on the American coast in our history."[28] In fact, however, pollution damage was small. The CRS reported a "general scientific consensus that classifying the incident as an ecological catastrophe had no factual basis."[29]

🐝 In 1979 an oil well in the Bay of Campeche, Mexico, exploded. Oil and gas spewed from the pipe and the platform burned up. This turned out to be the largest oil spill in the history of offshore drilling or tanker transportation. Yet by the end of 1980, said the CRS, the only oil left was "scattered patches of tar mats along the Texas barrier island beaches,"[30] and some of these may have been natural oil seeps.

🐝 In sum, the environmental impact of the spills studied was "relatively modest and . . . of relatively short duration,"[31] said the CRS. It also found that "short-term impacts on marine animal life are dramatic but recovery of species populations in almost every case studied has been swift." [32]

In addition to perpetuating exaggerated fears, the books are misguided about policy. After discussing the Exxon Valdez spill off the Alaska coast in 1989, the D. C. Heath text *Earth Science: The Challenge of Discovery* says: "Some people want to stop off-shore drilling and seek other sources of energy in order to protect the environment. How would you vote on such issues?"[33]

The implication is that laws against off-shore drilling will avoid oil spills.

In fact, they will encourage them. The Exxon Valdez was carrying oil that had been drilled in Alaska. Bans on off-shore drilling encourage more on-shore drilling. That means increased shipping of oil in ocean vessels rather than pipelines to reach refineries.

QUESTIONS AND ANSWERS

Experts think that water quality is improving in the United States. It is, however, difficult to be sure since there was not a good base of information when the Clean Water Act was passed in 1972.

We do know of specific examples of major improvements in water quality. Sometimes, people have joined together to clean up a body of water so that people can swim and fish in it—the way that the children in Everett, Washington, did at the beginning of this chapter.

As for water availability, we know that there is enough water for everyone. But unrealistic prices make it hard for the people who really want it to get it.

Now you can answer your children's questions:

Are We Running Out of Water?

No. The amount of water on the Earth stays the same. However, some places do not have enough water to let people live comfortably during periods of drought. Usually this is because of government policies that provide water at less than its cost.

Why Do Some Places Have Too Little Water?

In the western United States, most of the water is sold to farmers or ranchers for a price that is much lower than the cost of supplying it. The price is also much lower than the price that people in cities are willing to pay for the water. However, government regulations often prevent the farmers from selling their water to cities.

Is Our Water Getting More Polluted?

Probably not. It appears that many lakes and streams have better water quality than they used to. Laws require industry and sewage plants to clean their water before sending it to streams or rivers. But the laws do not really address the water that flows over streets and fields, picking up pollutants. Primarily because of this pollution, some bodies of water remain seriously polluted.

ACTIVITIES

The following activities will help young people think realistically about water supplies and water pollution.

Reading a Utility Bill

Ask your children to look at the two sample utility bills on the next page, which charge residents for water, sewage, and trash pick-up.

Ask them to compute the price per gallon of water from the information on these two water bills. They will quickly notice that Bill #2 lumps water together with other services and doesn't charge on the basis of the amount of water you use. (That bill does charge for trash volume, however, as we will discuss in chapter 17.)

Discuss how these two billing procedures can influence how a person or family will use water. Which bill is more likely to encourage conservation? *(The first bill, because you can reduce your water bill by using less.)* Which leads to more usage? *(The second, because usage doesn't affect the amount you are charged.)*

Have the children compare their own families' water bills to the two above. Would their families save money if everyone conserved on water?

UTILITY BILL #1   UTILITY BILL #2

Anytown, USA Utilities Service Office			Ourtown, USA City Services Department		
Account Number 00-0000-00	Present Reading Date 11/22/99	Present Reading 467	Account Number 00-0000-00	Billing Date 10/3/99	
	Previous Reading Date 10/22/99	Previous Reading 463	Service From: 9/1/99	Service To: 9/30/99	
Water Rate/ 1000 gal $5.50	Sewer Rate/ 1000 Gal $5.30	Consumption 4	Trash Service Rate $1.50/Can	# Cans 6	Trash Charge $9.00
	Charges: Water $22.00 Sewer $21.20 Trash $15.00			Charges: Water Service $15.00 Sewer Service $10.00 Trash Service $ 9.00	
Due Date 12/10/99	Amount Due $58.20		Due Date 10/30/99	Amount Due $34.00	

Water for Sale

Talk to young people about products that help people get cleaner or better water.

At the grocery store, they can find bottled water for sale. Have them note a typical price per gallon. Ask them to compare the price of bottled water to the price of tap water, using their water bill (if it supplies these figures). They will probably find that the price is much higher at the store.

Ask why people are willing to pay more for bottled water. For one thing, the higher price is for drinking water or specialized water such as distilled water, while the water from the faucet has many uses. In addition, some people want a certain kind of taste in their water and they are willing to pay for it.

Children might also ask the manager of a plumbing supply store about products that homeowners use to purify their tap water or to soften it. The point of these discussions is to show that people can take action on their own to make sure that their drinking water is to their liking.

Rivers and Streams

Stopping at a river or a stream gives you a chance to point out the problem of lack of ownership. In most places in the country, no one "owns" the water in the stream, unless it is a small stream on private property. Fishermen can fish in streams but they do not "own" the right to fish in clean water. If someone pollutes the stream, the users of the water have little recourse.

In contrast, if someone dumped trash in your backyard, you could sue that person for polluting your property (so people rarely do such a thing). Similarly, if people owned a stream, they could sue polluters to protect their property.

This process works in England, where the right to fish is something that a person can own. Do you know of any private fishing lakes or ponds? A visit to them might help explain why public streams and lakes are often dirty. To encourage discussion, you might look back at the "tragedy of the commons" section in chapter 3.

CHAPTER FIFTEEN

Don't Eat That Apple!

....

LEIGH BRADFORD, A SIXTH-GRADER in Wheaton, Maryland, planted a garden. But it wasn't an ordinary garden. It was "organic." Leigh fertilized the plants with compost rather than chemicals and applied no pesticides while they were growing. (She did use a bug killer for the aphids on the vegetables when they were harvested.)

Leigh went to the trouble of planting a chemical-free garden because she had been taught that agricultural chemicals were dangerous. They "poison birds, animals and water supplies and also get in the food," she explained.[1]

Leigh had probably read about pesticides. Perhaps she had seen:

🐝 *The Kids' Environment Book,* which talks about the 2.5 billion pounds of "toxic gunk" on our crops,[2] and recommends organic gardening or, at least, buying organic foods.

🐝 Or *This Planet Is Mine: Teaching Environmental Awareness and Appreciation to Children,* which says that the "lack of toxic substances" makes organic foods safer. "Logically, what's less risky for humans to consume is also a safer choice for the environment," this book states.[3]

Our children's books treat farm chemicals as dangerous by-products of technology that should be banned or severely restricted. To many authors, pesticides are killers and should be eliminated at all costs:

- Pesticide residues are "building up in the soil and entering the water supply,"[4] says *Your Health!*, a Prentice Hall text.

- The Environmental Protection Agency ranked pesticide residues as the "third most important environmental problem in the United States in terms of cancer risk...,"[5] says Diane MacEachern, author of the children's book, *Save Our Planet: 750 Everyday Ways You Can Help Clean Up the Earth*. Between 1982 and 1985, "federal and state monitoring programs detected more than 110 different pesticides on commonly eaten fruit and vegetables." (The fact that most of these residues are harmless is ignored.)

- Anne Pedersen advises that if you can't grow your own garden "the next best thing is to buy organic produce.... It's usually more expensive and maybe doesn't look quite as picture-perfect,...but it's probably safer."[6]

THE OTHER SIDE OF THE STORY

Chemicals have transformed farming. Pesticides have nearly eliminated the ancient scourge of insect infestation, and fertilizer allows farmers to restore the nutrients that plants take from the soil as they grow. According to the National Research Council, the use of these chemicals "has increased the quantity of fresh fruits and vegetables in the diet, thereby contributing to improvements in public health."[7]

But chemicals have disadvantages, too. Pesticides that harm insects can also harm humans and animals. The nutrients from fertilizers, while vital to crops, also spill over into waterways, where they encourage the growth of algae that can smother other plant life and fish. Some chemicals may reach pools of underground water that provide drinking water.

These days, what worries people the most is whether pesticide residues on food can cause cancer. Some scientists think that small amounts of pesticide left on food—amounts usually measured in parts per million or parts per billion—increase the risk of cancer. Yet the evidence for this is extremely weak. In 1996 a National Academy of Sciences report said that levels of synthetic chemicals in Americans' diet are "so low that they are unlikely to pose an appreciable cancer risk."[8]

DDT: SCARE NO. 1

Much of the fear about pesticides stems from concern about one product, DDT. The fear began with Rachel Carson's 1962 book, *Silent Spring*.

Carson treated DDT as a dangerous chemical that had killed wildlife and might be causing cancer to humans. Carson's attack on DDT shocked the world because it contradicted what everyone had believed about this "miracle" chemical.

DDT had saved many lives by killing mosquitos that carried malaria and typhus. By the time it entered commercial use in 1947, says historian Thomas R. Dunlap, it "had a reputation for effectiveness, power and safety unmatched by any other material."[9] Unlike most insecticides of the day, it caused no acute harm to people and its effect was long-lasting, so that repeated applications were not necessary. DDT appeared to be so safe that farmers, foresters, and municipal authorities quickly adopted it after the war.

Clearly, DDT was safe for people to use in the short run. But what about the long run? DDT builds up in the tissues of animals and people, and Carson raised concern that it could cause cancer.

This fear has been refuted to most scientists' satisfaction. In 1989, three public health scientists who had followed nearly one thousand people for a decade reported that they had found "no relation between either overall mortality or cancer mortality and increasing serum DDT levels [that is, levels of DDT in body fluids]."[10]

The strongest case against DDT was not that it caused cancer in humans but that it was causing birds to die. Carson's book evoked the image of a "silent spring" in which no birds would sing. She suggested that DDT accumulated in the tissues of birds, especially predatory and fish-eating birds like eagles and falcons. By causing their eggshells to thin, DDT was destroying their ability to reproduce.

The question of whether DDT does hurt the reproductive ability of bird populations is still not completely resolved. A thorough review of scientific literature revealed that while some studies show a correlation between eggshell thinning and DDT, others did not.[11] However, the evidence, plus the fact that many birds at the top of the food chain like falcons and eagles have recovered in number since DDT was banned, strongly suggest that DDT was at least partly responsible. (It is also possible, though, that other chemicals, such as polychlorinated biphenols [PCBs], which are used in electrical transformers, contributed to eggshell thinning.)[12]

In 1972, due more to political pressure rather than to clear scientific evidence, the Environmental Protection Agency imposed a nearly complete ban on DDT in the United States. This ban is viewed as an important victory in the texts, a triumph of environmental activism over the evils of modern technology. But some of the consequences were unfortunate.

Pesticides that are more toxic to humans replaced DDT and they had to be applied more often. Some of these posed (and continue to pose) serious dangers to farm workers.[13]

In at least one country, Sri Lanka, a DDT spraying program, which had virtually eliminated malaria in Sri Lanka, was stopped. When Sri Lanka stopped using DDT, the number of malaria cases rose again to 2.5 million in the years 1968-9.[14] Today, throughout the world, malaria kills two million people per year.[15]

APPLE HYSTERIA

One legacy of *Silent Spring* is periodic hysteria over small amounts of chemicals. In early 1989, the CBS show "60 Minutes" called Alar, a chemical used on apples, "the most potent cancer-causing agent in our food supply." And the elegant actress Meryl Streep appeared on the "Phil Donahue Show" to alert parents to its dangers.

The EPA had been considering a ban on Alar because of animal tests suggesting that it broke down into a possibly carcinogenic substance. But an environmental group, the Natural Resources Defense Council, didn't want to wait for the EPA to decide. It orchestrated a public relations campaign against Alar that scared nearly everyone. Parents inundated pediatricians with phone calls and schools stopped serving apples.

As the furor mounted, the EPA, the Food and Drug Administration, and the Department of Agriculture issued a statement assuring parents that eating apples did not pose "an imminent hazard" to children.[16]

Alar is a growth regulator, not a pesticide—it keeps apples on trees so that they can stay crisp and attain a deep red color. It is regulated by the Environmental Protection Agency.

While a few tests on animals had shown that Alar's breakdown product could cause tumors in animals, the doses were so massive that some animals died simply because the dose overwhelmed their systems, not because of cancer.[17] According to one source, a human being would have to eat twenty-eight thousand pounds of apples daily for seventy years to produce tumors like the ones the mice developed.[18] Yet the Alar hysteria was so intense and the political pressures so great that the manufacturer halted production.

FACTS, NOT FEARS

What are the facts about pesticide residues? British researchers Richard Doll and Richard Peto are highly respected for their studies of the causes of cancer.[19] In 1986, they concluded that all environmental pollution, taken together, may have contributed to 2 percent of all recent cancer deaths. As for pesticide residues, they are "unimportant" as an explanation for any cancer today, these experts said.[20]

Lifestyle, smoking, and diet appear to have a lot more to do with whether people develop cancer. When cancer rates in the United States are adjusted to take into account the changing age of the population and to exclude the contribution of smoking, the risk of death from cancer is either the same or decreasing.[21]

It is ironic that people are so concerned about synthetic pesticides and yet ignore natural ones. Plants produce natural toxins to protect themselves against insects and other predators. When natural chemicals are tested on animals, some turn out to be carcinogenic, just as do some synthetic chemicals. (About the same percentage of the natural pesticides—about 50 percent—cause tumors in animals as do synthetic pesticides.)[22] Based on animal tests, scientists know that coffee and cocoa, spices such as cinnamon and mustard, and fruits such as pineapples and plums all have natural carcinogens.[23]

Plants that are naturally pest-resistant have higher natural pesticides.[24] In fact, the 1996 National Research Council report quoted earlier, which said we shouldn't worry much about chemicals in our foods, also stated that natural components may be of "greater concern" than synthetic ones.[25]

In creating and using synthetic pesticides, human beings can control the amounts and kinds of pesticides that are used. When toxins are made naturally by the plants themselves, humans cannot control them very well.

Bruce Ames and Lois Swirsky Gold at the University of California at Berkeley point out that people ingest about ten thousand times more of these natural pesticides than synthetic ones! The reason these don't harm us, they explain, is that "the many layers of general defenses in humans and other animals protect against toxins, without distinguishing whether they are synthetic or natural." These natural defenses can't tell whether toxins are plant-made or laboratory-made. They protect humans against both.[26]

Bans on pesticides may actually have serious health consequences. An impressive array of studies indicates that fruits and vegetables reduce the risk of most cancers, and synthetic pesticides have made a major contribution to health by reducing the cost of producing fruits and vegetables.[27] Prohibiting the use of many chemicals is likely to decrease the supply and raise the price of fruits and vegetables. This will reduce the consumption of these healthful foods, especially by poor people.

QUESTIONS AND ANSWERS

Agricultural chemicals can benefit society as well as have bad consequences. That simple fact is often ignored in the textbooks. Here are some questions that you can now answer:

Do Pesticides on our Food Cause Cancer in Humans?

This is very unlikely. While some scientists speculate that pesticide residues can increase our risk of cancer, the evidence to support this is very weak, as a recent National Research Council report indicates. Some pesticides have caused tumors in animals when tested at near-toxic doses, but it is difficult to know if humans would react in similar ways at the low-exposure levels of pesticide residues in our diet.

What Was Wrong with DDT?

The buildup of DDT in the environment may have contributed to the serious decline in the numbers of birds such as falcons and eagles. However, the claim that DDT is a human carcinogen is not supported by the evidence.

Should We Buy Only Organic Food?

No. There is no reason to believe that organic food is safer than food grown and processed under the usual conditions. Naturally pest-resistant crops have their own powerful toxins. Health experts emphasize the importance of eating fruits and vegetables, and pesticides and herbicides help keep the costs of these foods low and the supply high. Organic foods are often more expensive than other foods, and this discourages people from eating them.

ACTIVITIES

Here are some activities that will help put agricultural chemicals into perspective.

At the Organic Food Store

Encourage your children to visit an organic food store. Have them look at the fruits and vegetables, and record some of the prices. Then they should go to a regular grocery store and look at the appearance of the same fruits and vegetables, and record their prices. Discuss the differences in price and quality.

They might find something like this:

PRODUCE PRICES AT GROCERY STORES VS. ORGANIC FOOD STORES
(Prices: June 12, 1999; Tucson, Arizona)

Price per 1 pound	Non-Organic Safeway	Non-Organic Albertson	Organic Wild Oats	Organic Food Conspiracy	Organic New Life
Red Delicious Apples	.89	.99	1.49	.99	1.09
Yellow Onions	.46	.39	.49	.79	.79
Large Tomatoes	1.19	1.49	2.99	1.99	2.39
Celery	.79	.89	1.69	.79	
Carrots	.79	.49	1.49	1.59	.59
Broccoli	.89	.79	1.69	1.89	1.19
Green Peppers	.69 each	.89	2.29	1.99	1.89
Green Beans	1.99	1.49	2.99	3.49	3.39

When farmers do not use pesticides, insects may destroy more of the crop. This lowers the supply and causes prices to be higher. Also, since the quality is lower, demand for organic products is lower, and "organic" farmers cannot obtain the cost savings that come from producing large quantities.

If all fruits and vegetables were as expensive as those in some organic food stores, families, especially poor families, would be less able to afford them. Thus, these people would have poorer diets, which would contribute to many health problems. Young people could call the American Cancer Society (800-227-2345) and ask for its "Guidelines for Nutrition and Cancer Prevention." The National Cancer Institute has information about the importance of eating furits and vegetables on its web site, http://www.nci.nih.gov.

At a Nursery or Garden Center

Encourage children to visit a nursery or garden center. There they can see the various pesticides and herbicides that are available for sale. Ask them to read (or read to them) the safety instructions on the containers. These instructions are there to ensure that the products are used safely to protect both the person handling the chemicals and the environment. They should learn that many products are dangerous if used improperly, but, if used according to the instructions, the products are safe.

Agricultural Progress

The following table compares several characteristics of various countries. They show the extent to which these countries use modern farming methods, including tractors and fertilizers. Looking at the data, young people will see that there seems to be a connection between modern farming methods and longer life expectancy and higher incomes. Many factors influence income levels and life expectancy, but one important factor is the abundance of inexpensive food provided by modern agriculture.

Country	Life Expectancy 1994	Tractors per Million Population	Million Tons Fertilizer per Million Population	Per Capita Income 1991 (Annual Income in US GNP/Pop)
Switzerland	78.5	17,703	26.2	$33,510
Canada	78.5	30,819	82.0	$21,260
Austria	76.5	46,518	39.7	$20,380
USA	76	19,095	74.1	$22,560
Denmark	76	31,724	123.7	$23,660
Portugal	75.5	13,932	28.3	$5,620
Chile	75	3,155	26.1	$2,160
Bulgaria	73.5	5,934	80.2	$1,840
Mexico	73	2,095	33.5	$2,870
Argentina	71.5	7,264	5.9	$2,780
Thailand	68.5	2,897	19.1	$1,580
China	68	713	23.3	$370
Iran	66	2,326	23.5	$2320
Peru	65.5	941	7.3	$1020
Philippines	65.5	176	9.7	$740
Guatemala	64.5	694	21.8	$930
Brazil	62	5,943	25.9	$2,920
India	58.5	1,171	14.9	$330
Bangladesh	55	60	10.7	$220
Somalia	54.5	299	0.4	$150
Kenya	53	463	5.4	$340
Ethiopia	52.5	92	2.6	$120
Haiti	45	43	0.2	$370
Zimbabwe	42	2,703	22.7	$620
Chad	41	51	1.8	$220
Rwanda	40	19	0.6	$260

Sources: Marlita Reddy, ed. *Statistical Abstract of the World* (New York: Gale Research, Inc., 1994), Table 57 (tractors), p. 449; Tables 58, 59, 60 (fertilizers), pp. 457, 464, 471, and *Encyclopedic World Atlas* (New York: Oxford University Press, 1994), Per Capita Income in U.S. Dollars, V1, Life Expectancy, V3.

CHAPTER SIXTEEN

A Garbage Crisis?

·······························

TANJA VOGT, A STUDENT at West Milford High School (N.J.), read a newspaper article about a local school-board decision. The board had decided to continue using food trays made of Styrofoam (a trade name for foamed polystyrene plastic) in the school cafeteria. The cafeteria served food on polystyrene trays because they cost a nickel less than paper ones.

Tanja had learned that polystyrene was dangerous. "I asked myself, why would we use these things if they're harmful to the environment?" Tanja said. She and her friends campaigned to get rid of the plastic trays and even persuaded students to pay an extra nickel. The school board changed its mind.[1]

Most teachers and parents would be proud of Tanja and her classmates, and they should be. The students perceived an environmental hazard and took action. The only problem is that their action was based on inaccurate information. Plastic trays are not necessarily more harmful than pressed paper trays. By some measures, they are more environmentally sound.

TOO MUCH TRASH

Our children are taught that the United States faces a garbage crisis. They learn that our wasteful lifestyles produce too much trash and there is no place to bury it.

- Several textbooks tell the story of a garbage barge that left New York City in 1988 looking for a place to dump its cargo of three thousand tons of garbage. Rejected by states all along the East Coast, the barge cruised to Mexico, Belize, and the Bahamas, seeking a place for its garbage. It finally returned to New York and was allowed to deposit its cargo, which was incinerated in Brooklyn.[2] The story conveys the idea that space for garbage is scarce and getting scarcer.

- One text reports that the United States has about 6,500 landfills, "down from 10,000 in 1980," and that almost one-third of the dumps are due to close soon. "Few sites are planned because finding space for them is getting more difficult,"[3] says the Addison-Wesley text *Civics: Participating in Our Democracy.*

Students are also taught that products that "biodegrade" or decompose are environmentally preferable to those that don't.

- Organic materials "will be broken down over time by the action of bacteria,"[4] says the seventh grade text by Silver Burdett & Ginn, *General Science: Book One.*

- But "many modern products, such as plastic, do not decay. They will remain in the environment for a long time,"[5] says another text, *Being Healthy.*

WHERE DOES IT GO?

The truth is that there is no garbage crisis. And plastic isn't really Public Enemy No. 1.

Municipal solid waste is the term used for waste produced by households. Modern societies like our own produce more waste than traditional societies, but throughout history all societies have had to deal with garbage. Some amount of waste is a natural by-product of living. The best we can do is figure out how to manage it with minimal harm to ourselves and the environment.

There are four principal approaches to disposing of solid waste: Reducing the amount of waste, recycling or composting, incinerating, and putting it in landfills. Although textbooks discuss all of these, most children's textbooks emphasize landfills, the major repositories of solid waste.

A landfill is a place where garbage is deposited and then covered up. There are two kinds of landfills for municipal garbage.

- Older landfills are essentially holes in the ground where garbage is placed and then covered with dirt. (Some are located in clay soils, because clay reduces leakage.)

- Newer landfills are also holes in the ground, but the hole is lined with plastic to prevent chemicals from leaking into groundwater, methane gas is vented, fluids are caught and purified, and garbage is covered daily with dirt.[6] Modern landfills are a big improvement over most earlier ones.

Most people don't really know much about landfills. But Dr. William Rathje does. He's an archaeologist at the University of Arizona who studies modern civilization the same way that archaeologists study ancient ones—by digging up waste sites. (He cheerily calls himself a "garbologist.") Rathje has learned a lot of things. Some of these are surprises. For example, in his "digs" in the 1980s he learned that:

- Fast-food packaging of all kinds makes up less than 1 percent of the materials in landfills, whether measured by weight or volume.[7]

- Expanded polystyrene foam (Styrofoam) represents no more than 1 percent of the volume of trash.[8]

- Disposable diapers represent only 1.4 percent of the volume.[9]

- All plastic products account for less than 16 percent of landfill space; Rathje found that this percentage hadn't gone up over the previous twenty years.[10]

- Paper takes up well over 40 percent of landfill space. Newspapers alone average about 13 percent.[11]

- Rathje has found in his digging more than two thousand readable newspapers, some of them from as far back as 1952.[12]

A LANDFILL CRISIS?

While there is no garbage crisis, in some places there is a shortage of land-fills. New ones must be continually developed since most only last for about ten years. (Newer landfills tend to be much larger than older ones.)

The problem isn't space. Clark Wiseman of Gonzaga University points out that all the trash produced by the United States for the next one thousand years could fit in a landfill forty-four miles square by 300 feet deep. That's right. One thousand years![13] This is only one twenty-fifth of 1 percent of all the land area of the continental United States.

Rather, the problem is simply that people are not eager to have a landfill next door. The reason has more to do with the possible effect on property values than on risk to health. Landfills are no longer built in areas where the water table is shallow or the soil is permeable and thus the chemicals can leak out.

Even the old landfills rarely pose much risk. A U.S. General Accounting Office report found that only 107 landfill sites out of 7,682 landfills operating in 1988 (less than 2 percent) were either the object of state cleanup efforts or identified as Superfund sites. Most of these are older municipal landfills built long before the advent of technological improvements.[14]

And some citizens and towns are willing to put up with having a landfill nearby—for a price. Private landfill operators can produce a package of incentives that benefit cities and individuals.

> Clark Wiseman of Gonzaga University points out that all the trash produced by the United States for the next one thousand years could fit in a landfill forty-four miles square by 300 feet deep. That's right. One thousand years!

The government in Charles City County, Virginia, allowed a regional landfill to be built in return for $1.1 million per year. This fee allowed property taxes to be cut by 20 percent. Local residents were willing to allow a landfill in the area in exchange for lower property taxes.[15]

In fact, in 1995 the *Wall Street Journal* concluded that the supposed landfill crisis is a myth. "New capacity, it turns out, hasn't been hard to come by because expanding old dumps isn't terribly difficult," wrote reporter Jeff Bailey. Siting new ones isn't impossible, either. Bailey noted that WMX Technologies Inc. opened a new landfill in Arlington, Oregon, in 1990. The company overcame local resistance with "small per-ton fees paid to local government" and by giving better information to local citizens.[16]

PUBLIC ENEMY NO. 1?

As William Rathje discovered, neither plastic nor paper is likely to "biodegrade"—that is, break apart into its original "natural" components—in a typical landfill. The inertness of plastic is actually an advantage, since it won't produce chemicals that can leak out. And when environmental impacts other than landfill space are considered, plastic may have some advantages.

 A study published in *Science* magazine compared the manufacture of paper and polystyrene cups. Martin Hocking concluded that producing paper cups required more chemicals, more steam, more electricity, and more cooling water, and produced more air pollution and wastewater.

🐝 Another study, this one by Franklin Associates, found that plastic bags can be produced for 20 to 40 percent less energy than paper bags, and produce less air and water pollution than do paper bags.[17]

Although textbooks criticize polystyrene because it does not biodegrade, it gained its status as a "public enemy" because some foamed polystyrene products were formerly produced using CFCs (chlorofluorocarbons). These chemicals may be depleting the ozone layer. (The problem of ozone depletion was discussed in chapter 12.)

But polystyrene is no longer made with CFCs,[18] although some substitutes (HCFCs) still may have a depleting effect. Rather than praise this development, many activists shifted to criticizing polystyrene because it fills up landfills.

MCDONALD'S AND THE "CLAMSHELL"

In the late 1980s, McDonald's came under pressure to get rid of the polystyrene "clamshell" container that kept hamburgers hot. Initially, the foamed polystyrene was attacked because its production required CFCs, which have been linked to the possible loss of ozone in the stratosphere. But when the suppliers to McDonald's stopped using CFCs in the manufacture of polystyrene, it came under fire for other reasons. Polystyrene doesn't biodegrade in a landfill. (Of course, as we have seen, hardly anything biodegrades in a landfill.) Also, people think that plastic takes up a great deal of room (it doesn't).

Concerned about the public image surrounding its "clamshell," McDonald's made plans to start a polystyrene recycling program. But in the autumn of 1990, McDonald's chairman changed his mind. McDonald's abandoned the clamshell and replaced it with a "quilt-wrap" made of paper coated with plastic. The Environmental Defense Fund, an

MOUNTAINS OF WASTE

A major theme of environmental texts is that Americans are wasteful. Discussions of solid waste elaborate on this theme.

🐝 Textbooks typically state that Americans produce between four and eight pounds of trash per person per day.[19] This includes not just household waste but everything that is thrown away.

🐝 The Addison-Wesley text *The United States and Its People* displays a chart showing that a typical household in New York produces 1,450 pounds of garbage per year (about four pounds per day), while a household in Rome produces 550 pounds, and Calcutta, 410 pounds.[20]

🐝 *Save the Earth: An Action Handbook for Kids* urges children to emulate students at Dartmouth College. They carried around a garbage

environmental group that had been working with McDonald's to reduce the environmental impact of its business, had pressed for the switch.

McDonald's received public acclaim for this change, which was reported on the front page of the *New York Times* (Nov. 2, 1990). But there were several ironies in this decision. For one thing, the "quilt wrap" is difficult to recycle, while the polystyrene was well on the way to being recycled.

Second, polystyrene represented only 4 percent (by weight) of all McDonald's solid waste. (Most of the waste, even when the clamshell was in use, was paper.) And, finally, by returning to paper, McDonald's was going back to a product it had abandoned, partly on environmental grounds, in the 1970s. At that time, environmentalists thought that using so much paper meant logging too many trees and producing too much pollution in the paper-making process. In 1990, by returning to paper, the company came full circle.

(This discussion is based primarily on *Rubbish! The Archaeology of Garbage* by William Rathje and Cullen Murphy [New York: HarperCollins Publishers, 1992], 221-28.)

bag for one week to put all the trash they produced so they could see how much they personally created.[21]

Figures on waste seem to be mostly guesswork. William Rathje says he has seen estimates ranging from 2.9 pounds to 8 pounds per person per day. His own studies suggest that in some parts of the country households produce less than three pounds of garbage per day.[22]

Lynn Scarlett, a researcher for the Reason Foundation, estimates that American households produce 3.2 pounds of trash per day. One reason American figures may be higher than Japanese or European figures is that recycled products such as aluminum cans, newspapers, and glass are included in U.S. solid waste figures, but Japanese and European statistics include only items that actually go to the dump.[23]

William Rathje actually measured garbage thrown out by households in the United States and Mexico (he wasn't digging into landfills in this experiment; he and his associates examined household trash cans). He found that American households produce one-third less garbage than Mexican households.[24]

Why? Modern packaging actually reduces waste, he explains. When vegetables are bought frozen in cardboard boxes, very little is wasted. In contrast, in Mexican households, vegetables are more often bought raw, so rinds, husks, leaves, stems, and other materials must be removed and discarded.[25] (In the United States, food processing companies often make animal feed and other products from these materials.)

QUESTIONS AND ANSWERS

Thanks to the pioneering work of Rathje and others, we know more about the composition of solid waste than we used to. Our texts should teach that each product has its environmental benefits and its environmental costs. While glass bottles can be re-used, for example, juice boxes take up far less space, especially when they are crushed. Furthermore, our texts should teach the lesson that good solid waste management can minimize the environmental harm caused by any product.

Now you can answer these questions:

Are We Running Out of Landfills?

No. While there may be a shortage of space in some places, it is likely to be temporary. The much-talked-about landfill shortage of the late 1980s has disappeared. Even though people don't want landfills "in their backyards," they may welcome them if the owners provide benefits such as lower property taxes.

Does Plastic Hurt a Landfill?

No. Since it is inert, plastic isn't going to produce chemicals in a landfill that could leak out. And while it does not biodegrade or decompose, the fact is that hardly anything decomposes in a landfill because there is not enough oxygen and water to cause biodegradation.

Are Americans Too Wasteful?

This is a question that each individual or family should answer for itself. But claims that Americans throw out far more than others are exaggerated.

ACTIVITIES

The following activities may help children think more carefully about solid waste.

Orange Juice: Fresh or Frozen?

Packaging may not be as wasteful as it seems. A simple activity will make this clear. Purchase a can of frozen orange juice concentrate and some fresh oranges. Have children make the frozen orange juice according to the package instructions and save all of the packaging from the frozen orange juice. Then make the same amount of juice from fresh oranges. Save all the orange rinds as you make the juice.

Weigh the squeezed orange peels and compare them with the weight of the empty orange juice container (or just look at the space they take up). Ask the young people which form of packaging produces more waste that will go into a landfill.

(Michael's eight-year-old son Devin made twenty-four ounces of fresh orange juice, and had twenty-eight ounces of empty orange rinds when he was through. When he made the same amount of juice from concentrate, the only waste was the empty can, which weighed one ounce.)

Once the juice has been fresh-squeezed, ask the children what happens to the skin and pulp. Of course, unless you have a compost pile, it will be thrown away. Tell them how commercial juice producers use the pulp and skin for animal feed, orange extracts, and flavoring oils. In the light of that reuse, which method of delivering orange juice is less wasteful?

Make Your Own Landfill

Some books for children have an experiment that is supposed to show that some things, like food scraps, will decompose in a landfill and other things, like plastic, will not. These experiments are flawed because very little actually decomposes in a landfill. The essential elements for decomposition—air, high moisture levels, and microbes—are missing from most landfills.

The following experiment more accurately reflects what happens in a landfill.

Get a small plastic food container or glass jar with an airtight lid. Select small quantities of the following: newspaper, foam plastic cup, food scraps (orange or potato peel), and a plastic bag. Make a list of these items and their condition. Pack these items into the container as tightly as possible and pack it as full as possible. The objective is to leave as little air in the container as you can. Then wrap the container in aluminum foil so that no light can get in.

Leave the container tightly sealed for four to six weeks. After that time, open the container and examine each item. Can you read the newspaper? Even items that are considered "biodegradable" rarely degrade under landfill conditions.

A Short History of the Soda Can

Most children do not understand or appreciate how competitive market forces often cause producers to reduce the amount of material they use in their packages. For example, plastic grocery bags were 70 percent thinner in 1989 than they were in 1976.[26] Here is another example—beverage cans.

In the 1960s, producers used steel to make beverage cans. They switched to lighter aluminum in the late 1960s and 1970s and since then have gradually reduced the amount of aluminum per can. Today, soda pop cans are extremely light. The following graph illustrates this history. You may wish to discuss its implications.

**POUNDS OF METAL REQUIRED PER 1,000 CANS,
1965 VS. 1990**

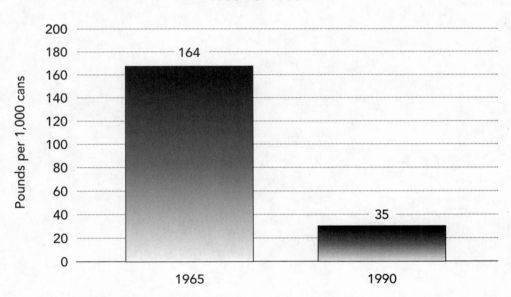

Source: James D. Gwartney and Richard L. Stroup, *Economics: Public and Private Choice* (Fort Worth: The Dryden Press, 1997), p. 741.

CHAPTER SEVENTEEN

The Recycling Myth

BRUCE VAN VOORST, A writer for *Time* magazine, noticed the problem a few years ago.[1] In apartments and in homes around the country, he observed, Americans were washing glass bottles and separating them into piles of green, clear, and amber. They were bundling up newspapers in one container, putting mixed white paper in another, and placing computer paper in a third. They were hauling the whole collection out to the curb or over to the local recycling center.

But Van Voorst had discovered a "dirty secret." A lot of the carefully separated materials were never actually recycled. "More than 10,000 tons of old newspapers have piled up in waterfront warehouses in New Jersey," he wrote, and for the entire country the figure could exceed 100 million tons. In Seattle, a recycler pondered what to do with six thousand tons of bottles that couldn't be reused.

Swamped by waste, the recycling centers couldn't handle all the debris that dutiful citizens were saving from the landfill. A lot ended up in incinerators, landfills, or storage areas.

THE PRESSURE IS ON

Children are taught that the Earth faces disaster. The chief hope for preventing catastrophe is recycling. The pressure on children to recycle—and to persuade their parents to recycle—is enormous.

- "Recycle, or reuse, aluminum cans, glass bottles, newspapers, cardboard boxes, and magazines,"[2] says the health text *Being Healthy*.

- "It is estimated that 80 percent of the solid waste that is thrown out could be recycled,"[3] says the Glencoe text *Teen Health: Decisions for Healthy Living*.

- "Recycling would eliminate much of the need for burning and landfill space,"[4] says the D. C. Heath text *Life Science: The Challenge of Discovery*.

- Recycling is considered the "solid waste solution of the future by most environmentalists,"[5] says the Prentice Hall text *General Science: A Voyage of Exploration*.

- The eighth-grade D. C. Heath text *Earth Science: The Challenge of Discovery*[6] asks students to:
    "Write to your state legislator and explain your position on mandatory recycling. Ask the legislator to explain his or her position on the issue. If your state does not have any recycling laws, ask if there are plans for new recycling legislation."

A MAJOR MISUNDERSTANDING

Children learn that recycling consists of separating aluminum cans, glass, newspaper, and some plastics and taking them to the curb or to a neighborhood recycling center. Of course, as Bruce Van Voorst discovered, that is only half the story. Nothing is truly recycled until a new product made of recycled materials is purchased by a willing customer.

Yet not everything can be turned into new products. Consider paper. It accounts for 40 percent or more of landfill volume. William Rathje of the University of Arizona points out that there isn't a market for this amount of recycled newspaper. Nor are there enough mills to process all the paper that could be collected.

In 1987 New Jersey passed legislation that required every community in the state to recycle, and the recycling rate for newspapers jumped from 50 percent to 62 percent. This created such a glut that the price of newsprint fell from $45 per ton to minus $25 per ton. That's right. Recyclers had to pay $25 per ton for someone to haul the newspapers away![7]

In Europe, the recycling craze has gone further, and the results have not been good. In 1991, the German government enacted a recycling law. It requires businesses to take back from customers and recycle all forms of packaging, including bottles, cans, containers, cartons, and sacks. By 1994, the nonprofit company that collects and sorts the items was $412 million in debt,[8] and in 1993 the government admitted that some of the returned packaging would be incinerated or landfilled.[9]

EVEN MORE LAWS

Weak demand for recycled products has led several state governments to pass laws requiring that certain products, such as newspapers and other paper goods, contain a minimum percentage of recycled material. Congress has also considered such legislation and the White House has issued executive orders to encourage the use of recycled products.

The goal is understandable—no one wants piles of yellowing newspapers or mountains of unsanitary glass bottles stuck in warehouses with nowhere to go. But forcing people to buy all the recycled material that is piling up creates its own problems.

Often, recycled material is already more expensive than virgin material due to the cost of collecting all the dispersed material and because recycling requires different processing equipment. To require every item to contain a specific amount of recycled material raises prices even more. Manufacturers must make costly investments in plants and equipment that wouldn't otherwise be necessary.

These laws also discourage innovative ways of dealing with waste. Manufacturers and packagers must be more concerned with whether the material can be recycled than with other characteristics. For example:

🌰 Lynn Scarlett of the Reason Foundation points out that recycling laws could eliminate the one-pound coffee "brick packs" you now find in retail stores. These packages hold the same amount of coffee as metal cans, but weigh less than one-third of traditional metal cans, and they take up little space. Recycled-content laws would force the use of the cans instead.[10]

🌰 Christopher Boerner and Kenneth Chilton of the Center for the Study of American Business point out that single-layered packaging for food is easier to recycle than packages that have several layers of plastic and paper, but the multilayered packaging extends the shelf life of food, and eliminating it will increase food waste.[11]

THE POINT OF IT ALL

So, we have people forced to separate their trash, and now we have people forced to use recycled products. We should at least stop and ask what we are getting for all this mandatory effort. As we saw in chapter 16, the answer is: Not very much. Recycling may reduce somewhat the amount of paper and other materials that go into landfills, but as we saw, space for landfills is not a very pressing problem.

And there are other real concerns.

🌰 Most texts declare that recycling newspapers and other paper saves trees. "If the newspapers thrown out in a medium-sized city in a month were recycled, 34,000 trees would be saved,"[12] says *Teen Health: Decisions for Healthy Living*. The D. C. Heath text *Life Science: The Challenge of Discovery* claims that "by recycling paper products, people can save thousands of trees."[13]

🐝 But the trees that will be "saved" are usually those planted specifically to make pulpwood for paper. More recycling would reduce the incentive to maintain and plant such trees. Economist Clark Wiseman estimates that if paper recycling reaches 40 percent (it is about 30 percent now), demand for paper from trees would fall by about 7 percent, and some owners would convert their land to other uses.[14]

No one is being forced to recycle—or buy—aluminum cans or tabs. Recycling happens because people can earn money by supplying them.

There are some environmental problems with recycling, too.

🐝 Transporting recyclables to processing plants requires additional collection trucks, and producing the finished goods consumes energy and causes pollution, just as production of paper from wood does.[15]

🐝 De-inking of newspaper produces sludge that may contain chlorinated organic chemicals, which are often considered toxic. Toxic or not, the sludge must end up somewhere, probably in a landfill.

So, although it is technically possible to recycle almost all trash, doing so would itself waste resources—labor, energy, and materials. And it would pose its own environmental stresses.

ON A BRIGHTER NOTE

In 1995, 62 percent of all aluminum cans were recycled.[16] The reason for this high figure is economics.

Producing aluminum from raw ore requires enormous amounts of energy.[17] Producing new cans from old ones uses much less energy. Making new cans from old ones saves money. Although the price varies from time to time, returned aluminum cans fetch between $400 and $600 per ton.[18]

Recycling aluminum cans began in 1968 when the Reynolds Metals Company started a pilot recycling center. The company was responding to public concerns about litter and wanted to forestall expensive bottle deposit bills. The rapid rise in energy prices during the 1970s plus fears of energy cutoffs soon made recycling permanent.[19]

Over ten years ago, members of a Veterans of Foreign Wars chapter outside St. Paul, Minnesota, learned that the small push-pull tabs that are used to open aluminum cans are of a higher quality than the rest of the aluminum can. Per pound, they are worth more than returned aluminum cans, and collecting them is less cumbersome. The veterans began to raise funds for the Minneapolis Ronald McDonald House (the building sponsored by McDonald's that provides housing for families of hospitalized children). The Minneapolis house now raises $80,000 a year from tabs, and the program has spread to other parts of the country, and to other charities.[20]

No one is being forced to recycle—or buy—aluminum cans or aluminum tabs. Recycling happens because the used products (the cans and tabs) have value, and people can earn money if they go to the trouble of collecting them.

Other materials are recycled voluntarily, too. About 45 percent of all corrugated boxes, for example, are recycled.[21] One reason is that collection costs are low, since places such as grocery stores and shopping malls always have lots of boxes.

Junkyards recycle cars, metals, glass, paper, and plastic. Members of the Institute of Scrap Recycling Industries, a trade association, recycled 9 million cars in 1990, nearly the same as the number of new cars sold that year. These businesses also recycled 60 million tons of ferrous metals, 7 million tons of nonferrous metals, and 30 million tons of paper, glass, and plastic.[22]

In sum, when it is economically feasible, recycling can be an excellent alternative to hauling discards to the landfill. However, recycling does not always represent the best use of resources. Our children's textbooks should reflect the complexity of the recycling issue.

QUESTIONS AND ANSWERS

Children often think that recycling is the closest thing we have to a solution to our environmental problems. You can now respond to their questions with a more realistic view of recycling.

How Much Should We Recycle?

We should recycle when it makes sense to do so. For one thing, we want to be sure that recycling actually takes place. Separating materials and putting them in a recycling box does not mean that materials are being recycled or that landfill space is being saved. If real recycling is to occur, the collected materials must be turned into new products that people want to buy.

When Does Recycling Make Sense?

Recycling makes sense if people are using it to make products that others want, and if all the costs associated with recycling are not higher than the price people are willing to pay for the recycled product. Clearly, recycling aluminum cans is working. So is recycling cardboard and scrap steel. Businesses exist to recycle these products, and no one is being forced to save them or take them.

Will Recycling Save Trees?

Not over the long run. Much of our paper comes from trees that are planted specifically to grow pulpwood for paper. If the demand for paper declines, some owners will stop growing those trees.

Why Not Force People to Buy Recycled Materials?

Such laws will make products more expensive and discourage innovative ways of dealing with waste (such as reducing the amount of packaging). You may also want to discuss whether such interference in normal activities is what we want from our government.

ACTIVITIES

The following activities will also help put recycling into perspective.

A Visit to the Recycling Center

Take your children to the local recycling center and have them talk to the manager. Recycling may help conserve resources and alleviate disposal problems but it also has its drawbacks. What happens to the glass, newspaper, or other recyclables that are sorted and collected? Where do they go? What are they used for? How much does it cost?

Garbage Bills

Show your children the two city utility bills on the next page (the same ones we saw in chapter 14). Ask them to examine the numbers carefully.

Point out that with Utility Bill #1 the family pays the same amount each month for garbage collection no matter how much trash the family leaves at the curb. In this case, recycling does not change the price the family pays for trash. A family that produces just a little trash pays as much as the family that produces large bundles.

Now have the children look at Utility Bill #2. This city charges a fee ($1.50) for each trash can it picks up. A family that produces a lot of trash pays more than a family that produces a little. The family's cost can change every week, depending on how many cans of trash the family uses. Which bill is likely to encourage recycling? (*Bill #2.*)

Now have the children compare their family's bill to these two bills. (Of course, they may not have any bill for trash other than their property tax bill.)

Families that are charged fees reflecting the amount of trash they produce can save money by cutting down on their trash. If they are not charged this way, however, they have little incentive to reduce the amount of trash they throw out. Some cities have reduced landfill usage by the "pay-as-you-throw" method.

UTILITY BILL #1   UTILITY BILL #2

Anytown, USA
Utilities Service Office

Ourtown, USA
City Services Department

Account Number 00-0000-00	Present Reading Date 11/22/99	Present Reading 467	Account Number 00-0000-00	Billing Date 10/3/99	
	Previous Reading Date 10/22/99	Previous Reading 463	Service From: 9/1/99	Service To: 9/30/99	
Water Rate/ 1000 gal $5.50	Sewer Rate/ 1000 Gal $5.30	Consumption 4	Trash Service Rate $1.50/Can	# Cans 6	Trash Charge $9.00
	Charges: Water $22.00 Sewer $21.20 Trash $15.00			Charges: Water Service $15.00 Sewer Service $10.00 Trash Service $ 9.00	
Due Date 12/10/99	Amount Due $58.20		Due Date 10/30/99	Amount Due $34.00	

Costs of Recycled Products

Take your children to a stationery store and compare the costs of recycled versus nonrecycled paper. Sometimes recycled paper is more expensive (but not always). Discuss whether they will purchase recycled paper if it is more expensive. If so, how much more are they willing to pay?

Discuss why recycled products may be more expensive than normal products. Often, collecting paper from many different sources is more difficult than cutting down trees and making pulp at a mill near the trees. Higher prices suggest that the recycled product uses more resources—more labor, more materials, or more energy (or perhaps more of all three). Is this really what we want?

As markets for recycled paper increase, the prices of recycled paper should go down as companies benefit from economies of scale. Some paper companies have already designed plants that do a better job of manufacturing paper from recycled paper. But is all that effort and expense really helping the environment? This is a difficult question to answer.

CHAPTER EIGHTEEN

What We Can Do

....

MOST OF THE EDUCATIONAL MATERIALS DISCUSSED in this book have one major flaw: lack of balance. Although we have found factual errors, the key problem is usually that environmental books tell only one side of an often complicated story. They are remarkably consistent in presenting material that supports exaggerated views of environmental problems, pessimistic forecasts, and political action based on this one-sided information.

In this concluding chapter, we would like to suggest steps that teachers, parents, and anyone interested in quality education can take to offset the myths and half-truths that pass for environmental education. Let's begin with what we see as the proper goals of environmental education.

THE PURPOSE OF ENVIRONMENTAL EDUCATION

Environmental education should help students understand the complex living world and the natural laws or principles that govern it—that is, it should be grounded in science. In addition, it should be taught with an understanding of economics, which is simply the study of why people make the choices they do.

Environmental study offers an opportunity to help children develop critical thinking and decision-making skills that will help them make wise choices.

Understanding Science

Too often, the science conveyed in our texts gives a false impression of certainty. This is especially misleading with environmental issues, because the science surrounding them is often ambiguous and in a state of flux. The impression of certainty stunts children's curiosity and denies them awareness of the excitement of scientific discovery.

Children should be encouraged to view current debates over environmental issues as part of the search for truth, not as morality plays. These debates can make science interesting and can introduce children to the way knowledge is obtained, how its validity is established, and the tentative nature of many of our conclusions.

Scientists use rigorous methods to collect and analyze information, but they do not always draw the same conclusions from these data. For example, some scientists think that higher CO_2 levels will make the world hotter, creating regional droughts. Some think that the increase will make the world warmer, wetter, and greener. Still others point to factors that could make the planet cooler. By exploring these controversies, all of us have an opportunity to meld the classroom with the real world and introduce children to the puzzles that have yet to be solved. This, we believe, is much better preparation for becoming responsible adults than the crisis-based approach prevalent in many, if not most, textbooks and curriculum materials.

Understanding Economics

Unlike science, economics is rarely taught in schools, and when it is, the classes are usually at the high school level. Yet an understanding of a few simple economic principles is essential to an understanding of environmental problems. People have to make choices about how to use our land, air, and water. In making these choices, people respond to incentives. Sometimes incentives help the environment and sometimes they hurt it.

Many of our environmental problems stem from the fact that no one owns the water or the air or the fish or the wildlife. They are a "common pool" resource. Common pools create some harmful incentives.

🌲 People may choose to use a lake or river as a waste dump. There is no owner of the water who can insist that the pollution be stopped.

🌲 People may capture too many animals and fish, sometimes leading to extinction. In parts of the world where wildlife is not owned or managed, no one can be sure that a tiger or elephant that isn't captured will be there in the future. Anyone has a right to take it.

Over time, societies have figured out ways to provide incentives for protecting the environment. In some cases, we have laws that limit emissions of waste or prohibit excessive hunting of animals. But sometimes laws designed to protect the environment create harmful incentives. We saw in chapter 3 that the Endangered Species Act can actually discourage people from protecting wildlife. And the ban on CFCs to protect the ozone layer has caused a black market in illegally imported CFCs. Economics helps us to understand the unintended consequences of well-meaning legislation. It also helps us understand why the industrialized countries often have more attractive environments than poor developing countries. The textbooks generally ignore the fact, but economic growth leads to increases in environmental protection.

Why? People want an attractive natural environment. When they are poor, other demands take precedence. But when basics such as food and shelter have been satisfied, people often seek to improve their environment. With economic growth, societies have the wherewithal and the ability to protect the environment and restore it where it has been damaged.

EVALUATING CURRICULA

Evaluating school materials is a job for everyone: teachers, parents, school board members, librarians, PTA members, and textbook adoption committees.

Educators should critically review environmental curricula, and parents should keep alert to the materials used in their children's environmental education. Fortunately, one-sided presentations, such as the ones identified in this book, are easy to detect. Just ask questions such as the following:

- In general, are theories presented as theories or as scientifically established "facts"?

- Is there a pervasive bias against economic growth and technology?

- Are human beings presented as being "against" nature rather than part of it?

- Is there an effort to make children feel guilty about the material advantages Americans enjoy?

- Is the overall presentation of environmental problems gloomy and pessimistic?

- Are children being scared into becoming environmental activists?

On any specific environmental issue, the curriculum can be compared with the information in this book. For example:

- Does the curriculum on acid rain mention the findings of the NAPAP study?

- Do the global warming materials discuss both the criticisms of and the arguments for the idea that the world will get much warmer?

If the information contained in this book is not covered, the curriculum is ignoring legitimate debates and presenting only one side.

Be alert for activities that urge students to engage in political action. It's not uncommon for texts to recommend that students write their city, state, and federal representatives about environmental laws. While such letters have some merit, these activities often cross the line between education and political activism. When they are based on biased information, they are not appropriate for schools.

REVIEWING MATERIALS

We all know that textbooks are just one aspect of education. Supplemental materials, library books, and outside speakers are also important. To improve the quality of education, all these sources of information should be considered.

Textbooks generally fall into three categories: those that contain very little environmental information, those that cover environmental information outside the main subject of the text (usually as extra features or specific chapters), and those with environmental education as a main focus. (See Appendix A for the texts we reviewed, which are typical of the texts produced by the major publishers for children at the 6-10 grade levels.)

Texts provide only a general guideline for teachers, who are usually free to cover material in the text or ignore it. They are also free to bring in additional materials. A good teacher can use an inadequate text and still provide good education. This book could be a good source of balance.

Supplemental materials often come from environmental organizations. While some of the materials fall into the "learning about nature" category and are useful, others are based on emotion, not facts. Sometimes corporations also sponsor environmental education materials and activities that are inaccurate and misleading.

Schools often bring in outside speakers. These may range from a local Forest Service employee to the local president of a radical group like Earth First! Many advocate the same environmental messages presented in the texts.

Many schools also include field trips, outdoor work projects, and even overnight camps in their environmental curriculum. Some of these programs teach children about nature, but others promote the views of activist environmental groups.

HOW TO IMPROVE ENVIRONMENTAL EDUCATION

After evaluating the curricula used in schools, some teachers and parents may be dissatisfied. This section will recommend some steps to take.

SUCCESS IN ARIZONA

Given the severity of the problems documented in this book, it might seem that improvement is impossible. In Arizona, however, parents, teachers, and legislators are charting a new course for environmental education. Michael, one of the authors of this book, has been following this process closely.

Parents became aware of problems in environmental education in 1993 when a statewide reading exam used a passage about rain forest deforestation that was filled with inaccuracies and exaggerations. Upset about this exam, parents took their concerns to the state legislature.

Under the leadership of Representative Rusty Bowers, the legislature changed the law governing environmental education. Today, Arizona law requires that when schools teach about environmental topics, they must ensure that the programs are "conducted in a balanced manner" and based on "current scientific information," and they must include a discussion of "economic and social implications."

The changes put environmental education on a sounder footing. The state has a large grants program (funded from sales of environmental license plates). In fiscal year 1998 the state spent more than $500,000 on grants for environmental education. This amount places Arizona among the national leaders in spending on such programs.

The Arizona Advisory Council on Environmental Education, a ten-member citizen's committee, has statutory responsibility to see that funded projects are balanced and based on current science. The council has established three grant programs. The first funds traditional grants (up to $10,000) for new curricula, teacher training, and field trips. The second establishes environmental education sites that teach outdoor environmental education, resource management, and related issues.

Seek Out Balance

The experience of Jack Stauder, a college teacher at the University of Massachusetts-Dartmouth, is instructive. He taught an environmental issues

---

The third program is an innovative environmental research contest. High school and middle school classes compete by writing balanced papers on controversial environmental topics, choosing from five or six topics that change each school year. Recent topics include global warming, logging on national forests, recycling, the Endangered Species Act, and urban air pollution. Students are expected to apply the latest scientific and economic research and present the issue in a balanced way. For each topic, the winning high school and middle school classes receive $10,000 for an educational field trip. (Second and third place winners receive educational field trips worth $5000 and $2500.)

Students and teachers are ecstatic about this contest. "This contest is the single best teaching tool I have, without a doubt," says one teacher. When students in a winning class were informed of their win by speaker phone, they began yelling and cheering at the news. Students also recognize that winning the contest requires hard work. "The hardest part was understanding the scientific journals," said Kelsie Knutson, whose team won a $10,000 field trip.

The Arizona experience has established a very clear goal for environmental education: teaching balanced lessons based on current science and economics. Where scientific controversies exist, students are exposed to all sides of these debates. This clearly stated goal helps those in the educational system develop practical programs that can be measured against the goal.

In sum, Arizona is moving from a history of bickering over the politicizing of children on environmental issues to a reasoned discussion over the content and methods for teaching science-based environmental issues. It creates a model that other states can copy.

210 FACTS, NOT FEAR

course for several years before discovering that scientific disagreements exist about issues such as global warming, acid rain, and pesticides. Once he began delving into the subjects himself, he found to his amazement "another side that could not be dismissed easily as representing only ignorance and greed."[1] His discoveries led him to change his course in environmental issues from lectures to research and discussion. He found so much material he wanted to explore that he had his students conduct some of the research he didn't have time for. "The new course was a success," he reports.

Not every teacher has time to research these topics, nor does every teacher have students capable of extensive research. However, more books and articles offering balanced views of environmental issues are available today than just a few years ago. (See Appendix C for a list of such books.) Teachers and parents can urge the school librarian or the school board to buy additional books that provide balance.

Bring In Outside Speakers

Many private organizations, not as well known as the activist organizations that lobby in Washington, D.C., are accomplishing genuine environmental improvements. These may include organizations such as Ducks Unlimited, the Nature Conservancy, a local arboretum or land trust, an organization that protects injured wildlife, or even a local electric utility that is using some of its land to protect an endangered species. Their representatives could tell students about their work. Such speakers would emphasize the positive side of environmental protection.

The Broader Picture

Every school is guided by a network of laws, regulations, and standards. Many states have passed laws mandating environmental education and laying out specific requirements. Such laws usually reflect a strong constituency of environmentalist or environmental-education activists who are influential in school policy. These individuals tend to promote one-sided information and political activism.

Countering such pressures is difficult, and it involves political organization. See the sidebar on pages 208-209 in this chapter to learn about the experience in Arizona. There, state legislators, responding to parents' concerns, have revolutionized environmental education mandates. New laws require that environmental material be science-based and balanced. For some readers of this book, such a political course of action may be the only route to genuine change.

Education For Life

The goal of this book has been to emphasize the spirit of inquiry. By treating environmental issues as subjects to be explored, not positions to be advocated, teachers, parents, and all who are interested in quality education can offset the exaggeration and pessimism so typical of the texts we have reviewed. While maintaining an objective view of these emotion-laden issues is not always easy, such an approach is more accurate and scientific and more conducive to critical thinking.

Such an approach will also convey an important message to young people. They will learn that studying the environment can be an adventure that takes them to frontiers that await investigation and understanding. By learning facts, not fear, and guided by people they respect, young people will experience the excitement that is an integral part of genuine education.

Appendix A

....

TEXTBOOKS REVIEWED

The authors reviewed these textbooks for their coverage of environmental issues only. The authors did not review the subject matter content of the nonenvironmentally related information in these texts. Criticisms of the environmental content does not imply criticism of the nonenvironmental content of these texts.

The textbooks reviewed for this book were published by many of the top-selling publishing companies in the country. Textbook publishers do not release sales figures on individual textbooks so it is impossible to determine the exact proliferation of specific textbooks. By selecting the top publishing firms, we believe that we have selected many of the most commonly used texts in the country.

Addison-Wesley

Chiras, Daniel D. *Environmental Science: A Framework for Decisionmaking.* 2d ed. Menlo Park, CA: Addison-Wesley Publishing Co., 1989.

Davis, James E., and Phyllis Maxey Fernlund. *Civics: Participating in Our Democracy.* Menlo Park, CA: Addison-Wesley Publishing Co., 1993.

Dispezio, Linner, and Lisowski Lube. *Science Insights: Exploring Earth and Space.* Reading, MA: Addison-Wesley Publishing Co., 1995.

Essnfeld, Bernice, Carol Gontag, and Randy Moore. *Biology.* Reading, MA: Addison-Wesley Publishing Co., 1994.

Fariel, Robert E., et al. *Earth Science.* Menlo Park, CA: Addison-Wesley Publishing Co., 1984.

King, David C., Norman McRae, and Jaye Zola. *The United States and Its People.* Menlo Park, CA: Addison-Wesley Publishing Co., 1993.

D. C. Heath (A Raytheon Company)

Bailey, Thomas A., and David M. Kennedy. *The American Pagent.* Lexington, MA: D. C. Heath and Co., 1991.

Carle, Mark A., et al. *Physical Science: Challenge of Discovery.* Lexington, MA: D. C. Heath and Co., 1991.

Gritzner, Charles. *World Geography.* Lexington, MA: D. C. Heath and Co., 1989.

Snyder, Robert E., et al. *Earth Science: The Challenge of Discovery.* Annotated Teacher's Edition. Lexington, MA: D. C. Heath and Co., 1991.

Spaulding, Nancy, and Samuel Namowitz. *Heath Earth Science.* Indianapolis, IN: D. C. Heath, 1994.

Ver Steeg, Clarence L., and Carol Ann Skinner. *Exploring Regions Near and Far.* Lexington, MA: D. C. Heath and Co., 1991.

Warner, Linda A., et al. *Life Science: The Challenge of Discovery.* Lexington, MA: D. C. Heath and Co., 1991.

Glencoe (Macmillan/McGraw-Hill)

Boehm, Richard G., and James L. Swanson. *Glencoe World Geography*. Mission Hills, CA: Glencoe Publishing Co., 1989.

Boehm, Richard G., and James L. Swanson. *World Geography: A Physical and Cultural Approach*. 3d ed. Lake Forest, IL: Glencoe Publishing Co., 1992.

Daniel, Lucy, et al. *Merrill Life Science*. Columbus, OH: Glencoe Publishing Co., 1994.

Farah, Mounir, and Andrea Berens Karls. *World History: The Human Experience*. 3d ed. Lake Forest, IL: Glencoe Publishing Co., 1992.

Jackson, Carlton L., and Vito Perrone. *Two Centuries of Progress*. Mission Hills, CA: Glencoe Publishing Co., 1991.

Jones, Henke L., Ted Tsumura, and T. Bonekemper *Health and Safety for You*. Columbus, OH: Glencoe Publishing Co., 1987.

LaRaus, Roger, Harry P. Morris, and Robert Sobel. *Challenge of Freedom*. Mission Hills, CA: Glencoe Publishing Co., 1990.

Merki, Mary Bronson. *Teen Health: Decisions for Healthy Living*. Annotated Teacher's Edition. Mission Hills, CA: Glencoe Publishing Co., 1990.

Merki, Mary Bronson, and Don Merki. *Health: A Guide To Wellness*. 3d ed. Mission Hills, CA: Glencoe Publishing Co., 1993.

Nash, Gary B. *American Odyssey: The United States in the Twentieth Century*. Lake Forest, IL: Glencoe Publishing Co., 1991.

Remy, Richard C. *U. S. Government: Democracy in Action*. New York: Glencoe Publishing Co., 1994.

Welty, Paul Thomas, and Miriam Greenblatt. *The Human Expression: World Religions and Cultures*. 4th ed. Lake Forest, IL: Glencoe Publishing Co., 1992.

Globe (Simon & Schuster, A Paramount Communications Co.)

Bernstein, Leonard, et al. *Concepts and Challenges in Earth Science*. 3d ed. Annotated Teacher's Edition. Englewood Cliffs, NJ: Globe Book Co., 1991.

O'Conner, John R., and Robert M. Goldberg. *Exploring American Citizenship*. Englewood Cliffs, NJ: Globe Book Co., 1992.

Schwartz, Melvin, and John O'Conner. *Exploring a Changing World*. Englewood Cliffs, NJ: Globe Book Co., 1993.

Harcourt Brace Jovanovich (Holt, Rinehart and Winston)

Bacon, Phillip. *World Geography: The Earth and Its People*. Orlando, FL: Harcourt Brace Jovanovich, 1989.

Emiliani, Cesare, Linda B. Knight, and Mark Handwerker. *Earth Science*. Orlando: Harcourt Brace Jovanovich, 1989.

Olsen, Larry K., Richard W. St. Pierre, and Jan M. Ozlas. *Being Healthy*. Annotated Teacher's Edition. Orlando: Harcourt Brace Jovanovich, 1990.

Poehler, David, et al. *Health*. Orlando, FL: Harcourt Brace Jovanovich, 1987.

Swanson, John Colby, et al. *Essentials of Health*. Orlando: Harcourt Brace Jovanovich, 1986.

Watkins, Patricia, et al. *Life Science*. Orlando, FL: Harcourt Brace Jovanovich, 1989.

Holt, Rinehart and Winston (Harcourt Brace Jovanovich)

Arms, Karen, and Pamela Camp. *Biology*. Austin, TX: Holt, Rinehart and Winston, Inc., 1995.

Bacon, Phillip. *States and Regions*. Orlando, FL: Holt, Rinehart and Winston, Inc., 1991.

Boyer, Paul. *The American Nation*. Austin, TX: Holt, Rinehart and Winston, Inc., 1995.

Budziszewski, J., and Lawrence J. Pauline. *We the People*. Austin, TX: Holt, Rinehart and Winston, Inc., 1989.

Cuevas, Lamb, et al. *Holt Physical Science*. Austin, TX: Holt, Rinehart and Winston, Inc., 1994.

Garraty, John A. *The Story of America*. Austin, TX: Holt, Rinehart and Winston, Inc., 1991.

Garraty, John A. *The Story of America: Beginnings to 1877*. Annotated Teacher's Edition. Austin, TX: Holt, Rinehart and Winston, Inc., 1992.

Garraty, John A. *The Story of America: 1865 to the Present*. Volume 2. Austin, TX: Holt, Rinehart and Winston, Inc., 1992.

Goodman, Harvey D., et al. *Biology Today*. Annotated Teacher's Edition. Austin, TX: Holt, Rinehart and Winston, Inc., 1991.

Greenberg, Jerrold, and Robert Gold. *Holt Health*. Orlando, FL: Holt, Rinehart and Winston, Inc., 1994.

Hartley, William H., and William S. Vincent. *American Civics*. Freedom Edition. Austin, TX: Holt, Rinehart and Winston, Inc., 1992.

Israel, Saul, Douglas Johnson, and Dennis Wood. *World Geography Today*. Holt, Rinehart and Winston, Inc., 1980.

McFadden, Charles, and Robert Yager. *Science Plus: Technology and Society*. Blue Edition, Austin, TX: Holt, Rinehart and Winston, Inc., 1993.

McFadden, Charles, and Robert Yager. *Science Plus: Technology and Society*. Green Edition, Austin, TX: Holt, Rinehart and Winston, Inc., 1993.

McFadden, Charles, and Robert Yager. *Science Plus: Technology and Society*. Red Edition, Austin, TX: Holt, Rinehart and Winston, Inc., 1993.

Sager, Robert J., David M. Helgren, and Saul Israel. *World Geography Today*. Revised Edition. Austin, TX: Holt, Rinehart and Winston, Inc., 1992.

Towle, Albert. *Modern Biology*. Annotated Teacher's Edition. Austin, TX: Holt, Rinehart and Winston, Inc., 1993.

Houghton Mifflin Co.

Armento, Beverly J., et al. *From Sea to Shining Sea*. Boston: Houghton Mifflin Co., 1991.

DiBacco, Thomas V., Lorna C. Mason, and Christian G. Appy. *History of the United States*. Boston: Houghton Mifflin Co., 1993.

Getchell, Bud, Rusty Pippin, and Jill Varnes. *Health*. Boston: Houghton Mifflin Co., 1987.

Getchell, Bud, Rusty Pippin, and Jill Varnes. *Perspectives on Health*. Boston: Houghton Mifflin Co., 1987.

Macmillan/McGraw-Hill (Harcourt Brace Jovanovich)

Audesirk, Gerald, and Teresa Audesirk. *Biology: Life on Earth*. New York: Macmillan/McGraw-Hill, 1993.

Banks, James A., et al. *United States and Its Neighbors*. New York: Macmillan/McGraw-Hill, 1993.

Banks, James A., et al. *The World Around Us: Regions Near and Far*. New York: Macmillan/McGraw Hill, 1993.

Banks, James A., et al. *World Regions*. Riverside, NJ: Macmillan/McGraw-Hill, 1993.

Jantzen, Michel, et al. *Life Science*. New York: Macmillan/McGraw-Hill, 1986.

Merrill (Macmillan/McGraw-Hill)

Biggs, Alton, et al. *Biology: The Dynamics of Life*. Columbus, OH: Merrill Publishing Co., 1991.

Feather, Ralph M., et al. *Earth Science*. Lake Forest, IL: Merrill/Glencoe, 1993.

Feather, Ralph M., et al. *Science Connections*. Blue ed. Columbus, OH: Merrill Publishing Co., 1990.

Feather, Ralph M., et al. *Science Connections*. Red Ed. Columbus, OH: Merrill Publishing Co., 1990.

Hantula, James Neil, et al. *Global Insights*. Columbus, OH: Merrill Publishing Co., 1988.

Heimler, Charles H. *Focus on Life Science*. Columbus, OH: Merrill Publishing Co., 1989.

Heimler, Charles H., and Charles D. Neal. *Principles of Science: Book 2*. Columbus, OH: Merrill Publishing Co., 1986.

Hunkins, Francis P. and David G. Armstrong. *World Geography: People and Places*. Columbus, OH: Merrill Publishing Co., 1984.

Kaskel, Albert, Paul J. Hummer, Jr., and Lucy Daniel. *Biology: An Everyday Experience*. Lake Forest, IL: Merrill/Glencoe, 1992.

Meeks, Linda, and Philip Heit. *Health: A Wellness Approach*. Columbus, OH: Merrill Publishing Co., 1991.

Meeks, Linda, and Philip Heit. *Health: Focus on You*. Columbus, OH: Merrill Publishing Co., 1990.

Oram, Raymond F. *Biology: Living Systems*. Annotated Teacher's Edition. Columbus, OH: Merrill Publishing Co., 1989.

Turner, Mary Jane, et al. *American Government: Principles and Practices*. Columbus, OH: Merrill Publishing Co., 1991.

Prentice Hall
(Simon & Schuster, A Paramount Communications Co.)

Baerwald, Thomas J., and Celeste Fraser. *World Geography*. Needham, MA: Prentice Hall, 1993.

Beers, Burton F. *World History: Patterns of Civilization*. Englewood Cliffs, NJ: Prentice Hall, 1993.

Cobel, Charles R., et al. *Earth Science*. Englewood Cliffs, NJ: Prentice Hall, 1991.

Cormler, Robert J., et al. *Magruder's American Government*. Englewood Cliffs, NJ: Prentice Hall, 1992.

Davidson, James West, and John E. Batchelor. *The American Nation*. 3d ed. Englewood Cliffs, NJ: Prentice Hall, 1991.

Davidson, James West, and Mark H. Lytle. *The United States: A History of the Republic*. 5th ed. Englewood Cliffs, NJ: Prentice Hall, 1990.

Donatelle, Rebecca J., Lorraine G. Davis, and Carolyn F. Hoover. *Access to Health*. Englewood Cliffs, NJ: Prentice Hall, 1988.

Gray, Pamela Lee, et al. *America: Pathways to the Present*. Englewood Cliffs, NJ: Prentice Hall, 1995.

Haber-Shaim, Yuri. *Introduction to Physical Science*. Englewood Cliffs, NJ: Prentice Hall, 1987.

Hurd, Dean, et al. *General Science: A Voyage of Adventure*. 3d ed. Englewood Cliffs, NJ: Prentice Hall, 1992.

Hurd, Dean, et al. *General Science: A Voyage of Discovery*. Englewood Cliffs, NJ: Prentice Hall, 1992.

Hurd, Dean, et al. *General Science: A Voyage of Exploration.* Englewood Cliffs, NJ: Prentice Hall, 1992.

Hurd, Dean, et al. *Prentice Hall Physical Science.* Englewood Cliffs, NJ: Prentice Hall, 1991.

Leinwand, Gerald. *The Pageant of World History.* Needham, MA: Prentice Hall, 1990.

Luckmann, Joan. *Your Health!* Englewood Cliffs, NJ: Prentice Hall, 1990.

Maton, Anthea. *Ecology: Earth's Natural Resources.* 2d ed. Englewood Cliffs, NJ: Prentice Hall, 1994.

Maton, Anthea. *Human Biology and Health.* 2d ed. Englewood Cliffs, NJ: Prentice Hall, 1994.

Maton, Anthea. *Matter: Building Block of the Universe.* 2d ed. Englewood Cliffs, NJ: Prentice Hall, 1994.

Miller, Kenneth R., and Joseph Levine. *Biology.* Englewood Cliffs, NJ: Prentice Hall, 1991.

Pruitt, Crumpler, et al. *Health: Skills for Wellness.* Englewood Cliffs, NJ: Prentice Hall, 1994.

Schraer, William D., and Herbert J. Stoltze. *Biology: The Study of Life.* 4th ed. Needham, MA: Prentice Hall, 1991.

Seehafer, Roger Wayne, Carol Bershad, and Deborah S. Haber, Program Consultants. *Health: Choosing Wellness.* Needham, MA: Prentice Hall, 1989.

Seehafer, Roger Wayne, Carol Bershad, and Deborah S. Haber, Program Consultants. *Health: Choosing Wellness.* 2d ed. Needham, MA: Prentice Hall, 1992.

Wright, Jill, et al. *Life Science.* Englewood Cliffs, NJ: Prentice Hall, 1991.

Wright, Nebel J., and Richard T. Wright. *Environmental Science: The Way the World Works.* 4th ed. Englewood Cliffs, NJ: Prentice Hall, 1991.

Scott Foresman
(A Division of HarperCollins Publishers)

Alexander, Gretchen M. *Life Science.* Teacher's Edition. Palo Alto, CA: Scott Foresman and Co., 1983.

Barber, Kissamis, et al. *Earth Science*. Glenview, IL: Scott Foresman and Co., 1990.

de Blij, Harm J., et al. *World Geography: A Physical and Cultural Study*. Glenview, IL: Scott Foresman and Co., 1989.

Divine, Robert A., et al. *America: The People and the Dream*. Vol. II: The Later Years. Glenview, IL: Scott Foresman and Co., 1991.

Patrick, John J., and Richard C. Remy. *Civics for Americans*. 2d ed. Glenview, IL: Scott Foresman and Co., 1991.

Richmond, Julius B., Elenore T. Pounds, and Charles B. Corbin. *Health for Life*. Glenview, IL: Scott Foresman and Co., 1990.

Wallbark, T. Walter, et al. *History and Life*. Updated Edition. Glenview, IL: Scott Foresman and Co., 1993.

Silver Burdett & Ginn
(Simon & Schuster, A Paramount Communications Co.)

Ainsley Jr., W. Frank, et al. *Comparing Regions*. From the series: People in Time and Place. Morristown, NJ: Silver Burdett & Ginn, 1993.

Alexander, Fiegel, et al. *Silver Burdett Earth Science*. Morristown, NJ: Silver Burdett & Ginn, 1990.

Alexander, Fiegel, et al. *Silver Burdett Physical Science*. Morristown, NJ: Silver Burdett & Ginn, 1990.

Alexander, Peter, et al. *General Science, Book One*. Needham, MA: Silver Burdett & Ginn, 1989.

Alexander, Peter, et al. *General Science, Book Two*. Needham, MA: Silver Burdett & Ginn, 1989.

Bass, John C. *Our Country*. Morristown, NJ: Silver Burdett & Ginn, 1993.

Cooper, Kenneth S. *The Eastern Hemisphere*. Morristown, NJ: Silver Burdett & Ginn, 1991.

Greenlow, Linda L., W. Frank Ainsley, Jr., and Gary S. Elbow. *World Geography: People in Time and Place*. Morristown, NJ: Silver Burdett & Ginn, 1992.

Hatfield, Claudette Butler, et al. *World Geography*. Teacher's Edition. Morristown, NJ: Silver Burdett & Ginn, 1992.

Helmus, Timothy M., et al. *The United States Yesterday and Today*. Morristown, NJ: Silver Burdett & Ginn, 1990.

Miscellaneous Publishers

Brockway, Carolyn Sheets, Robert Gardner, and Samuel F. Howe. *General Science*. Newton, MA: Allyn and Bacon, 1985.

BSCS, Green Version. *Biological Science: An Ecological Approach*. Dubuque, IA: Kendall/Hunt Publishing Co., 1992.

Camp, William, and Roy Donahue. *Environmental Science: For Agriculture and the Life Sciences*. Albany, NY: Delmar Publishers, Inc., 1994.

Campbell, Neil A. *Biology*. Redwood City, CA: The Benjamin/Cummings Publishers Co., Inc., 1993.

Chiras, Daniel D. *Environmental Science: A Framework for Decisionmaking*. 2d ed. Menlo Park, CA: The Benjamin/Cummings Publishing Co., Inc., 1988.

Christensen, John W. *Global Science*. 3rd ed. Dubuque, IA: Kendall/Hunt Publishing Co., 1991.

Curtis, Helena, and Sue N. Barnes. *Biology*. New York: Worth Publishing Company, 1989.

Daley, Robert B., W. John Higham, and George F. Matthias. *Earth Science: A Study of a Changing Planet*. Newton, MA: Cebco, A Division of Allyn and Bacon, Inc., 1986.

Jordan, Winthrop D., Miriam Greenblatt, and John S. Bowes. *The Americans: A History*. Evanston, IL: McDougal/Littell, 1994.

Kane, William M., Senior Consultant. *Understanding Health*. 2d ed. New York: Random House School Division, 1987.

Lineberry, Robert, George C. Edwards III, and Martin P. Wattenberg. *Government In America: People, Politics, and Policy*. 5th ed. New York: HarperCollins Publishers, 1991.

May, Ernest R. *A Proud Nation*. Evanston, IL: McDougal, Littell & Company, 1989.

Milani, Jean P., Revision Coordinator. *Biological Science: An Ecological Approach*. 6th ed. Dubuque, IA: Kendall/Hunt Publishing Co., 1987.

Person, Jane L. *Environmental Science, How the World Works and Your Place in It*. New York: J. M. LeBel Enterprises Inc., 1989.

Turk, Jonathan. *Introduction to Environmental Studies*. 3d ed. Philadelphia: Saunders College Publishing, 1989.

Turk, Jonathan, Amos Turk, and Karen Arms. *Environmental Science*. 3d ed. Philadelphia, Saunders College Publishing, 1988.

Wallace, Robert A., Gerald P. Sanders, and Robert J. Ferl. *Biology: The Science of Life*. New York: HarperCollins Publishers, 1991.

West's American Government. St. Paul, MN: West Publishing Co., 1993.

Appendix B

....

ENVIRONMENTAL BOOKS FOR CHILDREN

These books were reviewed by the authors. They vary in the quality of their coverage of environmental issues, and we are not recommending them. See Appendix C for books that we recommend.

Aaseng, Nathan. *Ending World Hunger*. New York: Franklin Watts, 1991.

Anderson, Madelyn Klein. *Oil Spills*. New York: Franklin Watts, 1990.

Baines, John. *Acid Rain* (Conserving Our World Series). Austin, TX: Steck-Vaughn Library, 1989.

Baker, Jeannie. *Where the Forest Meets the Sea*. New York: Scholastic, Inc., 1987.

Banks, Martin. *Conserving Rain Forests*. Austin, TX: Steck-Vaughn Library, 1990.

Becklake, John. *The Climate Crisis: Greenhouse Effect and Ozone Layer.* New York: Franklin Watts, 1989.

Becklake, John, and Sue Becklake. *The Population Explosion.* London: Gloucester Press, 1990.

Bloyd, Sunni. *Endangered Species* (Our Endangered Planet). San Diego: Lucent Books, Inc., 1989.

Bright, Michael. *Pollution and Wildlife.* New York: Gloucester Press, 1987.

Bruchac, Joseph. *Native American Stories.* Golden, CO: Fulcrum Publishing, 1991.

Caduto, M. J., and J. Bruchac. *Keepers of the Earth: Native American Stories & Environmental Activities for Children.* Golden, CO: Fulcrum, Inc, 1988.

Carr, Terry. *Spill! The Story of Exxon Valdez.* New York: Franklin Watts, 1991.

Cherry, Lynne. *The Great Kapok Tree: A Tale of the Amazon Rain Forest.* San Diego: Harcourt Brace Jovanovich Publishers, 1990.

Condon, Judith. *Recycling Paper.* New York: Franklin Watts, 1990.

Cowcher, Helen. *Antarctica.* New York: Scholastic, Inc., 1990.

Cowcher, Helen. *Rain Forest.* New York: Farrar, Straus and Giroux, 1988.

Crutchins, Judy, and Ginny Johnston. *The Crocodile and the Crane: Surviving in a Crowded World.* New York: William Morrow and Company, Inc., 1986.

Dee, Catherine, ed. *Kid Heroes of the Environment.* Berkeley, CA: Earth Works Press, 1991.

Dehr, Roma, and Ronald M. Bazar. *Good Planets Are Hard to Find: An Environmental Information Guide, Dictionary and Action Book for Kids (and Adults).* Vancouver, BC: Earth Beat Press, 1989.

Dolan, Edward. *Our Poisoned Sky.* New York: Dutton Children's Books, 1991.

Dolan, Edward F. *Drought: The Past, Present and Future Enemy.* New York: Franklin Watts, 1990.

Dorros, Arthur. *Rain Forest Secrets.* New York: Scholastic, Inc., 1990.

Drutman, A. D. *Protecting Our Planet: Activities to Motivate Young Students to a Better Understanding of Our Environmental Problems* (For Primary Grades). Carthage, IL: Good Apple Publications, 1991.

Duden, Jane. *The Ozone Layer*. New York: Crestwood House, 1990.

Duggleby, John. *Pesticides*.New York: Crestwood House, 1990.

Elkington, John, et al. *Going Green: A Kid's Handbook to Saving the Planet*. New York: Puffin Books, 1990.

Facklam, Howard, and Margery Facklam. *Plants: Extinction or Survival?* Hillside, NJ: Enslow Publishers, Inc., 1990.

Facklam, Margery, and Howard Facklam. *Changes in the Wind: Earth's Shifting Climate*. San Diego: Harcourt Brace Jovanovich Publishers, 1986.

Facklam, Margery. *And Then There Was One: The Mysteries of Extinction*. San Francisco: Sierra Club Books, 1990.

Fine, Charles Christopher. *The Hunger Road*. New York: Atheneum, 1988.

Foreman, Michael. *One World*. New York: M&S, 1990.

Fradin, Dennis B. *Disaster! Famines*. Chicago: Children's Press Inc., 1986.

Freeman, Don. *The Seal and the Slick*. New York: Viking Press, 1974.

Gallant, Ray A. *The Peopling of Planet Earth: Human Population Growth Through the Ages*. New York: Macmillan Publishing Company, 1990.

Galle, Janet, and Patricia Warren. *Ecology Discovery Activities List: A Complete Teaching Unit for Grades 4–8*. West Nyack, New York: Center for Applied Research in Education, 1989.

Gang, Paul. *Our Planet, Our Home: Teacher's Guide*. Tucson, AZ: Zephyr Press, 1992.

Gay, Kathlyn. *Garbage and Recycling* (Issues in Focus). Hillside, NJ: Enslow Publishers, Inc., 1991.

Gay, Kathlyn. *The Greenhouse Effect*. (A Science Impact Book). New York: Franklin Watts, 1986.

Gay, Kathlyn. *Water Pollution*. New York: Franklin Watts, 1990.

Gertson, Rich. *Just Open the Door: A Complete Guide to Experiencing Environmental Education*. Danville, IL: Industake Printers and Publishers, Inc., 1983.

Gold, Susan Dudley. *Toxic Waste*. New York: Crestwood House, 1990.

Goodman, Billy. *A Kid's Guide to How to Save the Planet*. New York: Avon Books, 1990.

Greene, Carole. *Caring for Our Water* (Caring for Our Earth). Hillside, NJ: Enslow Publishers, Inc., 1991.

Gutnik, Martin J. *Ecology*. New York: Franklin Watts, 1984.

Hadingham, Evan, and Janet Hadingham. *Garbage! Where it Comes From, Where it Goes*. New York: Simon & Schuster, 1990 (A NOVA Book).

Hare, Tony. *Acid Rain* (Save Our Earth Series). London: Gloucester Press, 1990.

Hare, Tony. *The Ozone Layer* (Save Our Earth Series). London: Gloucester Press, 1990.

Hare, Tony. *Polluting the Sea* (Save Our Earth Series). London: Glouchester Press, 1991.

Hare, Tony. *Rainforest Destruction* (Save Our Earth Series). London: Gloucester Press, 1990.

Harris, Jack C. *The Greenhouse Effect*. New York: Crestwood House, 1990.

Herman, Maring Lachecki et al. *Teaching Kids to Love the Earth*. Duluth, MN: Pfiefer-Hamilton Publishing, 1991.

Hirschi, Ron. *Where Are My Prairie Dogs and Black-footed Ferrets?* New York: Bantam Books, 1992 (National Audubon Society).

Hocking C., C. Sneider, J. Erickson, and R. Golden. *Global Warming and the Greenhouse Effect* (Great Explorations in Math and Science GEMS). Berkeley, CA: Lawrence Hall of Science, 1990 (A Teacher's Guide).

Hocking, C., J. Barber, and J. Coonrod. *Acid Rain: A Teacher's Guide*. Berkeley, CA: Lawrence Hall of Science UC, Berkeley, 1990 (LHS GEMS Series).

Hoff, Mary King, and Mary M. Rodgers. *Our Endangered Planet: Groundwater*. Minneapolis, MN: Lerner Publications Company, 1991.

Hoff, Mary King, and Mary M. Rodgers. *Our Endangered Planet: Oceans*. Minneapolis, MN: Lerner Publications Company, 1991.

Hoff, Mary King, and Mary M. Rodgers. *Our Endangered Planet: Rivers and Lakes*. Minneapolis, MN: Lerner Publications Company, 1991.

Hoose, Phillip. *It's Our World, Too! Stories of Young People Who are Making A Difference*. Boston: Little, Brown and Company, 1993.

Javna, John. *50 Simple Things Kids Can Do to Save the Earth*. Kansas City, MO: Andrews and McMeel, 1990.

Johnson, Rebecca. *The Greenhouse Effect: Life on a Warmer Planet*. Minneapolis, MN: Lerner Publications Company, 1990.

Kalbacken, Joan, and Emilie U. Lepthien. *Recycling* (A New True Book). Chicago: Childrens Press, Inc., 1991.

Knapp, Brian. *World Disasters: Drought*. Austin, TX: Steck-Vaughn Library, 1990.

Koral, April. *Our Global Greenhouse*. New York: Franklin Watts, 1989.

Kronewetter, Michael. *Managing Toxic Wastes* (Issues for the 90s). Englewood Cliffs, NJ: Julian Messner, 1989.

Lambert, David. *Pollution and Conservation*. New York: Bookwright Press, 1986.

Landau, Elaine. *Tropical Rain Forests Around the World*. New York: Franklin Watts, 1990.

Lee, Sally. *Throwaway Society*. New York: Franklin Watts, 1990.

Lefkowitz, R. J. *Save It! Keep It! Use It Again! A Book about Conservation and Recycling*. New York: Parents Magazine Press, 1977.

Leinwand, Gerald. *The Environment* (American Issues Series). New York: Facts on File, 1990.

Lewis, Barbara A. *Kid's Guide to Environmental Action: How to Solve the Social Problems You Choose—and Turn Creative Thinking into Positive Action*. Minneapolis, MN: Free Spirit Publishing, 1991.

Lucas, Eileen. *Water: A Resource in Crisis*. Chicago: Childrens Press, 1991.

Luoma, Jon R. *Troubled Skies, Troubled Waters: The Story of Acid Rain*. New York: Penquin Books, 1984.

MacEachern, Diane. *Save Our Planet: 750 Everyday Ways You Can Help Clean Up the Earth*. New York: A Dell Trade Paperback, 1990.

MacRae-Campbell, Linda, and Micki McKisson. *Our Only Earth: A Curriculum for Global Problem Solving*. Tucson, AZ: Zephyr Press, 1992.

McCoy, J. J. *How Safe Is Our Food Supply?* (An Impact Book). New York: Franklin Watts, 1990.

McGrath, Susan. *Saving Our Animal Friends*. Washington, DC: National Geographic, 1986.

McGraw, Eric. *Population Growth*. Vero Beach, FL: Rourke Enterprises, Inc., 1987.

Metzger, Mary, and Cinthya P. Whittaker. *This Planet Is Mine: Teaching Environmental Awareness and Appreciation to Children*. New York: A Fireside Book, 1991.

Miles, Betty. *Save the Earth: An Ecology Handbook for Kids*. New York: Alfred A. Knopf, 1991.

Miller, Christina G., and Louise A. Berry. *Jungle Rescue: Saving One New World Tropical Rain Forest*. New York: Atheneum, 1991.

Miller, Christina G., and Louise A. Perry. *Acid Rain: A Source Book for Young People*. New York: Julian Messner, 1986.

Miller, Christina G., and Louise A. Perry. *Coastal Rescue: Preserving our Seashores*. New York: Atheneum, 1989.

Miller, Christina G., and Louise A. Perry. *Wastes* (A First Book). New York: Franklin Watts, 1986.

Mutel, Cornelia Fleischer, and Mary M. Rodgers. *Our Endangered Planet: Tropical Rain Forests*. Minneapolis, MN: Lerner Publications Co., 1991.

O'Connor, Karen. *Garbage* (Our Endangered Planet). San Diego: Lucent Books, 1989.

Pearce, Fred. *The Big Green Book*. New York: Grosset & Dunlap, 1991.

Peckham, Alexander. *Global Warming*. New York: Gloucester Press, 1991.

Pederson, Anne. *The Kid's Environment Book: What's Awry and Why*. Santa Fe: John Muir Publications, 1991.

Pringle, Laurence. *Ecology: Science of Survival*. New York: Macmillan Publishers, 1971.

Pringle, Laurence. *Global Warming: Assessing the Greenhouse Threat*. New York: Arcade Publishing, 1990.

Pringle, Laurence. *Living in a Risky World*. New York: Morrow Junior Books, 1989.

Pringle, Laurence. *Living Treasure: Saving Earth's Threatened Biodiversity*. New York: Morrow Junior Books, 1991.

Pringle, Laurence. *Rain of Troubles: The Science and Politics of Acid Rain*. New York: Macmillan Publishing Company, 1988.

Pringle, Laurence. *Restoring Our Earth*. Hillsdale, NJ: Enslow Publishers, Inc., 1987.

Pringle. Laurence. *Saving Our Wildlife*. Hillside, NJ: Enslow Publishers, Inc., 1990. #3

Pringle, Laurence. *Throwing Things Away: From Middens to Resource Recovery*. New York: Thomas Y. Crowell, 1986.

Pringle, Laurence. *Water: The Next Great Resource Battle*. New York: Macmillan Publishers, 1982.

Pringle, Laurence. *What Shall We Do With the Land? Choices for America*. New York: Thomas Y. Crowell, 1981.

Rinard, Judith E. *Wildlife Making a Comeback: How Humans Are Helping*. Washington, DC: National Geographic Society, 1987.

Ross, Bonnie. *Waste Away: Information and Activities for Investigating Trash Problems and Solutions*. Woodstock, VT: Vermont Institute of Natural Science, 1989.

Schwartz, Linda. *Earth Book for Kids: Activities to Help Heal the Environment*. Santa Barbara, CA: Learning Works, Inc., 1990.

Simon, Noel. *Vanishing Habitats*. New York: Gloucester Press, 1987.

Simons, Robin. *Recyclopedia: Games, Science Equipment, and Crafts from Recycled Materials*. New York: Houghton Mifflin Co., 1976.

Sobel, David, ed. *The Ocean Book: Aquarium and Seaside Activities and Ideas for All Ages*. (Center for Marine Conservation) New York: John Wiley & Sons, Inc., 1989.

Stille, Darlene R. *The Greenhouse Effect* (A New True Book). Chicago: Childrens Press, Inc., 1990.

Stille, Darlene R. *Water Pollution* (A New True Book). Chicago: Childrens Press, Inc., 1990.

Stone, Lynn M. *Endangered Animals* (A New True Book). Chicago: Childrens Press, 1984.

Student Environmental Action Coalition. *The Student Environmental Action Guide*. Berkeley, CA: EarthWorks Press, 1991.

Szumski, Bonnie, and JoAnne Buggey. *Toxic Wastes: Examining Cause and Effect Relationships* (Juniors Opposing Viewpoints Series). San Diego: Greenhaven Press, Inc., 1989.

Tesar, Jenny E. *Global Warming* (Our Fragile Planet Series). New York: Facts on File, 1991.

Tesar, Jenny E. *Shrinking Forests* (Our Fragile Planet Series). New York: Facts on File, 1991.

Tesar, Jenny E. *Threatened Oceans* (Our Fragile Planet Series). New York: Facts on File, 1991.

Tesar, Jenny E. *The Waste Crisis* (Our Fragile Planet). New York: Facts on File, 1991.

Tilsworth, Debbie J. *Raising an Earth Friendly Child: The Keys to Your Child's Happy, Healthy Future* (Level I). Fairbanks, AK: Raven Press, 1991.

Timberlake, Lloyd. *Famine in Africa*. New York: Gloucester Press, 1986.

Versfield, Ruth. *Why Are People Hungry?* New York: Gloucester Press, 1988.

Wilcox, Charlotte. *Trash!* Minneapolis: Carolrhoda Books, Inc, 1988.

Winckler, Suzanne, and Mary M. Rodgers. *Our Endangered Planet: Population Growth*. Minneapolis, MN: Lerner Publications Co., 1991.

Zipko, Stephen J. *Toxic Threat: How Hazardous Substances Poison Our Lives*. Englewood Cliffs, NJ: Julian Messner, 1990.

Appendix C

....

BOOKS FOR A WELL-STOCKED ENVIRONMENTAL LIBRARY

The books in this appendix should be in junior high school or high school libraries. Some offer a more balanced view of environmental issues; others offer insights that are often ignored in environmental teaching today. Generally written in nontechnical language, they will broaden children's understanding of environmental issues.

Avery, Dennis. *Global Food Progress 1991*. Indianapolis: Hudson Institute, 1991.

Bailey, Ronald, ed. *Earth Report 2000: The True State of the Planet Revisited*. New York: The Free Press, 1999.

Balling, Robert C., Jr. *The Heated Debate: Greenhouse Predictions Versus Climate Reality*. San Francisco: Pacific Research Institute, 1992.

Bast, Joseph L., Peter J. Hill, and Richard Rue. *Eco-Sanity: A Common Sense Guide to Environmentalism*. Lanham, MD: Madison Books, 1994.

Bernstam, Mikhail S. *The Wealth of Nations and the Environment*. London: Institute for Economic Affairs, 1991.

Budiansky, Stephen. *Nature's Keepers: The New Science of Nature Management*. New York: The Free Press, 1995.

Clawson, Marion. *Forests: For Whom and For What?* Baltimore: Johns Hopkins University Press, 1975.

Field, Barry. *Environmental Economics: An Introduction*. New York: McGraw-Hill, 1994.

Frederick, Kenneth D., and Roger A. Sedjo, eds. *America's Renewable Resources: Historical Trends and Current Challenges*. Washington, DC: Resources for the Future, 1991.

Fumento, Michael. *Science Under Siege: Balancing Technology and the Environment*. New York: William Morrow and Company, Inc., 1993.

Glickman, Theodore S., and Michael Gough, eds. *Readings in Risk*. Washington, DC: Resources for the Future, 1990.

Goudie, Andrew. *The Human Impact on the Natural Environment*. 4th ed. Cambridge: The MIT Press, 1994.

Mann, Charles C., and Mark L. Plummer. *Noah's Choice: The Future of Endangered Species*. New York: Alfred A. Knopf, 1995.

Rathje, William, and Cullen Murphy. *Rubbish! The Archaeology of Garbage: What Our Garbage Tells Us About Ourselves*. New York: HarperCollins Publishers, 1992.

Shaw, Jane S., ed. *A Blueprint for Environmental Education*. Bozeman, MT: Political Economy Research Center, 1999.

Simon, Julian L., ed. *The State of Humanity*. Cambridge, MA: Blackwell Publishers, Inc., 1996.

Wildavsky, Aaron. *But Is It True? A Citizen's Guide to Environmental Health and Safety Issues*. Cambridge: Harvard University Press, 1995.

About the Authors

....

MICHAEL SANERA EARNED HIS Ph.D. in political science from the University of Colorado at Boulder in 1979. He currently serves as the Director of and a Senior Fellow at the Center for Environmental Education Research in Tucson, Arizona, a project of the Competitive Enterprise Institute. For seventeen years, he was a professor teaching political science and public administration at Northern Arizona University in Flagstaff. He has published two previous books. During the 1980s, he held several positions in Washington, D.C., including Assistant Director at the Office of Personnel Management and consultant at the U. S. Department of Education. He is a native of Arizona. Currently, he resides in Tucson with his wife, Wendy, and his youngest son, Devin.

JANE S. SHAW IS A Senior Associate of PERC (the Political Economy Research Center) in Bozeman, Montana. PERC is a nonprofit institute that applies innovative approaches to environmental problems. Shaw directs PERC's editorial outreach program, which prepares and distributes articles about economics and the environment for the popular and non-academic press. Before joining PERC in 1984, Shaw was an Associate Economics Editor of *Business Week,* and before that was a correspondent for McGraw-Hill Publications in Washington, D.C., and Chicago. Shaw received her B.A. degree from Wellesley College. She lives in Bozeman with her husband, Richard Stroup, and their son, David.

Notes

....

CHAPTER 1: A LETTER TO PARENTS

1. M. A. Maxwell, "Save the Planet, But Don't Forget Humans," *New York Times*, April 24, 1997.
2. Elliot Zaret, "Activist Accused of 'Highjacking' Earth Day Group," *Denver Post*, April 22, 1998, and Berny Morson, "Sorry About Environment Rally, Principal Tells Campbell," *Rocky Mountain News*, April 22, 1998.
3. Illustrated newsletter of Kids FACE, Nashville, TN: Kids FACE, March/April 1991, 3.
4. Leonard Bernstein, et al., *Concepts and Challenges in Earth Science*, 3d ed., Annotated Teacher's Edition (Englewood Cliffs, NJ: Globe Book Company, 1991), 270.
5. J. J. Houghton, L.G. Meiro Filho, B.A. Callander, N. Harris, A. Kattenberg, and K. Maskell, eds., *Climate Change 1995: The Science of Climate Change*. Contribution of Working Group I to the Second Assessment Report of the Intergovernmental Panel on Climate Change. (New York: Cambridge University Press, 1996).
6. Helen Cowcher, *Rainforest* (New York: Farrar, Straus and Giroux, 1988), no page numbers.
7. National Wildlife Federation, *Pollution: Problems and Solutions*, Ranger Rick's *NatureScope,* ed. Judy Braus (Washington, D.C.: National Wildlife Federation, 1990), 44.
8. National Acid Precipitation Assessment Program, *Integrated Assessment, External Review Draft* (Washington, DC, August 1990).

9. Bonnie Ferraro and Karen Brumley, *Saving Our Planet* (Columbus, OH: American Education Publishing, Weekly Reader, 1992), 5.

10. W. A. Dart, "Viewpoint: Pitching in the Foam Cup to Save the Planet," *Miami Herald*, April 22, 1990, and letter from David Jolly, Environmental Affairs Representative, Dart Container Corporation, September 11, 1992.

11. "What On Earth Are We Doing?" *Time*, January 2, 1989, 26–71.

12. Eliot Marshall, "A Is for Apple, Alar, and...Alarmist?" *Science*, Vol. 254 (October 4, 1991), 22.

13. Reported in S. Robert Lichter, Linda S. Lichter, and Daniel R. Amundson, "Doomsday Kids: Environmental Messages on Children's Television" (Washington, D.C.: Center for Media and Public Affairs, April 1995).

14. Stephen H. Schneider, Ph.D., "Dealing With the Greenhouse Effect," *Good Housekeeping*, April 1991, 78–79.

15. Sharon Begley, "He's Not Full of Hot Air," *Newsweek*, January 22, 1996, 24.

16. Ronald Bailey, *Eco-Scam: The False Prophets of Ecological Apocalypse* (New York: St. Martin's Press, 1993), 120.

17. Marc K. Landy, Marc J. Roberts, Stephen R. Thomas, *The Environmental Protection Agency: Asking the Wrong Questions* (New York: Oxford University Press, 1990), 133–171.

18. Letter from Vawter "Buck" Parker, acting president, Sierra Club Legal Defense Fund, 180 Montgomery Street, Suite 1400, San Francisco CA 94104, n.d.

19. Letter from Randall L. Hayes, executive director, Rainforest Action Network, 301 Broadway, San Francisco CA 94133, n.d.

20. Letter from Russell E. Train, chairman of the board, World Wildlife Fund & The Conservation Foundation, 1250 Twenty-fourth St. NW, Washington, DC 20037 (1991 or 1992).

21. *National Air Pollutant Emission Trends, 1900–1994* (Washington, DC: U.S. Environmental Protection Agency, October 1995) EPA-454/R-95-011, Executive Summary, ES8.

22. Roger A. Sedjo and Marion Clawson, "Global Forests Revisited," in *The State of Humanity,* ed. by Julian Simon (New York: Basil Blackwell, 1995), 332–3.

23. Winston Harrington, "Severe Decline and Partial Recovery," in *America's Renewable Resources: Historical Trends and Current Challenges*, Kenneth D. Frederick and Roger A. Sedjo, eds. (Washington DC: Resources for the Future, 1991), 237–8.

CHAPTER 2: AT ODDS WITH SCIENCE

1. Robert E. Snyder et al., *Earth Science: The Challenge of Discovery* (Lexington, MA: D.C. Heath and Co., 1991), 536.

2. National Acid Precipitation Assessment Program, *1992 Report to Congress*, Washington, D.C., June 1993. Also K. Mellanby, ed., *Air Pollution, Acid Rain and the Environment* (Elsevier Applied Science Publishers for the Watt Committee on Energy).

3. Pamela S. Zurer, "Antarctic Ozone Hole: Complex Picture Emerges," *Chemical & Engineering News*, November 2, 1987, 22–26.

4. Andrew Solow, "Is There a Global Warming Problem?" in *Global Warming: Economic Policy Responses*, ed. by Rudiger Dornbusch and James M. Poterba (Cambridge, MA: The MIT Press, 1991), 18.

5. Robert Jastrow, William A. Nierenberg, and Frederick Seitz, "An Overview," *Scientific Perspectives on the Greenhouse Problem* (Ottawa, IL:Jameson Books, Inc., 1990), 11.

6. Richard S. Lindzen, "Global Warming: The Origin and Nature of the Alleged Scientific Consensus," *Regulation*, Spring 1992, 89.

7. Al Gore, *Earth in the Balance: Ecology and the Human Spirit* (Boston: Houghton Mifflin Company, 1992), 39.

CHAPTER 3: WHAT ARE THE COSTS?

1. David G. Cameron, Testimony before the Task Force on Private Property Rights of the Committee on Resources of the U.S. House of Representatives, July 17, 1995.

2. National Wildlife Federation, *Pollution: Problems and Solutions*, Ranger Rick's *NatureScope,* ed. Judy Braus (Washington, D.C.: National Wildlife Federation, 1990), 70.

3. Judy Edelson Halpert, "Freon Smugglers Find Big Market," *New York Times*, April 30, 1994, A1ff.

4. See Tim Beardsley, "Better Than a Cure," *Scientific American,* January 1995, 88-95.

5. William Rathje and Cullen Murphy, *Rubbish! The Archaeology of Garbage* (New York: HarperCollins Publishers, Inc., 1992), 206.

6. Jeff Bailey, "Curbside Recycling Comforts the Soul, But Benefits Are Scant," *Wall Street Journal*, January 19, 1995, A8.

7. Jane S. Shaw, "Recycling," *The Fortune Encyclopedia of Economics*, ed. by David R. Henderson (New York: Warner Books, Inc., 1993), 459.

8. Federal Highway Administration figure reported in *The Milwaukee Journal*, January 15, 1995.

9. Council on Environmental Quality, *22nd Annual Report* (Washington, DC: Superintendent of Documents, U.S. Government Printing Office, March 1992), 10.

10. E. Calvin Beisner and Julian L. Simon, "Editors' Appendix," in *The State of Humanity,* ed. by Julian L. Simon (Cambridge, MA: Blackwell Publishers Inc., 1995), 469.

11. Robert W. Crandall, *Controlling Industrial Air Pollution: The Economics and Politics of Clean Air* (Washington, DC: The Brookings Institution, 1983), 19.

12. This term was coined by Garrett Hardin in "The Tragedy of the Commons," *Science,* Vol. 162 (1968), 1243–48.

13. J. Dirck Stryker, "Technology, Human Pressure, and Ecology in the Arid and Semi-Arid Tropics," in *Environment and the Poor: Development Strategies for a Common Agenda*, ed. by H. Jeffrey Leonard (New Brunswick, NJ: Transaction Books, 1989), 95.

14. *World Development Report 1992*, 12.

15. Richard L. Stroup and Jane S. Shaw, "Environmental Harms from Federal Government Policy," in *Taking the Environment Seriously,* ed. by Roger E. Meiners and Bruce Yandle (Lanham, MD: Rowman & Littlefield Publishers, Inc., 1993), 51–72, esp. p. 55.

16. Peter Passell, "Experts Question Staggering Costs of Toxic Cleanups," *New York Times*, September 1, 1991, A1.

17. Richard L. Stroup and Jane S. Shaw, 56.

18. Frederic H. Wagner et al., *Wildlife Policies in the U.S. National Parks* (Washington, D.C.: Island Press, 1995), 62.

19. Gene M. Grossman and Alan B. Krueger, *Environmental Impacts of a North American Free Trade Agreement*, Discussion Paper in Economics, Woodrow Wilson School of Public and International Affairs, Princeton University, Princeton, NJ, February 1992, 5. This paper has been published in *The U.S. Mexico Free Trade Agreement*, ed. by P. Garber (Cambridge, MA: MIT Press, 1993), 13–56.

20. Lynn Scarlett, "Make Your Environment Dirtier—Recycle," *Wall Street Journal*, January 14, 1991.

CHAPTER 4: WILL BILLIONS STARVE?

1. Herbert I. London, *Why Are They Lying to Our Children?* (New York: Stein and Day Publishers, 1984), 31-2.
2. Mounir Farah and Andrea Berens Karls, *World History: The Human Experience*, 3d ed. (Lake Forest, IL: Glencoe, 1992), 961–2.
3. Jean P. Milani, *Biological Science: An Ecological Approach*, 6th ed. (Dubuque, IA: Kendal/Hunt, 1987), 932–3.
4. Indur M. Goklany, "Feeding the World's Billions Without Crowding Out the Rest of Nature" (Washington, DC: Department of the Interior, Office of Policy Analysis, November 1995).
5. Dennis T. Avery, *Global Food Progress 1991: A Report from Hudson Institute's Center for Global Food Issues* (Indianapolis: The Hudson Institute, 1991), 72, fig. 1–5.
6. United Nations, *1998 Revision of the World Population Estimates and Projections.* Available at: http://www.popin.org/pop1998.
7. United Nations, *idem.*
8. Jacqueline R. Kasun, *Population and Environment: Debunking the Myths* (Baltimore: Population Research Institute, 1991), 3.
9. Avery, 16.
10. Julian Simon, *The Ultimate Resource* (Princeton: Princeton University Press, 1981), 67.
11. Alexandratos, Nikos, *World Agriculture: Towards 2010* (Chichester, England: Food and Agriculture Organization of the United Nations and John Wiley & Sons, 1995), 124.
12. Alexandratos, 130.
13. Thomas T. Poleman, "Income and Dietary Change," in *Food Policy*, Vol. 20, No. 2 (1995), 49–159.
14. William H. Hartley and William S. Vincent, *American Civics*, Freedom Ed. (Austin: Holt, Rinehart and Winston, Inc., 1992) 509.
15. Francis P. Hunkins and David G. Armstrong, *World Geography: People and Places* (Columbus, OH: Merrill Publishing Company, 1984), 120.
16. Leonard Bernstein et al., *Concepts and Challenges in Life Science*, 3rd ed., Annotated Teacher's Edition (Englewood Cliffs, NJ: Globe Book Co., 1991), 59.
17. William D. Schraer and Herbert J. Stoltze, *Biology: The Study of Life*, 4th ed. (Needham, MA: Prentice Hall, 1991), 864.
18. See the discussion of carrying capacity in Julian Simon, 177.
19. Colin Clark, *Population Growth and Land Use* (New York: Macmillan, 1968), 153.
20. Avery, 90.
21. Avery, 10.
22. Avery, 18.
23. Roger LaRaus et al., *Challenge of Freedom*, 3rd ed. (Mission Hills, CA: Glencoe Publishing Co., 1990), 702.
24. Anne Pedersen, *The Kids' Environment Book: What's Awry and Why* (Santa Fe, NM: John Muir Publications, 1991), 136.
25. World Bank, *World Development Report 1993* (Oxford University Press, 1993), Table 1.
26. Robert J. Sager et al., *World Geography Today*, rev. ed. (Austin: Holt, Rinehart and Winston, Inc., 1992), 620.

27. Allen C. Kelley, "Economic Consequences of Population Change," *Journal of Economic Literature*, 26 (December 1988), 1685–1728.

28. Quoted in Julian Simon, *Population Matters: People, Resources, Environment, and Immigration* (New Brunswick, NJ: Transaction Publishers, 1990), 230.

29. Farah and Karls, 962. Also see Richard G. Boehm and James L. Swanson, *World Geography: A Physical and Cultural Approach*, 3d ed. (Lake Forest, IL: Glencoe, 1992), 491–4.

30. Milani, 932-3.

31. Linda L. Greenlow, et al., *World Geography: People in Time and Place* (Morristown, NJ: Silver Burdett & Ginn, 1992), 435.

32. Farah and Karls, 961.

33. Thomas T. Poleman, *Population: Past Growth and Future Control*, Working Paper, Department of Agricultural, Resource, and Managerial Economics, Cornell University, Ithaca, NY, September 1994, 8.

34. Poleman, 8.

35. Lant H. Pritchett, "Desired Fertility and the Impact of Population Policies," *Population and Development Review*, March 1994, 55.

36. Avery, 70.

37. Alexandratos, 53.

38. Avery, 53.

39. Avery, 47.

40. Avery, 20.

CHAPTER 5: NATURAL RESOURCES—ON THE WAY OUT?

1. Quoted in Stephen Moore, *Doomsday Delayed: America's Surprisingly Bright Natural Resource Future*, IPI Policy Report No. 118 (Lewisville, TX: The Institute for Policy Innovation, August 1992), 35.

2. Ralph M. Feather et al., *Science Connections*, Red ed., Annotated Teacher's Edition (Columbus, OH: Merrill Publishing, 1990), 493.

3. Robert E. Snyder et al., *Earth Science: The Challenge of Discovery*, Annotated Teacher's Edition (Lexington, MA: D. C. Heath and Co., 1991), 212.

4. David C. King et al., *The United States and Its People* (Menlo Park, CA: Addison-Wesley, 1993), 876.

5. Leonard Bernstein et al., *Concepts and Challenges in Earth Science*, 3d ed., Annotated Teacher's Edition (Englewood Cliffs, NJ: Globe Book Co., 1991), 290.

6. Peter Alexander et al., *General Science*, Book One (Needham, MA: Silver Burdett & Ginn, 1989), 401.

7. Robert E. Snyder et al., 410.

8. William H. Hartley and William S. Vincent, *American Civics*, Freedom ed. (Austin: Holt, Rinehart and Winston, Inc., 1992), 516.

9. James E. Davis and Phyllis Maxey Fernlund, *Civics: Participating in Our Democracy* (Menlo Park, CA: Addison-Wesley Publishing Co., 1993), 565.

10. John R. O'Conner and Robert M. Goldberg, *Exploring American Citizenship* (Englewood Cliffs, NJ: Globe Book Co., 1992), 329.

11. Robert E. Snyder et al., 436.

12. Albert Kaskel et al., *Biology, An Everyday Experience* (Lake Forest, IL: Glencoe, 1992), 677.

13. J. Clayburn LaForce, "The Energy Crisis: The Moral Equivalent of Bamboozle," Original Paper 11 (Los Angeles, International Institute for Economic Research, April 1978).
14. Quoted in Julian Simon, *The Ultimate Resource* (Princeton: Princeton University Press, 1981), 93.
15. Energy Information Administration figures available at: http://www.eia.doe.gov/pub/energy.overview/monthly.energy/mer9-1.
16. U.S. Bureau of Mines, *Mineral Facts and Problems* (Washington, D.C.: Government Printing Office, 1985), 3.
17. David Osterfeld, *Prosperity Versus Planning: How Government Stifles Economic Growth* (New York: Oxford Press, 1992), 95.
18. Osterfeld, 95.
19. Julian Simon entitled a book on population and natural resources *The Ultimate Resource* to convey this point.
20. John Tierney, "Betting the Planet," *New York Times Magazine,* December 2, 1990, 52–3ff.

CHAPTER 6: ARE OUR FORESTS DYING?

1. Anne Pedersen, *The Kids' Environment Book: What's Awry and Why* (Santa Fe, NM: John Muir Publications, 1991), 73.
2. Daniel D. Chiras, *Environmental Science: A Framework for Decision Making*, 2d ed. (Menlo Park, CA: The Benjamine/Cummings Publishing Co., Inc., 1988), 193.
3. Raymond F. Oram, *Biology: Living Systems*, Annotated Teacher's Edition (Columbus, OH: Merrill Publishing Co., 1989), 758.
4. Carlton L. Jackson and Vito Perrone, *Two Centuries of Progress* (Mission Hills, CA: Glencoe/McGraw-Hill, 1991), 382.
5. Alton Biggs et al., *Biology: The Dynamics of Life* (Columbus, OH: Merrill Publishing Co., 1991), 769.
6. Evergreen Foundation, *The Truth About America's Forests,* Special Bonus Issue (Washington, D.C.: Island Press, 1991), 4.
7. Roger A. Sedjo, "Forests," in *The True State of the Planet*, ed. by Ronald Bailey (New York: The Free Press, 1995), 178–209 at 185.
8. Roger A. Sedjo, "Forest Resources: Resilient and Serviceable," in *America's Renewable Resources*, ed. by Kenneth D. Frederick and Roger A. Sedjo (Washington, DC: Resources for the Future, 1991), 113.
9. D. S. Powell, D. R. Darr, Z. Zhu, and D.W. MacCleery, *Forest Resources of the U. S., 1992.* General Technical Report RM-234 (USDA/Forest Service, September 1993).
10. Sedjo (1991), 109.
11. Bill McKibben, "An Explosion of Green," *The Atlantic Monthly*, April 1995, 61–83.
12. Marion Clawson, "Forests in the Long Sweep of American History," *Science*, Vol. 204, July 15, 1979, 1168.
13. Sedjo (1991), 87.
14. Sedjo (1991), 87.
15. See Clawson, op. cit., and Sedjo (1995), 185.
16. Evergreen Foundation (1991), Table, "U.S. Forest Area," 3.
17. Quoted in Terry L. Anderson and Donald R. Leal, *Free Market Environmentalism* (San Francisco: Pacific Research Institute for Public Policy and Westview Press, 1991), 38.

18. Sedjo (1991), 90.
19. Gary B. Nash, *American Odyssey: The United States in the Twentieth Century* (Lake Forest, IL: Glencoe, 1991), 180.
20. Mary Jane Turner et al., *American Government: Principles and Practices* (Columbus, OH: Merrill Publishing Co., 1991), 423.
21. See Robert H. Nelson, *Public Lands and Private Rights: The Failure of Scientific Management* (Lanham, MD: Rowman & Littlefield Publishers, Inc., 1995), 43–90.
22. D. S. Powell, et al., op cit.
23. Private communication from Douglas W. MacCleery, U. S. Forest Service, Aug. 29, 1996.
24. D.S. Powell, et al., op cit.
25. Lance R. Clark and R. Neil Sampson, *Forest Ecosystem Health in the Inland West: A Science and Policy Reader* (Washington, D.C.: Forest Policy Center, 1995), 2-3.
26. Roger A. Sedjo, "Local Logging—Global Effects," *Journal of Forestry*, Vol. 93, No. 7 (1995), 25-27.
27. See Sedjo (1991), 92–7.
28. Sedjo (1991), 96.
29. Sedjo (1991), 107.
30. Sedjo (1991), 104–6.
31. Sedjo (1991), 104–6.

CHAPTER 7: THE RAIN FOREST—ONE HUNDRED ACRES A MINUTE?

1. Linda L. Greenlow, et al., *World Geography: People in Time and Place* (Morristown, NJ: Silver Burdett & Ginn, 1992), 241-4.
2. John Javna, ed., *50 Simple Things Kids Can do to Save the Earth* (Kansas City, MO: Andrews and McMeel, 1990), 96.
3. T. Walter Wallbark, et al., *History and Life*, updated ed. (Glenview, IL: Scott Foresman and Co., 1993), 766.
4. Thomas J. Baerwald and Celeste Fraser, *World Geography* (Needham, MA: Prentice Hall, 1993), 250.
5. Karen Arms, *Environmental Science*, Annotated Teacher's Edition (Austin, TX: Holt, Rinehart and Winston, 1996), 83.
6. Anne Pedersen, *The Kids' Environment Book: What's Awry and Why* (Sante Fe, New Mexico: John Muir Publications, 1991), 71–78.
7. Charles H. Heimier, *Focus on Life Science* (Columbus, OH: Merrill Publishing Co., 1989), 215.
8. Daniel D. Chiras, *Environmental Science: A Framework for Decision Making* (Menlo Park, CA: The Benjamin/Cummings Publishing Co., Inc., 1988), 200–3.
9. Roger A. Sedjo and Marion Clawson, "Global Forests Revisited," in *The State of Humanity*, ed. by Julian Simon (Cambridge, MA: Blackwell Publishers, 1995), 332.
10. Sedjo and Clawson, 329.
11. See Food and Agriculture Organization of the United Nations, *Forest Resources Assessment 1990, Tropical Countries #112*, Tables 3, 4, 7, 8.
12. Food and Agriculture Organization of the United Nations, Tables 3, 4, 7, 8.
13. Sedjo and Clawson, 334.

14. Peter H. Raven, Linda R.Berg and George B. Johnson, *Environment* (Fort Worth TX: Harcourt Brace College Publishing, 1993), 379.
15. See Baerwald and Fraser, 250-1, and Melvin Schwartz and John O'Conner, *Exploring a Changing World* (Englewood Cliffs, NJ: Globe Book Co., 1993), 243.
16. Robert Repetto, *The Forest for the Trees? Government Policies and the Misuse of Forest Resources* (Washington, D.C.: World Resources Institute, 1988), 1.
17. Repetto, 13.
18. Repetto, 16.
19. Repetto, 16.
20. Dennis J. Mahar, *Government Policies and Deforestation in Brazil's Amazon Region*, (Washington, D.C.: World Bank, 1989), 9.
21. Mahar, 11.
22. Mahar, 37.
23. Mahar, 13–20.
24. John O. Browder, "The Social Costs of Rain Forest Destruction," *Interciencia,* Vol. 13, No. 3, May/June 1988, 115–120 at 118.
25. Sedjo and Clawson, 333.
26. Evergreen Foundation, *The Truth About America's Forests,* Special Bonus Issue (Washington, D.C.: Island Press, 1991), 4.
27. Sedjo and Clawson, 334.
28. Robert T. Deacon and Paul Murphy, "Swapping Debts for Nature: Direct International Trade in Environmental Services," in *NAFTA and the Environment*, ed. by Terry L. Anderson (San Francisco: Pacific Research Institute, 1993), 69–90.
29. Deacon and Murphy, 77.
30. Harvey K. Goodman et al., *Biology Today*, Annotated Teacher's Edition (Austin: Holt, Rinehart and Winston, Inc., 1991), 76.
31. Beau Fly Jones, *Rain Forests: The Lungs of the Earth*, Teachers' Edition (Columbus, OH: Zaner-Bloser, Inc., 1990), 25.
32. Wallbark et al., 766.
33. Pedersen, 71–8.
34. Richard A. Houghton and George M. Woodwell, "Global Climatic Change," *Scientific American*, Vol. 260, No. 4, April 1989, 36–44.
35. Beau Fly Jones, *Rain Forests: The Lungs of the Earth*, Teacher's Edition (Columbus, OH: Zaner-Bloser, Inc., 1990), 25.
36. Thomas J. Baerwald and Celeste Fraser, *World Geography* (Needham, MA: Prentice Hall, 1993), 250.
37. Albert Kaskel et al., *Biology: An Everyday Experience* (Lake Forest, IL: Merrill, 1992), 675.
38. Linda Schwartz, *Earth Book for Kids: Activities to Help Heal the Environment* (Santa Barbara, CA: The Learning Works, Inc., 1990), 114.
39. Deacon and Murphy, 73.
40. Deacon and Murphy, 74.
41. Roger A. Sedjo and Marion Clawson, "Global Forests," in *The Resourceful Earth*, ed. by Julian Simon and Herman Kahn (New York: Basil Blackwell, 1984), 151.

CHAPTER 8: AMERICAN WILDLIFE—ON THE EDGE?

1. Catherine Dee, ed., *Kid Heroes of the Environment* (Berkeley, CA: Earth Works Press, 1991), 63–4.
2. Harvey D. Goodman et al., *Biology Today*, Annotated Teacher's Edition (Austin: Holt, Rinehart and Winston, Inc., 1991), 874.
3. Charles H. Heimier, *Focus on Life Science* (Columbus, OH: Merrill Publishing Co., 1989), 571.
4. William D. Schraer and Herbert J. Stoltze, *Biology: The Study of Life*, 4th ed. (Needham, MA: Prentice Hall, 1991), 867.
5. Thomas J. Baerwald and Celeste Fraser, *World Geography* (Needham, MA: Prentice Hall, 1993), 570.
6. Winston Harrington, "Severe Decline and Partial Recovery," in *America's Renewable Resources: Historical Trends and Current Challenges*, Kenneth D. Frederick and Roger A. Sedjo, eds. (Washington DC: Resources for the Future, 1991), 238.
7. Harrington, 238.
8. Harrington, 238.
9. Harrington, 237–8.
10. Harrington, 238.
11. Alston Chase, *Playing God in Yellowstone: The Destruction of America's First National Park* (Boston: The Atlantic Monthly Press, 1986), 126.
12. Bill Heard, "Supply Side Management: Alaska's Success Story?" Paper presented at Fraser Institute Conference, "Would Quotas Solve the Problems Facing the West Coast Fishery?" Vancouver, British Columbia, May 30-31, 1966, 10.
13. Charles C. Mann and Mark L. Plummer, *Noah's Choice: The Future of Endangered Species* (New York: Alfred A. Knopf, Inc., 1995), 75–6.
14. Robert M. McClung, *Lost Wild America: The Story of Our Extinct and Vanishing Wildlife* (Hamden, CT: Linnet Books, 1993), 33.
15. James A. Tober, *Who Owns the Wildlife? The Political Economy of Conservation in Nineteenth-Century America* (Westport, CT: Greenwood Press, 1981), 95.
16. McClung, 35.
17. David A. Dary, *The Buffalo Book: The Full Saga of the American Animal* (Athens: Ohio University Press and Swallow Press, 1989), 234–40.
18. Robert J. Smith, *No Regrets for Great Egrets*, Working Paper 94-4, Political Economy Research Center, Bozeman, MT, 1994, 2–4.
19. Harrington, 215–6. See also Dean L. Lueck, "The Economic Organization of Wildlife Institutions" in *Wildlife in the Marketplace*, Terry L. Anderson and Peter J. Hill, eds. (Lanham, MD: Rowman & Littlefield Publishers, Inc., 1995), 1–24.
20. Bernard J. Nebel and Richard T. Wright, *Environmental Science: The Way the World Works*, 4th ed. (Needham, MA: Prentice Hall, 1993), 420.
21. Karen Arms, *Environmental Science* (Austin: Holt, Rinehart and Winston, Inc., 1996), 263.
22. Arms, 263.
23. Richard L. Stroup, *The Endangered Species Act: Making Innocent Species the Enemy* (Political Economy Research Center, Bozeman, MT, PS-3, April 1995).
24. Stroup, 2.

25. Robert J. Smith, "The Endangered Species Act: Saving Species or Stopping Growth," *Regulation* (Winter 1992), 85, plus personal communication by the author.

26. Robert J. Smith, personal communication.

27. Information from Ducks Unlimited, One Waterfowl Way, Long Grove, IL 60047.

28. Information from Delta Waterfowl Foundation, 102 Wilmot Road, Suite 410, Deerfield, IL 60015.

29. Jo Kwong, "Public and Private Benefits: The Case For Fee Hunting," *PERC Viewpoints*, No. 2, Political Economy Research Center, Bozeman MT, July/August 1987, 4.

30. Council on Environmental Quality, "Special Report: The Public Benefits of Private Conservation," *Fifteenth Annual Report* (Washington, D.C., 1984), 387–94.

CHAPTER 9: WHERE HAVE ALL THE SPECIES GONE?

1. Kenneth Miller and Joseph Levine, *Biology*, 2nd ed. (Englewood Cliffs, NJ: Prentice Hall, 1993), 1065.

2. Anne Pedersen, *The Kids' Environment Book: What's Awry and Why* (Santa Fe, NM: John Muir Publications, 1991), 136–42.

3. Ralph M. Feather et al., *Science Connections*, Red ed. (Columbus, OH: Merrill Publishing Co., 1990), 479.

4. Jonathan Turk, *Introduction to Environmental Studies*, 3d ed. (Philadelphia: Saunders College Publishing, 1989), 143.

5. Jill Wright et al., "Wildlife Conservation: Which Animals Should Be Saved?" *Life Science* (Englewood Cliffs, NJ: Prentice Hall, 1991), 268–9.

6. Leonard Bernstein et al., *Concepts and Challenges in Earth Science*, 3d ed., Annotated Teacher's Edition (Englewood Cliffs, NJ: Globe Book Co., 1991), 294.

7. National Wildlife Federation, *Pollution and Solutions*, Ranger Rick's *NatureScope*, ed. Judy Braus (Washington, D.C.: National Wildlife Federation, 1990), 34.

8. Paul R. Ehrlich and Edward O. Wilson, "Biodiversity Studies: Science and Policy," *Science*, Vol. 253, 16 August 1991, 758–62 at 758.

9. U.S. Council on Environmental Quality and Department of State, *The Global 2000 Report to the President,* Vol. 2, 331.

10. Ehrlich and Wilson, 759.

11. Quoted in Charles C. Mann, "Extinction: Are Ecologists Crying Wolf?" *Science*, Vol. 253, August 16, 1991, 736-38, at 738.

12. 13. U.S. Council on Environmental Quality and Department of State, *The Global 2000 Report to the President,* Vol. 2, 331.

13. Julian L. Simon and Aaron Wildavsky, *Assessing the Empirical Basis of the "Biodiversity Crisis,"* Competitive Enterprise Institute, Washington, D.C., May 1993.

14. Simon and Wildavsky, 7.

15. Charles C. Mann and Mark L. Plummer, *Noah's Choice: The Future of Endangered Species* (New York: Alfred A. Knopf, Publisher, 1995), 60.

16. Mann and Plummer, 61.

17. Quoted in Mann, 737.

18. Lawrence B. Slobodkin, "Islands of Peril and Pleasure," *Nature*, Vol. 381, May 16, 1996, 205.

19. Mann, 738.

20. Mann and Plummer, 75-6.

21. T. C. Whitmore and J. A. Sayer, eds., *Tropical Deforestation and Species Extinction* (New York Chapman and Hall, 1992), quoted in Simon and Wildavsky, 9.

22. Randy T. Simmons and Urs P. Kreuter, "Herd Mentality," *Policy Review*, Fall 1989, 46–9.

23. Eugene Linden, "Tigers on the Brink," *Time*, March 28, 1994, 44-51.

24. Information from The Nature Conservancy, 815 North Lynn Street, Arlington, VA 22209.

25. Ike C. Sugg, "To Save an Endangered Species, Own One," *Wall Street Journal*, August 31, 1992.

CHAPTER 10: THE AIR WE BREATHE

1. Derek M. Elsom, "Atmospheric Pollution in the United Kingdom," in *The State of Humanity*, ed. by Julian L. Simon (Cambridge, MA: Blackwell Publishers, Inc., 1995), 476–490 at 478.

2. Julius B. Richmond et al., *Health for Life* (Glenview, IL: Scott, Foresman and Co., 1990), 295.

3. Robert E. Snyder et al., *Earth Science: The Challenge of Discovery*, Annotated Teacher's Edition (Lexington, MA: D. C. Heath and Co., 1991), 529.

4. Russell Seitz, "A War Against Fire: The Uses of 'Global Warming,'" *National Interest*, Summer 1990, 55.

5. Edward F. Dolan, *Our Poisoned Sky* (New York: Dutton, 1991), 4.

6. John R. O'Conner and Robert M. Goldberg, *Exploring American Citizenship* (Englewood Cliffs, NJ: Globe Book Co., 1992), 330.

7. Mary Metzger and Cinthya P. Wittacker, *This Planet Is Mine: Teaching Environmental Awareness and Appreciation to Children* (New York: Fireside, 1991), 18.

8. Council on Environmental Quality, *22nd Annual Report* (Washington, DC: Superintendent of Documents, U.S. Government Printing Office, March 1992), 10.

9. National Air Pollutant Emission Trends, 1900-1994 (Washington, DC: U.S. Environmental Protection Agency, October 1995) EPA-454/R-95-011, Executive Summary, ES8.

10. James M. Lents and William J. Kelly, "Clearing the Air in Los Angeles," *Scientific American*, October 1993, 32-9.

11. Environmental Protection Agency news release, supported by U.S. Congress, Office of Technology Assessment, *Catching Our Breath: Next Steps for Reducing Urban Ozone*, OTA-O-412 (Washington, D.C.: U.S. Government Printing Office, July 1989), 6.

12. *Statistical Abstract of the United States 1995* published as The *American Almanac 1995-96* (Austin, TX: The Reference Press, 1995), Table No. 376, 234.

13. Rick Henderson, "Insufficient Data," *Reason*, June 1992, 56.

14. Robert W. Crandall, *Controlling Industrial Pollution* (Washington, D.C.: The Brookings Institution, 1983), 18–19.

15. James M. Lents and William J. Kelly, "Clearing the Air in Los Angeles," *Scientific American* (October 1993), 38.

16. Philip J. Hilts, *New York Times*, July 19, 1993, 1.

17. John Javna, *50 Simple Things Kids Can Do to Save the Earth* (Kansas City: Andrews and McMeel, 1990), 114–5.

18. J. G. Calvert, et al., "Achieving Acceptable Air Quality: Some Reflections on Controlling Vehicle Emissions," *Science*, July 2, 1993, 37–45.

19. Rick Henderson, "Dirty Driving," *Policy Review*, Spring 1992, 56-60 at 57.

20. Henderson, 56–60.

CHAPTER 11: A HOTTER PLANET?

1. Dean Hurd, et al., *General Science: A Voyage of Exploration* (Englewood Cliffs, NJ: Prentice Hall, 1992), 401–2.

2. Mary Jane Turner, et al., *American Government: Principles and Practices* (Columbus, OH: Merrill Publishing, 1991), 427.

3. Leonard Bernstein et al., *Concepts and Challenges in Earth Science*, 3d ed., Annotated Teacher's Edition (Englewood Cliffs, NJ: Globe Book Co., 1991), 270.

4. J. J. Houghton, L. G. Meiro Filho, B. A. Callander, N. Harris, A. Kattenberg, and K. Maskell, eds., *Climate Change 1995: The Science of Climate Change*. Contribution of Working Group I to the Second Assessment Report of the Intergovernmental Panel on Climate Change. (New York: Cambridge University Press, 1996).

5. J. J. Houghton et al.

6. Gifford H. Miller and Anne de Vernal, Will Greenhouse Warming Lead to Northern Hemisphere Ice-sheet Growth?" *Nature*, Vol. 355 (January 16, 1992), 244–6.

7. Stephen H. Schneider, "The Greenhouse Effect: Science and Policy," *Science*, Vol. 243 (February 10, 1989), 771–81 at 774.

8. R. Monastersky, "Global Warming; Politics Muddle Policy," *Science News*, June 23, 1990, 391.

9. J. J. Houghton, et al.

10. R. W. Spencer and J. R. Christy, "Precise Monitoring of Global Temperature Trends from Satellites," in *Scientific Perspectives on the Greenhouse Problem* (Ottawa, IL: Jameson Books, Inc., 1990), 95-104, for figures through 1988. These figures were updated by R. W. Spencer.

11. James E. Hansen, Makiko Sato, Reto Ruedy, Andrew Lacis, and Jay Glascoe, "Global Climate Data and Models; A Reconciliation," *Science*, Vol. 281, August 14, 1998, 930-932, and Roy Spencer, "Scientist's Notebook," August 14, 1998. Available: http://science.nasa.gov (Aug 13, 1998).

12. See for example P. D. Jones, "Hemispheric Surface Air Temperature Variations: Recent Trends and an Update to 1987," *Journal of Climate*, Vol. 1 (1988), 654–660, and Philip D. Jones and Tom M. L. Wigley, "Global Warming Trends," *Scientific American*, August 1990, 84–91.

13. Personal communication from Robert C. Balling, Jr., Arizona State University, August 25, 1999.

14. Quoted on the dust jacket of Lowell Ponte, *The Cooling* (Englewood Cliffs, NJ: Prentice Hall, 1976).

15. Sylvan H. Wittwer, "The Greenhouse Effect" (Burlington, NC: Carolina Biological Supply Company, 1988), 3.

16. Balling, 23 (figures adjusted to reflect current CO_2 levels).

17. Robert Jastrow, William A. Nierenberg, and Frederick Seitz, "An Overview," *Scientific Perspectives on the Greenhouse Problem* (Ottawa IL: Jameson Books, Inc., 1990), 11.

18. Aaron Wildavsky, "Introduction" to *The Heated Debate: Greenhouse Predictions versus Climate Reality*, by Robert C. Balling, Jr. (San Francisco: Pacific Research Institute for Public Policy, 1992), xxiv.

19. Patrick J. Michaels, "Crisis in Politics of Climate Change Looms on Horizon," *Forum for Applied Research and Public Policy* (Winter 1989), 15.

20. Richard A. Kerr, "Study Unveils Climate Cooling Caused by Pollutant Haze," *Science*, Vol. 268 (May 12, 1995), 802.
21. Frederick Seitz, Robert Jastrow, William A. Nierenberg, *Scientific Perspectives on the Greenhouse Problem* (Ottawa, IL: Jameson Books, Inc., 1990),32-33.
22. J. D. Kahl, D. J. Charlevoix, N. A. Zartseva, R. C. Schnell and M. C. Serreze, *Nature*, Vol. 361 (1993), 335–337, cited in *Are Human Activities Causing Global Warming?* (Washington, D.C.: George C. Marshall Institute, 1996), 33.
23. Andrew R. Solow, "Is There a Global Warming Problem?" in Rudiger Dornbusch and James M. Poterba, *Global Warming: Economic Policy Responses* (Cambridge MA: The MIT Press, 1991), 7-28, at 26.
24. Thomas Gale Moore, *Climate of Fear: Why We Shouldn't Worry About Global Warming* (Washington, DC: Cato Institute, 1998), 84.
25. Sherwood B. Idso and Bruce A. Kimball, "Tree Growth in Carbon Dioxide Enriched Air and Its Implications for Global Carbon Cycling and Maximum Levels of Atmospheric CO_2," *Global Biogeochemical Cycles,* Vol. 7, No. 3, September 1993, 537–55.
26. J. Goudriaan and M. H. Unsworth, "Implications of Increasing Carbon Dioxide and Climate Change for Agricultural Productivity and Water Resources," in *Impact of Carbon Dioxide, Trace Gases, and Climate Change on Global Agriculture* (Madison, WI: American Society of Agronomy Special Publication Number 53, 1990), 111.

CHAPTER 12: SORTING OUT OZONE

1. Catherine Dee, ed., *Kid Heroes of the Environment* (Berkeley, CA: Earth Works Press, 1991), 79.
2. Tony Hare, *The Ozone Layer* (New York: Gloucester Press, 1990), 15.
3. Robert E. Snyder et al., *Earth Science: The Challenge of Discovery*, Annotated Teacher's Edition (Lexington, MA: D. C. Heath and Co., 1991), 532.
4. J. Budziszewski and Lawrence J. Pauline, *We the People* (Austin: Holt, Rinehart and Winston, Inc., 1989), 573.
5. Richard G. Boehm and James L. Swanson, *World Geography: A Physical and Cultural Approach*, 3d ed. (Lake Forest, IL: Glencoe, 1992), 83.
6. Betty Miles, *Save the Earth: An Action Handbook for Kids* (New York: Alfred A. Knopf, 1991), 17.
7. Sharon Roan, *Ozone Crisis: The 15-Year Evolution of a Sudden Global Emergency* (New York: Wiley, 1990), 8.
8. Miles, 17.
9. S. Fred Singer, "My Adventures in the Ozone Layer," *National Review* (June 30, 1989), 36.
10. "Daily Total Ozone As Measured by TOMS During 1980," chart prepared by M. R. Schoeberl, Goddard Space Flight Center, NASA, in *Science Summary* by Fluorocarbon Program Panel, Chemical Manufacturers' Association, Washington, D.C. (April 1989), 19.
11. Anne Pedersen, *The Kids' Environment Book: What's Awry and Why* (Santa Fe, NM: John Muir Publications, 1991), 33–4.
12. J. D. Mahlman, "A Looming Arctic Ozone Hole?" *Nature*, Vol. 360, November 19, 1992, 209.

13. Richard S. Stolarski, "The Antarctic Ozone Hole," *Scientific American*, Vol. 258 (January 1988), 32.
14. Richard A. Kerr, "Ozone Destruction Worsens," *Science*, Vol. 252, April 12, 1991, 204.
15. Richard Stolarski, Rumen Bojkov, Lane Bishop, Christos Zerefos, Johannes Staehelin, Joseph Zawodny, "Measured Trends in Stratospheric Ozone," *Science*, Vol. 256, April 17, 1992, 342–349.
16. S. Fred Singer, "What Could Be Causing Global Ozone Depletion?" in *Climate Impact of Solar Variability*, ed. by K. H. Schalten and A. Arking, NASA Publication 3086 (Washington, D.C.: NASA, 1990).
17. Linwood B. Callis et al., "Ozone Depletion in the High Latitude Lower Stratosphere: 1979-1990," *Journal of Geophysical Research*, Vol. 96, No. D2, (February 20, 1991), 2921-37, on 2931.
18. Susan Solomon, R. W. Portmann, R. R. Garcia, L. W. Thomason, L. R. Poole, and M. P. McCormick, "The Role of Aerosol Variation in Anthropogenic Ozone Depletion at Northern Midlatitudes," *Journal of Geophysical Research*, Vol. 101, D3, March 20, 1996, 6713-6728.
19. Susan Solomon, "Progress Towards a Quantitative Understanding of Antarctic Ozone Depletion," *Nature,* Vol. 347, September 27, 1990, 347–354.
20. Joseph Scotto et al., "Biologically Effective Ultraviolet Radiation: Surface Measurements in the United States, 1974 to 1985," *Science*, Vol. 239 (1988), 762–4.
21. J. B. Kerr and C. T. McElroy, "Evidence for Large Upward Trends of Ultraviolet-B Radiation Linked to Ozone Depletion," *Science*, Vol. 262 (November 12, 1993), 1032–4, and John Maddox, "Can Evidence Ever Be Inconclusive?" *Nature*, Vol. 369, (May 12, 1994), 97.
22. Shaw Liu et al., "Effect of Anthropogenic Aerosols On Biologically Active Ultraviolet Radiation," *Geophysical Ressaerch Letters,* January 3, 1992, 2265.
23. Quoted in Ronald Bailey, *Eco-Scam: The False Prophets of Ecological Apocalypse* (New York: St. Martin's Press, 1993), 131.
24. The National Research Council studied the relationship and could not decide what connection there is between sun exposure and melanoma. National Research Council, *Causes and Effects of Changes in Stratospheric Ozone: Update 1983* (Washington, D.C.: National Academy Press, 1984), 189.
25. Richard B. Setlow, et al., "Wavelengths Effective in Induction of Malignant Melanoma," *Proceedings of the National Academy of Sciences U.S.A.*, Vol. 90 (July 1993), 6666.
26. Hugh W. Ellsaesser, "The Holes in the Ozone Hole II" paper presented at Cato Institute Conference, "Global Environmental Crises: Science or Politics?" Washington, D.C., June 5–6, 1991.
27. Arne Dahlback, et al., "Biological UV-Doses and the Effect of an Ozone Depletion," *Photochemistry and Photobiology*, Vol. 49 (1989), 621–5.
28. Quoted in Bailey, 128.
29. Osmund Holm-Hansen et al., "Ultraviolet Radiation in Antarctica: Inhibition of Primary Production," *Photochemistry and Photobiology*, Vol. 58, No. 4 (1993), 567–70.
30. *Consumer Economics in Action* by Roger LeRoy Miller and Alan D. Stafford (St. Paul, MN: West Publishing Co., 1993) does indicate the problem (p. 24).
31. Amal Kumar Naj, "CFC Substitute Might Be Toxic, Rat Study Finds," *Wall Street Journal,* July 2, 1991.

32. Steven E. Schwarzbach, "CFC Alternatives Under a Cloud," *Nature*, Vol. 376, July 27, 1995, 297–8.
33. Julie Edelson Halpert, "Freon Smugglers Find Big Market," *The New York Times*, April 30, 1995, A1ff.
34. Gary Stix, "Keeping Vaccines Cold," *Scientific American*, February 1996, 14–16.
35. Tim Beardsley, "Better Than a Cure," *Scientific American,* January 1995, 88–95.
36. Bailey, 138.

CHAPTER 13: ACID RAIN

1. Catherine Dee, ed., *Kid Heroes of the Environment* (Berkeley, CA: EarthWorks Press, 1991), 67-9.
2. Dean Hurd et al., *General Science: A Voyage of Discovery* (Englewood Cliffs, NJ: Prentice Hall, 1992), 498.
3. Leonard Bernstein et al., *Concepts and Challenges in Earth Science*, 3d ed., Annotated Teacher's Edition (Englewood Cliffs, NJ: Globe Book Co., 1991), 282.
4. Jill Wright et al., *Life Science* (Englewood Cliffs, NJ: Prentice Hall, 1991), 583.
5. Robert E. Snyder et al., *Earth Science: The Challenge of Discovery*, Annotated Teacher's Edition (Lexington, MA: D. C. Heath and Co., 1991), 540.
6. James E. Davis and Phyllis Maxey Fernlund, *Civics: Participating in Our Democracy* (Menlo Park, CA: Addison-Wesley Publishing Co., 1993), 546.
7. Thomas J. Baerwald and Celeste Fraser, *World Geography* (Needham, MA: Prentice Hall, 1993), 340.
8. National Wildlife Federation, *Pollution: Problems and Solutions*, Ranger Rick's NatureScope, ed. Judy Braus (Washington, D.C.: National Wildlife Federation, 1990), 44.
9. Martin J. Gutnik, *Ecology* (New York: Franklin Watts, 1984), 22–6.
10. D. W. Schindler, "Effects of Acid Rain on Freshwater Ecosystems," *Science*, Vol. 239, January 8, 1988, 149–157, at 149.
11. J. Laurence Kulp, "Acid Rain," in *The State of Humanity*, Julian Simon, ed. (Cambridge MA: Blackwell Publishers, Inc., 1995), 524.
12. National Acid Precipitation Assessment Program (NAPAP), "Assessment Highlights," September 5, 1990 (National Acid Precipitation Assessment Program, Washington, D.C., September 5, 1990), 4–7.
13. NAPAP, *1992 Report to Congress*, June 1993, 72.
14. J. Laurence Kulp, "Acid Rain: Causes, Effects, and Control," *Regulation*, Winter 1990, 43.
15. Edward C. Krug, "Fish Story," *Policy Review*, Spring 1990, 44–8, and Kulp, 44.
16. The U.S. National Acid Precipitation Program, *1990 Integrated Assessment Report* (Washington, D.C.: The NAPAP Office of the Director, November 1991), 33.
17. Krug, 48.
18. National Wildlife Federation, *Pollution: Problems and Solutions*, 33.
19. Dean Hurd, et al., *General Science: A Voyage of Discovery* (Englewood Cliffs, NJ: Prentice Hall, 1992), 500.
20. NAPAP, September 5, 1990, 19
21. Rose Gutfeld and Barbara Rosewicz, "Battle over Clean Air Looms in the House as Senate Finishes Up, *Wall Street Journal*, April 4, 1990, A1.

CHAPTER 14: NOT A DROP TO DRINK

1. Robert E. Snyder, et al., *Earth Science: The Challenge of Discovery*, Annotated Teacher's Edition (Lexington, MA: D. C. Heath and Co., 1991), 562.
2. National Wildlife Federation, *Pollution: Problems and Solutions*, Ranger Rick's *NatureScope*, ed. Judy Braus (Washington, D.C.: National Wildlife Federation, 1990), 65. The Adopt-a-Stream Foundation at the Northwest Stream Center is located at 600 128th St. S.E., Everett WA 98208 (telephone: 206-316-8592).
3. See Snyder, et al., 546, for example.
4. Snyder, et al., 546.
5. Snyder, et al., 559.
6. Jill Wright, et al. *Life Science*. Englewood Cliffs, NJ: Prentice Hall, 1991.
7. Snyder, et al., 557.
8. Leonard Bernstein, et al., *Concepts and Challenges in Earth Science*, 3d ed., Annotated Teacher's Edition (Englewood Cliffs, NJ: Globe Book Co., 1991), 284.
9. Snyder, et al., 586.
10. Mary Bronson Merki and Don Merki, *Health: A Guide to Wellness*, 2d ed. (Mission Hills, CA: Glencoe Publishing Co., 1989), 589.
11. Terry L. Anderson, "Water Options for the Blue Planet," in *The True State of the Planet*, ed. by Ronald Bailey (New York: The Free Press, 1995), 267–294 at 275.
12. B. Delworth Gardner and Ray G. Huffaker, "Cutting the Loss from Federal Water Subsidies," *Choices*, Fourth Quarter (1988), 24.
13. Anderson, 284.
14. James D. Gwartney and Richard L. Stroup, *Introduction to Economics: The Wealth and Poverty of Nations* (Fort Worth: The Dryden Press, 1994), 543.
15. Anderson, 284.
16. Anne Pedersen, *The Kids' Environment Book: What's Awry and Why* (Santa Fe: John Muir Publications, 1991), 63–4, is an example.
17. Erla Zwingle, "Ogallala Aquifer: Wellspring of the High Plains," *National Geographic*, Vol. 183, No. 3 (March 1993), 80–109.
18. Joan Luckmann, *Your Health!* (Englewood Cliffs, NJ: Prentice Hall, 1990), 530.
19. Amanda M. Phillips and Ellen K. Silbergeld, "Health Effects Studies of Exposure to Hazardous Waste Sites—Where Are We Today?" *American Journal of Industrial Medicine*, 1985, Vol. 8, 1–7.
20. Raymond F. Oram, *Biology: Living Systems*, Annotated Teacher's Edition (Columbus, OH: Merrill Publishing Co., 1989), 753.
21. Ralph M. Feather, *Earth Science* (Lake Forest, IL: Merrill/Glencoe, 1993), 535.
22. Terry L. Anderson and Donald R. Leal, *Free Market Environmentalism* (San Francisco: Pacific Research Institute, 1991), 148.
23. A. Myrick Freeman III, "Air Pollution Policy," in *Public Policies for Environmental Protection*, ed. by Paul R. Portney (Washington, D.C.: Resources for the Future, 1990), 97–149, at 120.
24. E. Calvin Beisner and Julian L. Simon, "Editors' Appendix," in *The State of Humanity*, ed. by Julian L. Simon (Cambridge, MA: Blackwell Publishers, Inc., 1995) 469–475.
25. Roger E. Meiners and Bruce Yandle, "Clean Water Legislation: Reauthorize or Repeal?" *Taking the Environment Seriously*, ed. by Meiners and Yandle (Lanham, MD: Rowman & Littlefield Publishers, Inc., 1993), 73-101, at 76.

26. Snyder, et al., 586.
27. James E. Mielke, "Oil in the Ocean: The Short- and Long-Term Impacts of a Spill," *Congressional Research Service Report for Congress*, July 24, 1990 (90-356 SPR).
28. Mielke, 18.
29. Mielke, 19.
30. Mielke, 22-24.
31. Mielke, Summary.
32. Mielke, Summary.
33. Snyder, et al., 586.

CHAPTER 15: DON'T EAT THAT APPLE!

1. Catherine Dee, ed., *Kid Heroes of the Environment* (Berkeley, CA: EarthWorks Press, 1991), 15–16.
2. Anne Pedersen, *The Kids' Environment Book: What's Awry and Why* (Santa Fe: John Muir Publications, 1991), 80, 82.
3. Mary Metzger and Cinthya P. Whittaker, *This Planet is Mine: Teaching Environmental Awareness and Appreciation to Children* (New York: Fireside, 1991), 146.
4. Joan Luckmann, *Your Health!* Englewood Cliffs, NJ: Prentice Hall, 1990.
5. Diane MacEachern, *Save Our Planet: 750 Everyday Ways You Can Help Clean Up the Earth* (New York: Dell Publishing, 1990), 8.
6. Pedersen, 84, 86.
7. National Research Council, *Pesticides in the Diets of Infants and Children* (Washington, D.C.: National Academy Press, 1993), 1.
8. National Research Council Committee on Comparative Toxicity of Naturally Occurring Carcinogens, *Carcinogens and Anticarcinogens in the Human Diet* (Washington, D.C.: National Academy Press, 1996), Executive Summary, 5.
9. Thomas R. Dunlap, *DDT: Scientists, Citizens, and Public Policy* (Princeton, NJ: Princeton University Press, 1981), 59.
10. Harland Austin, Julian E. Keil, and Philip Cole, "A Prospective Follow-Up Study of Cancer Mortality in Relation to Serum DDT," *American Journal of Public Health*, Vol. 79, No. 1 (January 1989), 43.
11. Holly Lippke, *DDT: An Overview*, PERC Working Paper 93–3, Political Economy Research Center, Bozeman, MT, 1993.
12. J. Gordon Edwards, "DDT Effects on Bird Abundance and Reproduction," in *Rational Readings on Environmental Concerns,* ed. by Jay H. Lehr (New York: Van Nostrand Reinhold, 1992), 195–216, at 205.
13. Kenneth Mellanby, "With Safeguards, DDT Should Still Be Used," *Wall Street Journal*, September 12, 1989, A30.
14. M. B. Green, *Pesticides—Boon or Bane?* (Boulder, CO: Westview Press, 1976), 101.
15. Robert S. Desowitz, "Yesterday's Malaria Wars," *Nature*, September 12, 1996, 135.
16. Michael Fumento, *Science Under Siege: Balancing Technology and the Environment* (New York: William Morrow and Company, Inc., 1993), 21-47.
17. Joseph D. Rosen, "The Death of Daminozide," in *Pesticides and Alternatives,* ed. by J. E. Casida (New York: Elsevier, 1990), 59.
18. Thomas Gale Moore, *Environmental Fundamentalism* (Stanford, CA: Hoover Institution, 1992), 6.

19. Richard Doll and Richard Peto, *The Causes of Cancer* (Oxford: Oxford University Press, 1986), 1245–1265.
20. Doll and Peto, 1250.
21. Bruce N. Ames and Lois Swirsky Gold, "Environmental Pollution and Cancer: Some Misconceptions," in *Rational Readings on Environmental Concerns*, ed. by Jay H. Lehr (New York, Van Nostrand Reinhold, 1992), 151–67.
22. Bruce N. Ames and Lois Swirsky Gold, "Pesticides, Risk, and Applesauce," *Science*, May 19, 1989, 755–757.
23. Lois Swirsky Gold, Thomas H. Slone, Bonnie R. Stern, Neela B. Manley, Bruce N. Ames, "Rodent Carcinogens: Setting Priorities," in *Science,* Vol. 258, October 9, 1992, 261–265, and Lois Swirsky Gold, Thomas H. Slone, and Bruce N. Ames, "Prioritization of Possible Carcinogenic Hazards in Food," in *Food Chemical Risk Analysis*, ed. by David Tennant (London: Chapman and Hall, forthcoming).
24. Ames and Gold, 756.
25. National Research Council Committee on Comparative Toxicity of Naturally Occurring Carcinogens, Executive Summary, 5–6.
26. Ames and Gold, 755.
27. Bruce N. Ames, Mark K. Shigenaga, and Tory M. Hagen, "Oxidants, Antioxidants, and the Degenerative Diseases of Aging," Proceedings of the National Academy of Sciences U.S.A., Vol. 90, September 1993, 7915–22.

CHAPTER 16: A GARBAGE CRISIS?

1. Catherine Dee, ed., *Kid Heroes of the Environment* (Berkeley, CA: EarthWorks Press, 1991), 73–5.
2. James E. Davis and Phyllis Fernlund, *Civics: Participating in Our Democracy* (Menlo Park, CA: Addison-Wesley Publishing Co., 1993), 505.
3. Davis and Fernlund, 507.
4. Peter Alexander, et al., *General Science: Book One* (Needham, MA: Silver Burdett & Ginn, 1989), 151.
5. Larry K. Olsen, et al., *Being Healthy*, Annotated Teacher's Edition (Orlando: Harcourt Brace Jovanovich Publishers, 1990), 378.
6. William Rathje and Cullen Murphy, *Rubbish! The Archaeology of Garbage* (New York: HarperCollins Publishers, 1992), 16.
7. Rathje and Murphy, 97.
8. Rathje and Murphy, 98.
9. Rathje and Murphy, 162
10. Rathje and Murphy, 101.
11. Rathje and Murphy, 103, 104, 106.
12. Personal conversation with William Rathje, July 1996.
13. Calculations by Clark Wiseman, Professor of Economics, Gonzaga University, sent to authors May 24, 1999.
14. Rodney Fort and Lynn Scarlett, "Too Little Too Late: Host-Community Benefits and Siting Solid Waste Facilities," Policy Study 157, The Reason Foundation, Los Angeles, April 1993, 6.
15. Lynn Scarlett, "A Consumer's Guide to Environmental Myths and Realities," Policy Report #99, National Center for Policy Analysis, Dallas, TX, September 1991, 37.

16. Jeff Bailey, "Curbside Recycling Comforts the Soul, But Benefits Are Scant," *Wall Street Journal*, January 19, 1995, A1ff.

17. Scarlett, 14.

18. Letter from David Jolly, Environmental Affairs Representative, Dart Container Corporation, September 11, 1992.

19. Davis and Fernlund, 506, and Charles R. Cobel et al. *Earth Science* (Englewood Cliffs, NJ: Prentice Hall, 1991), 552.

20. David C. King, et al., *The United States and Its People* (Menlo Park, CA: Addison-Wesley, 1993), 878.

21. Betty Miles, *Save the Earth: An Action Handbook for Kids* (New York: Alfred A. Knopf, 1991), 13.

22. William L. Rathje, "Rubbish!" *Atlantic Monthly*, December 1989, 101.

23. Scarlett, 8.

24. Rathje and Murphy, 217.

25. Rathje and Murphy, 217.

26. Scarlett, 32.

CHAPTER 17: THE RECYCLING MYTH

1. Bruce Van Voorst, "The Recycling Bottleneck," *Time*, September 14, 1992, 52–54.

2. Larry K. Olsen, et al., *Being Healthy*, Annotated Teacher's Edition (Orlando: Harcourt Brace Jovanovich Publishers, 1990), 378.

3. Mary Bronson Merki, *Teen Health: Decisions for Healthy Living*, Annotated Teacher's Edition (Mission Hills, CA: Glencoe, 1990), 434.

4. Linda A. Warner, et al., *Life Science: The Challenge of Discovery* (Lexington, MA: D. C. Heath and Company, 1991), 624.

5. Dean Hurd, et al., *General Science: A Voyage of Exploration* (Englewood Cliffs, NJ: Prentice Hall, 1992), 263.

6. Robert E. Snyder, et al., *Earth Science The Challenge of Discovery*, Annotated Teacher's Edition (Lexington, MA: D. C. Heath and Company, 1991), 248–9.

7. William Rathje and Cullen Murphy, *Rubbish! The Archaeology of Garbage* (New York: HarperCollins Publishers, Inc., 1992), 206.

8. James V. DeLong, *Wasting Away: Mismanaging Municipal Solid Waste*, Competitive Enterprise Institute, Washington, D.C., May 1994, 30.

9. Christopher Boerner and Kenneth Chilton, *Recycling's Demand Side: Lessons from Germany's "Green Dot,"* St. Louis, Washington University Center for the Study of American Business, August 1993.

10. Lynn Scarlett, "Recycling's Invisible Costs," *Wall Street Journal*, March 3, 1992.

11. Boerner and Chilton, 10.

12. Merki, 434.

13. Warner, et al., 615.

14. Quoted in Jane S. Shaw, "Recycling," *The Fortune Encyclopedia of Economics*, ed. by David R. Henderson (New York: Warner Books, Inc., 1993), 459.

15. Lynn Scarlett, "A Consumer's Guide to Environmental Myths and Realities," Policy Report #99, National Center for Policy Analysis, Dallas, TX, September 1991, 20.

16. Figure from the Aluminum Association, Washington, D.C., May 1996.

17. Rathje and Murphy, 204.
18. Rathje and Murphy, 200.
19. Shaw, 458.
20. For more information about the push-pull tab recycling program, you may contact NorthGreen Communications, Inc., 641 East Lake Street, Wayzata, Minnesota 55391.
21. Shaw, 458.
22. Rathje and Murphy, 202.

CHAPTER 18: WHAT WE CAN DO

1. Jack Stauder, "Changing Course," *Liberal Education,* Summer 1995, 36-40.

Index